50% OFF CBEST Test Prep Course!

Dear Customer,

We consider it an honor and a privilege that you chose our CBEST Study Guide. As a way of showing our appreciation and to help us better serve you, we have partnered with Mometrix Test Preparation to offer you **50% off their online CBEST Prep Course.** Many CBEST courses are needlessly expensive and don't deliver enough value. With their course, you get access to the best CBEST prep material, and **you only pay half price.**

Mometrix has structured their online course to perfectly complement your printed study guide. The CBEST Test Prep Course contains **in-depth lessons** that cover all the most important topics, over **700 practice questions** to ensure you feel prepared, more than **550 flashcards** for studying on the go, and over **190 instructional videos**.

Online CBEST Prep Course

Topics Include:

- Reading
  - Literary Analysis
  - Main Idea and Supporting Details
  - Elements of a Text
- Writing
  - Foundations of Grammar and Punctuation
  - Style and Form
  - Outlining and Organizing Ideas
- Mathematics
  - Numbers and Operations
  - Advanced Equations
  - Statistical Analysis
- And More!

Course Features:

- CBEST Study Guide
  - Get access to content from the best reviewed study guide available.
- Track Your Progress
  - Their customized course allows you to check off content you have studied or feel confident with.
- 7 Full-Length Practice Tests
  - With 700+ practice questions and lesson reviews, you can test yourself again and again to build confidence.
- CBEST Flashcards
  - Their course includes a flashcard mode consisting of over 550 content cards to help you study.

To receive this discount, visit their website at mometrix.com/university/cbest/ or simply scan this QR code with your smartphone. At the checkout page, enter the discount code: **TPBCBEST50**

If you have any questions or concerns, please contact Mometrix at support@mometrix.com.

SCAN HERE

FREE Test Taking Tips Video/DVD Offer

To better serve you, we created videos covering test taking tips that we want to give you for FREE. **These videos cover world-class tips that will help you succeed on your test.**

We just ask that you send us feedback about this product. Please let us know what you thought about it—whether good, bad, or indifferent.

To get your **FREE videos**, you can use the QR code below or email freevideos@studyguideteam.com with "Free Videos" in the subject line and the following information in the body of the email:

    a. The title of your product

    b. Your product rating on a scale of 1-5, with 5 being the highest

    c. Your feedback about the product

If you have any questions or concerns, please don't hesitate to contact us at info@studyguideteam.com.

Thank you!

CBEST Prep Book for California

4 CBEST Practice Tests with Study Guide Review for Reading, Math, and Writing [5th Edition]

Joshua Rueda

Written and edited by TPB Publishing.

TPB Publishing is not associated with or endorsed by any official testing organization. TPB Publishing is a publisher of unofficial educational products. All test and organization names are trademarks of their respective owners. Content in this book is included for utilitarian purposes only and does not constitute an endorsement by TPB Publishing of any particular point of view.

Interested in buying more than 10 copies of our product? Contact us about bulk discounts:
bulkorders@studyguideteam.com

ISBN 13: 9781637752630
ISBN 10: 1637752636

Table of Contents

Welcome

Dear Reader,

Welcome to your new Test Prep Books study guide! We are pleased that you chose us to help you prepare for your exam. There are many study options to choose from, and we appreciate you choosing us. Studying can be a daunting task, but we have designed a smart, effective study guide to help prepare you for what lies ahead.

Whether you're a parent helping your child learn and grow, a high school student working hard to get into your dream college, or a nursing student studying for a complex exam, we want to help give you the tools you need to succeed. We hope this study guide gives you the skills and the confidence to thrive, and we can't thank you enough for allowing us to be part of your journey.

In an effort to continue to improve our products, we welcome feedback from our customers. We look forward to hearing from you. Suggestions, success stories, and criticisms can all be communicated by emailing us at info@studyguideteam.com.

Sincerely,
Test Prep Books Team

FREE Videos/DVD OFFER

Doing well on your exam requires both knowing the test content and understanding how to use that knowledge to do well on the test. We offer completely FREE test taking tip videos. **These videos cover world-class tips that you can use to succeed on your test.**

To get your **FREE videos**, you can use the QR code below or email freevideos@studyguideteam.com with "Free Videos" in the subject line and the following information in the body of the email:

   a. The title of your product
   b. Your product rating on a scale of 1-5, with 5 being the highest
   c. Your feedback about the product
If you have any questions or concerns, please don't hesitate to contact us at info@studyguideteam.com.

Quick Overview

As you draw closer to taking your exam, effective preparation becomes more and more important. Thankfully, you have this study guide to help you get ready. Use this guide to help keep your studying on track and refer to it often.

This study guide contains several key sections that will help you be successful on your exam. The guide contains tips for what you should do the night before and the day of the test. Also included are test-taking tips. Knowing the right information is not always enough. Many well-prepared test takers struggle with exams. These tips will help equip you to accurately read, assess, and answer test questions.

A large part of the guide is devoted to showing you what content to expect on the exam and to helping you better understand that content. In this guide are practice test questions so that you can see how well you have grasped the content. Then, answer explanations are provided so that you can understand why you missed certain questions.

Don't try to cram the night before you take your exam. This is not a wise strategy for a few reasons. First, your retention of the information will be low. Your time would be better used by reviewing information you already know rather than trying to learn a lot of new information. Second, you will likely become stressed as you try to gain a large amount of knowledge in a short amount of time. Third, you will be depriving yourself of sleep. So be sure to go to bed at a reasonable time the night before. Being well-rested helps you focus and remain calm.

Be sure to eat a substantial breakfast the morning of the exam. If you are taking the exam in the afternoon, be sure to have a good lunch as well. Being hungry is distracting and can make it difficult to focus. You have hopefully spent lots of time preparing for the exam. Don't let an empty stomach get in the way of success!

When travelling to the testing center, leave earlier than needed. That way, you have a buffer in case you experience any delays. This will help you remain calm and will keep you from missing your appointment time at the testing center.

Be sure to pace yourself during the exam. Don't try to rush through the exam. There is no need to risk performing poorly on the exam just so you can leave the testing center early. Allow yourself to use all of the allotted time if needed.

Remain positive while taking the exam even if you feel like you are performing poorly. Thinking about the content you should have mastered will not help you perform better on the exam.

Once the exam is complete, take some time to relax. Even if you feel that you need to take the exam again, you will be well served by some down time before you begin studying again. It's often easier to convince yourself to study if you know that it will come with a reward!

Test-Taking Strategies

1. Predicting the Answer

When you feel confident in your preparation for a multiple-choice test, try predicting the answer before reading the answer choices. This is especially useful on questions that test objective factual knowledge. By predicting the answer before reading the available choices, you eliminate the possibility that you will be distracted or led astray by an incorrect answer choice. You will feel more confident in your selection if you read the question, predict the answer, and then find your prediction among the answer choices. After using this strategy, be sure to still read all of the answer choices carefully and completely. If you feel unprepared, you should not attempt to predict the answers. This would be a waste of time and an opportunity for your mind to wander in the wrong direction.

2. Reading the Whole Question

Too often, test takers scan a multiple-choice question, recognize a few familiar words, and immediately jump to the answer choices. Test authors are aware of this common impatience, and they will sometimes prey upon it. For instance, a test author might subtly turn the question into a negative, or he or she might redirect the focus of the question right at the end. The only way to avoid falling into these traps is to read the entirety of the question carefully before reading the answer choices.

3. Looking for Wrong Answers

Long and complicated multiple-choice questions can be intimidating. One way to simplify a difficult multiple-choice question is to eliminate all of the answer choices that are clearly wrong. In most sets of answers, there will be at least one selection that can be dismissed right away. If the test is administered on paper, the test taker could draw a line through it to indicate that it may be ignored; otherwise, the test taker will have to perform this operation mentally or on scratch paper. In either case, once the obviously incorrect answers have been eliminated, the remaining choices may be considered. Sometimes identifying the clearly wrong answers will give the test taker some information about the correct answer. For instance, if one of the remaining answer choices is a direct opposite of one of the eliminated answer choices, it may well be the correct answer. The opposite of obviously wrong is obviously right! Of course, this is not always the case. Some answers are obviously incorrect simply because they are irrelevant to the question being asked. Still, identifying and eliminating some incorrect answer choices is a good way to simplify a multiple-choice question.

4. Don't Overanalyze

Anxious test takers often overanalyze questions. When you are nervous, your brain will often run wild, causing you to make associations and discover clues that don't actually exist. If you feel that this may be a problem for you, do whatever you can to slow down during the test. Try taking a deep breath or counting to ten. As you read and consider the question, restrict yourself to the particular words used by the author. Avoid thought tangents about what the author *really* meant, or what he or she was *trying* to say. The only things that matter on a multiple-choice test are the words that are actually in the question. You must avoid reading too much into a multiple-choice question, or supposing that the writer meant something other than what he or she wrote.

5. No Need for Panic

It is wise to learn as many strategies as possible before taking a multiple-choice test, but it is likely that you will come across a few questions for which you simply don't know the answer. In this situation, avoid panicking. Because most multiple-choice tests include dozens of questions, the relative value of a single wrong answer is small. As much as possible, you should compartmentalize each question on a multiple-choice test. In other words, you should not allow your feelings about one question to affect your success on the others. When you find a question that you either don't understand or don't know how to answer, just take a deep breath and do your best. Read the entire question slowly and carefully. Try rephrasing the question a couple of different ways. Then, read all of the answer choices carefully. After eliminating obviously wrong answers, make a selection and move on to the next question.

6. Confusing Answer Choices

When working on a difficult multiple-choice question, there may be a tendency to focus on the answer choices that are the easiest to understand. Many people, whether consciously or not, gravitate to the answer choices that require the least concentration, knowledge, and memory. This is a mistake. When you come across an answer choice that is confusing, you should give it extra attention. A question might be confusing because you do not know the subject matter to which it refers. If this is the case, don't eliminate the answer before you have affirmatively settled on another. When you come across an answer choice of this type, set it aside as you look at the remaining choices. If you can confidently assert that one of the other choices is correct, you can leave the confusing answer aside. Otherwise, you will need to take a moment to try to better understand the confusing answer choice. Rephrasing is one way to tease out the sense of a confusing answer choice.

7. Your First Instinct

Many people struggle with multiple-choice tests because they overthink the questions. If you have studied sufficiently for the test, you should be prepared to trust your first instinct once you have carefully and completely read the question and all of the answer choices. There is a great deal of research suggesting that the mind can come to the correct conclusion very quickly once it has obtained all of the relevant information. At times, it may seem to you as if your intuition is working faster even than your reasoning mind. This may in fact be true. The knowledge you obtain while studying may be retrieved from your subconscious before you have a chance to work out the associations that support it. Verify your instinct by working out the reasons that it should be trusted.

8. Key Words

Many test takers struggle with multiple-choice questions because they have poor reading comprehension skills. Quickly reading and understanding a multiple-choice question requires a mixture of skill and experience. To help with this, try jotting down a few key words and phrases on a piece of scrap paper. Doing this concentrates the process of reading and forces the mind to weigh the relative importance of the question's parts. In selecting words and phrases to write down, the test taker thinks about the question more deeply and carefully. This is especially true for multiple-choice questions that are preceded by a long prompt.

9. Subtle Negatives

One of the oldest tricks in the multiple-choice test writer's book is to subtly reverse the meaning of a question with a word like *not* or *except*. If you are not paying attention to each word in the question, you can easily be led astray by this trick. For instance, a common question format is, "Which of the following is...?" Obviously, if the question instead is, "Which of the following is not...?," then the answer will be quite different. Even worse, the test makers are aware of the potential for this mistake and will include one answer choice that would be correct if the question were not negated or reversed. A test taker who misses the reversal will find what he or she believes to be a correct answer and will be so confident that he or she will fail to reread the question and discover the original error. The only way to avoid this is to practice a wide variety of multiple-choice questions and to pay close attention to each and every word.

10. Reading Every Answer Choice

It may seem obvious, but you should always read every one of the answer choices! Too many test takers fall into the habit of scanning the question and assuming that they understand the question because they recognize a few key words. From there, they pick the first answer choice that answers the question they believe they have read. Test takers who read all of the answer choices might discover that one of the latter answer choices is actually *more* correct. Moreover, reading all of the answer choices can remind you of facts related to the question that can help you arrive at the correct answer. Sometimes, a misstatement or incorrect detail in one of the latter answer choices will trigger your memory of the subject and will enable you to find the right answer. Failing to read all of the answer choices is like not reading all of the items on a restaurant menu: you might miss out on the perfect choice.

11. Spot the Hedges

One of the keys to success on multiple-choice tests is paying close attention to every word. This is never truer than with words like almost, most, some, and sometimes. These words are called "hedges" because they indicate that a statement is not totally true or not true in every place and time. An absolute statement will contain no hedges, but in many subjects, the answers are not always straightforward or absolute. There are always exceptions to the rules in these subjects. For this reason, you should favor those multiple-choice questions that contain hedging language. The presence of qualifying words indicates that the author is taking special care with their words, which is certainly important when composing the right answer. After all, there are many ways to be wrong, but there is only one way to be right! For this reason, it is wise to avoid answers that are absolute when taking a multiple-choice test. An absolute answer is one that says things are either all one way or all another. They often include words like *every*, *always*, *best*, and *never*. If you are taking a multiple-choice test in a subject that doesn't lend itself to absolute answers, be on your guard if you see any of these words.

12. Long Answers

In many subject areas, the answers are not simple. As already mentioned, the right answer often requires hedges. Another common feature of the answers to a complex or subjective question are qualifying clauses, which are groups of words that subtly modify the meaning of the sentence. If the question or answer choice describes a rule to which there are exceptions or the subject matter is complicated, ambiguous, or confusing, the correct answer will require many words in order to be expressed clearly and accurately. In essence, you should not be deterred by answer choices that seem

5

excessively long. Oftentimes, the author of the text will not be able to write the correct answer without offering some qualifications and modifications. Your job is to read the answer choices thoroughly and completely and to select the one that most accurately and precisely answers the question.

13. Restating to Understand

Sometimes, a question on a multiple-choice test is difficult not because of what it asks but because of how it is written. If this is the case, restate the question or answer choice in different words. This process serves a couple of important purposes. First, it forces you to concentrate on the core of the question. In order to rephrase the question accurately, you have to understand it well. Rephrasing the question will concentrate your mind on the key words and ideas. Second, it will present the information to your mind in a fresh way. This process may trigger your memory and render some useful scrap of information picked up while studying.

14. True Statements

Sometimes an answer choice will be true in itself, but it does not answer the question. This is one of the main reasons why it is essential to read the question carefully and completely before proceeding to the answer choices. Too often, test takers skip ahead to the answer choices and look for true statements. Having found one of these, they are content to select it without reference to the question above. Obviously, this provides an easy way for test makers to play tricks. The savvy test taker will always read the entire question before turning to the answer choices. Then, having settled on a correct answer choice, he or she will refer to the original question and ensure that the selected answer is relevant. The mistake of choosing a correct-but-irrelevant answer choice is especially common on questions related to specific pieces of objective knowledge. A prepared test taker will have a wealth of factual knowledge at their disposal, and should not be careless in its application.

15. No Patterns

One of the more dangerous ideas that circulates about multiple-choice tests is that the correct answers tend to fall into patterns. These erroneous ideas range from a belief that B and C are the most common right answers, to the idea that an unprepared test-taker should answer "A-B-A-C-A-D-A-B-A." It cannot be emphasized enough that pattern-seeking of this type is exactly the WRONG way to approach a multiple-choice test. To begin with, it is highly unlikely that the test maker will plot the correct answers according to some predetermined pattern. The questions are scrambled and delivered in a random order. Furthermore, even if the test maker was following a pattern in the assignation of correct answers, there is no reason why the test taker would know which pattern he or she was using. Any attempt to discern a pattern in the answer choices is a waste of time and a distraction from the real work of taking the test. A test taker would be much better served by extra preparation before the test than by reliance on a pattern in the answers.

Bonus Content

We host multiple bonus items online, including all four practice tests in digital format. Scan the QR code or go to this link to access this content:

testprepbooks.com/bonus/cbest

The first time you access the page, you will need to register as a "new user" and verify your email address.

If you have any issues, please email support@testprepbooks.com.

Introduction to the CBEST

Function of the Test

The California Basic Educational Skills Test (CBEST) was created by the government of the state of California as a way for teacher candidates to demonstrate proficiency in reading, writing, and mathematics. Individuals applying for their first California teaching credential, applying for admission to certain teacher preparation and credentialing programs, or seeking employment in a California school district or educational agency must meet the California Basic Skills Requirement. The California legislature has established eight different ways to meet this requirement, such as achieving certain scores on various tests, one of which is to pass the CBEST. The state of Nevada has also adopted the CBEST as a way to meet certain Nevada licensing requirements.

CBEST scores are generally used only for California and Nevada teacher licensing, credentialing and hiring. In the 2014-2015 school year, 32,890 individuals took the CBEST for the first time. 22,847 of these first-time test takers passed, for a passing rate of 69.5%. The passing rate over the last five years has ranged from 69.5% to 71.4%. Of the three sections, reading and math are generally a bit easier to pass, with passing rates of around 80%, while writing is a bit more difficult, with a passing rate around 73%. (http://www.ctc.ca.gov/commission/agendas/2016-04/2016-04-5C.pdf).

Test Administration

The computer-based version of the CBEST is offered year-round by appointment, Monday through Saturday, excluding certain holidays, at Pearson VUE testing centers. The paper-based version is available on a more limited basis, usually around five times per school year. Individuals who do not pass must wait 45 days to attempt the CBEST again on computer, or may attempt the test again on any scheduled paper-administered test day.

All CBEST test sites are wheelchair-accessible. Individuals with documented disabilities may receive additional accommodations such as allowance of a medical device in the testing room, additional breaks, and use of tools such as a magnifying glass or straight edge. Individuals seeking such accommodation should complete and submit an Alternative Testing Arrangements Request Form along with appropriate documentation prior to their scheduled test date. The form must be submitted each time a student seeking accommodations takes the CBEST exam.

Test Format

 A CBEST testing session will last four hours. Test takers may elect to take one, two, or all three of the sections offered. The reading section is made up of questions designed to assess the test takers ability to comprehend information in written passages, tables, and graphs. The mathematics section is primarily comprised of word problems to be solved without the use of a calculator. The writing section is composed of two essays, one in which the test taker is asked to analyze a given situation or statement and one in which the test taker is asked to describe a personal experience.

8

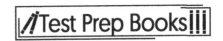

A summary of the content of the CBEST is as follows:

Section	Subsection	Approx # of Questions
Reading	Critical analysis and evaluation	20
	Comprehension and research skills	30
Mathematics	Estimation, measurement, and statistical principles	15
	Computation and problem solving	17
	Numerical and graphic relationships	17
Writing	Essay	2

Scoring

Scoring on the reading and math sections is done by calculating a raw score based on the number of correct answers with no penalty for guessing incorrectly and converting that raw score to a scaled score between 20 and 80. Similarly, the essays in the writing section are given a score between 1 and 4 by two readers for each of the two essays. The total raw score (between 4 and 16) is then converted to a scaled score between 20 and 80.

Test takers may pass the CBEST by *either* earning a scaled score on each section of at least 41, *or* earning a scaled score on each section of at least 37 and a total scaled score of at least 123. As discussed, the passing rate on individual sections ranges from the mid-70s to around 80%, and the overall passing rate hovers around 70%.

Study Prep Plan for the CBEST

1 **Schedule -** Use one of our study schedules below or come up with one of your own.

2 **Relax -** Test anxiety can hurt even the best students. There are many ways to reduce stress. Find the one that works best for you.

3 **Execute -** Once you have a good plan in place, be sure to stick to it.

One Week Study Schedule		
Day 1	Reading	
Day 2	Mathematics	
Day 3	Computation & Problem Solving	
Day 4	Writing	
Day 5	CBEST Practice Tests #1 & #2	
Day 6	CBEST Practice Tests #3 & #4	
Day 7	Take Your Exam!	

Two Week Study Schedule				
Day 1	Reading	Day 8	Numerical & Graphic Relationships
Day 2	Understanding the Effect of Word Choice	Day 9	Writing
Day 3	Comprehension and Context	Day 10	CBEST Practice Test #1
Day 4	Mathematics	Day 11	CBEST Practice Test #2
Day 5	Statistical Principles	Day 12	CBEST Practice Test #3
Day 6	Computation & Problem Solving	Day 13	CBEST Practice Test #4
Day 7	Solving Practical Math Problems	Day 14	Take Your Exam!

One Month Study Schedule						
Day 1	Reading	Day 11	Computation & Problem Solving	Day 21	Grammar, Usage, Syntax, and Mechanics Choices
Day 2	Understanding the Task, Purpose...	Day 12	Operations with Fractions, Decimals...	Day 22	CBEST Practice Test #1
Day 3	Understanding the Effect of Word Choice	Day 13	Decimals	Day 23	Answer Explanations for Practice Test #1
Day 4	Fallacies	Day 14	Solving Practical Math Problems	Day 24	CBEST Practice Test #2
Day 5	Comprehension and Context	Day 15	Solving Simple Algebraic Problems	Day 25	Answer Explanations for Practice Test #2
Day 6	Understanding the Use of Affixes, Context...	Day 16	Numerical & Graphic Relationships	Day 26	CBEST Practice Test #3
Day 7	Research and Reference Skills	Day 17	Mathematically Equivalent Expressions	Day 27	Answer Explanations for Practice Test #3
Day 8	Mathematics	Day 18	Data in Other Charts	Day 28	CBEST Practice Test #4
Day 9	Statistical Principles	Day 19	Writing	Day 29	Answer Explanations for Practice Test #4
Day 10	The Basic Principles of Probability...	Day 20	Understanding the Conventions of Standard English	Day 30	Take Your Exam!

Build your own prep plan by visiting:

testprepbooks.com/prep

11

As you study for your test, we'd like to take the opportunity to remind you that you are capable of great things! With the right tools and dedication, you truly can do anything you set your mind to. The fact that you are holding this book right now shows how committed you are. In case no one has told you lately, you've got this! Our intention behind including this coloring page is to give you the chance to take some time to engage your creative side when you need a little brain-break from studying. As a company, we want to encourage people like you to achieve their dreams by providing good quality study materials for the tests and certifications that improve careers and change lives. As individuals, many of us have taken such tests in our careers, and we know how challenging this process can be. While we can't come alongside you and cheer you on personally, we can offer you the space to recall your purpose, reconnect with your passion, and refresh your brain through an artistic practice. We wish you every success, and happy studying!

12

Reading

Critical Analysis and Evaluation

Comparison and Contrast

One writing device authors use is *comparison and contrast.* When authors take two objects and show how they are alike or similar, a comparison is being made. When authors take the same two objects and show how they differ, they are contrasting them. Comparison and contrast essays are most commonly written in nonfiction form. The Venn diagram below presents some of the common words or phrases used when comparing or contrasting objects.

Compare and Contrast Venn Diagram

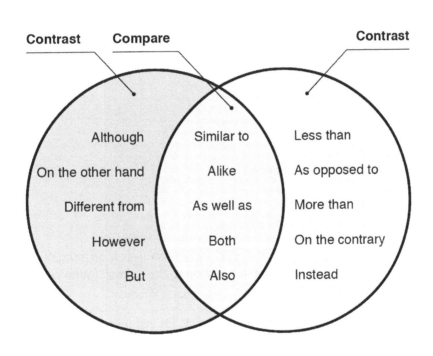

13

In order to understand the relationship between ideas, readers need to be able to *compare* and *contrast*. Comparing two things means identifying their similarities, while contrasting two things means finding their differences. Consider the following excerpt from "The Lamb" by William Blake:

> Little lamb, who made thee?
> Dost thou know who made thee,
> Gave thee life, and bid thee feed
> By the stream and o'er the mead;
> Gave thee clothing of delight,
> Softest clothing, woolly, bright;
> Gave thee such a tender voice,
> Making all the vales rejoice?
> Little lamb, who made thee?
> Dost thou know who made thee?

Consider that poem alongside an excerpt from another work by Blake called "The Tyger."

> Tyger! Tyger! burning bright
> In the forests of the night,
> What immortal hand or eye
> Could frame thy fearful symmetry?
> [...]
> What the hammer? what the chain?
> In what furnace was thy brain?
> What the anvil? what dread grasp
> Dare its deadly terrors clasp?
> When the stars threw down their spears,
> And watered heaven with their tears,
> Did he smile his work to see?
> Did he who made the Lamb make thee?

These poems have quite a few things in common. Each poem's subject is an animal—a lamb and a tiger, respectively—and each poem addresses the same question to the animal: "Who created you?" In fact, both poems are formed primarily of questions.

However, the poems also exhibit many differences. It's easy, for instance, to contrast the tone and word choice in each poem. Whereas "The Lamb" uses words with positive and gentle connotations to create a tone of innocence and serenity, "The Tyger" gives a completely different impression. Some strongly connotative words that stand out include "night," "fearful," and "deadly terrors," all of which contribute to a tone that's tense and full of danger.

When taken together, then, the two poems address the same question—who created the world and all of its creatures?—from two different perspectives. "The Lamb" considers all of the sweet and delightful things that exist, leaving "The Tyger" to ponder the problem of why evil exists. In fact, Blake relies on the contrast between the two poems to fully communicate his dilemma over the paradox of creation—"Did he who made the Lamb make thee?" Although the poems present a strong contrast to one another, it's also possible to find similarities in their subject matter.

14

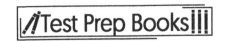

Authors often intentionally use contrast in order to ask readers to delve deeper into the qualities of the two things being compared. When an author deliberately places two things (characters, settings, etc.) side-by-side for readers to compare, it's known as *juxtaposition*. An example of juxtaposition can be found in Emily Bronte's *Wuthering Heights*, a novel in which the protagonist Cathy is caught in a love triangle between two romantic interests, Heathcliff and Edgar Linton, who are complete opposites. Cathy compares her feelings for each man in her memorable speech:

> *My love for Linton is like the foliage in the woods: time will change it, I'm well aware, as winter changes the trees. My love for Heathcliff resembles the eternal rocks beneath: a source of little visible delight, but necessary. Nelly, I* **am** *Heathcliff! He's always, always in my mind: not as a pleasure, any more than I am always a pleasure to myself, but as my own being.*

When these two characters are placed next to each other, it's easier for readers to grasp their notable characteristics. Edgar is gentle and sophisticated in comparison to Heathcliff, who is rough and wild. Here, Cathy also juxtaposes her feelings about each character. Her love for Edgar is fresh and harmless, like the new spring leaves on trees; but come winter, it will fade away. Her love for Heathcliff might be less conventionally appealing, like the rocks that form the earth; but, just like those rocks, that love forms the foundation of Cathy's being and is essential to her life. By juxtaposing these two men, Cathy is better able to express her thoughts about them.

Synthesize Information Across Multiple Sources

In any academic endeavor, it's essential to look to *many* sources of information to get a comprehensive and well-rounded view of the subject matter. Getting information from multiple texts, though, requires readers to synthesize their content—that is, to combine ideas from various sources and express it in an organized way.

In order to synthetize information, readers first need to understand the relationship between the different sources. One way to do so is comparing and contrasting, as described above. Comparison and contrast is also useful in evaluating non-literary sources. For example, if readers want to learn more about a controversial issue, they might decide to read articles from both sides of the argument, compare differences in the arguments on each side, and identify any areas of overlap or agreement. This will allow readers to arrive at a more balanced conclusion.

In addition to synthesizing information from persuasive sources with different opinions, readers can also combine information from different types of texts—for example, from entertaining and informative texts. Readers who are interested in medieval religious life in Europe, for instance, might read a text on medieval history by modern academics; a sociological research article about the role of religion in society; and a piece of literature from the Middle Ages such as Chaucer's *The Canterbury Tales*. By reading fiction written in that time period, readers can look at one writer's perspective on religious activities in their world; and by reading non-fiction texts by modern researchers, readers can further enhance their background knowledge of the subject.

Main Ideas and Supporting Details

Topics and main ideas are critical parts of writing. The **topic** is the subject matter of the piece. An example of a topic would be *the use of cell phones in a classroom*.

15

The **main idea** is what the writer wants to say about that topic. A writer may make the point that the use of cell phones in a classroom is a serious problem that must be addressed in order for students to learn better. Therefore, the topic is cell phone usage in a classroom, and the main idea is that it's *a serious problem needing to be addressed*. The topic can be expressed in a word or two, but the main idea should be a complete thought.

An author will likely identify the topic immediately within the title or the first sentence of the passage. The main idea is usually presented in the introduction. In a single passage, the main idea may be identified in the first or last sentence, but it will most likely be directly stated and easily recognized by the reader. Because it is not always stated immediately in a passage, it's important that readers carefully read the entire passage to identify the main idea.

The main idea should not be confused with the thesis statement. A **thesis statement** is a clear statement of the writer's specific stance and can often be found in the introduction of a nonfiction piece. The thesis is a specific sentence (or two) that offers the direction and focus of the discussion.

In order to illustrate the main idea, a writer will use **supporting details**, which provide evidence or examples to help make a point. Supporting details are typically found in nonfiction pieces that seek to inform or persuade the reader.

In the example of cell phone usage in the classroom, where the author's main idea is to show the seriousness of this problem and the need to "unplug", supporting details would be critical for effectively making that point. Supporting details used here might include statistics on a decline in student focus and studies showing the impact of digital technology usage on students' attention spans. The author could also include testimonies from teachers surveyed on the topic.

It's important that readers evaluate the author's supporting details to be sure that they are credible, provide evidence of the author's point, and directly support the main idea. Although shocking statistics grab readers' attention, their use may provide ineffective information in the piece. Details like this are crucial to understanding the passage and evaluating how well the author presents their argument and evidence.

Also remember that when most authors write, they want to make a point or send a message. This point or message of a text is known as the theme. Authors may state themes explicitly, like in *Aesop's Fables*. More often, especially in modern literature, readers must infer the theme based on text details. Usually after carefully reading and analyzing an entire text, the reader can identify the theme. Typically, the longer the piece, the more themes you will encounter, though often one theme dominates the rest, as evidenced by the author's purposeful revisiting of it throughout the passage.

Author's Intent

No matter the genre or format, all authors are writing to persuade, inform, entertain, or express feelings. Often, these purposes are blended, with one dominating the rest. It's useful to learn to recognize the author's intent.

Persuasive writing is used to persuade or convince readers of something. It often contains two elements: the argument and the counterargument. The argument takes a stance on an issue, while the counterargument pokes holes in the opposition's stance. Authors rely on logic, emotion, and writer credibility to persuade readers to agree with them. If readers are opposed to the stance before reading,

they are unlikely to adopt that stance. However, those who are undecided or committed to the same stance are more likely to agree with the author.

Informative writing tries to teach or inform. Workplace manuals, instructor lessons, statistical reports, and cookbooks are examples of informative texts. Informative writing is usually based on facts and is often void of emotion and persuasion. Informative texts generally contain statistics, charts, and graphs. Though most informative texts lack a persuasive agenda, readers still must examine the text carefully to determine whether one exists within a given passage.

Stories or narratives are designed to entertain. When you go to the movies, you often want to escape for a few hours, not necessarily to think critically. Entertaining writing is designed to delight and engage the reader. However, sometimes this type of writing can be woven into more serious materials, such as persuasive or informative writing to hook the reader before transitioning into a more scholarly discussion.

Emotional writing works to evoke the reader's feelings, such as anger, euphoria, or sadness. The connection between reader and author is an attempt to cause the reader to share the author's intended emotion or tone. Sometimes in order to make a piece more poignant, the author simply wants readers to feel the same emotions that the author has felt. Other times, the author attempts to persuade or manipulate the reader into adopting his stance. While it's okay to sympathize with the author, be aware of the individual's underlying intent.

Identifying Modes of Writing

Distinguishing Between Common Modes of Writing

To distinguish between the common modes of writing, it is important to identify the primary purpose of the work. This can be determined by considering what the author is trying to say to the reader. Although there are countless different styles of writing, all written works tend to fall under four primary categories: argumentative/persuasive, informative expository, descriptive, and narrative.

The table below highlights the purpose, distinct characteristics, and examples of each rhetorical mode.

Writing Mode	Purpose	Distinct Characteristics	Examples
Argumentative	To persuade	Opinions, loaded or subjective language, evidence, suggestions of what the reader should do, calls to action	Critical reviews Political journals Letters of recommendation Cover letters Advertising
Informative	To teach or inform	Objective language, definitions, instructions, factual information	Business and scientific reports Textbooks Instruction manuals News articles Personal letters Wills Informative essays Travel guides Study guides
Descriptive	To deliver sensory details to the reader	Heavy use of adjectives and imagery, language that appeals to any of the five senses	Poetry Journal entries Often used in narrative mode
Narrative	To tell a story, share an experience, entertain	Series of events, plot, characters, dialogue, conflict	Novels Short stories Novellas Anecdotes Biographies Epic poems Autobiographies

Identifying Common Types of Writing

The following steps help to identify examples of common types within the modes of writing:

1. Identifying the audience—to whom or for whom the author is writing
2. Determining the author's purpose—why the author is writing the piece
3. Analyzing the word choices and how they are used

To demonstrate, the following passage has been marked to illustrate *the addressee*, the author's purpose, and <u>word choices</u>:

> *To Whom It May Concern*:
>
> I am <u>extraordinarily excited</u> to be applying to the Master of Environmental Science program at Australian National University. I believe the richness in biological and cultural diversity, as well as Australia's close proximity to the Great Barrier Reef, would provide a <u>deeply fulfilling</u>

educational experience. *I am writing to express why I believe I would be an <u>excellent</u> addition to the program.*

While in college, I participated in a three-month public health internship in Ecuador, where I spent time both learning about medicine in a third world country and also about the Ecuadorian environment, including the Amazon Jungle and the Galápagos Islands. <u>My favorite experience</u> through the internship, besides swimming with sea lions in San Cristóbal, was helping to neutralize parasitic potable water and collect samples for analysis in Puyo.

Though my undergraduate studies related primarily to the human body, I took several courses in natural science, including a year of chemistry, biology, and physics as well as a course in a calculus. <u>I am confident</u> that my fundamental knowledge in these fields will prepare me for the science courses integral to the Masters of Environmental Science.

Having identified the *addressee*, it is evident that this selection is a letter of some kind. Further inspection into the author's purpose, seen in *bold*, shows that the author is trying to explain why he or she should be accepted into the environmental science program, which automatically places it into the argumentative mode as the writer is trying to persuade the reader to agree and to incite the reader into action by encouraging the program to accept the writer as a candidate. In addition to revealing the purpose, the use of emotional language—extraordinarily, excellent, deeply fulfilling, favorite experience, confident—illustrates that this is a persuasive piece. It also provides evidence for why this person would be an excellent addition to the program—their experience in Ecuador and with scientific curriculum.

The following passage presents an opportunity to solidify this method of analysis and practice the steps above to determine the mode of writing:

The biological effects of laughter have long been an interest of medicine and psychology. Laughing is often speculated to reduce blood pressure because it induces feelings of relaxation and elation. Participating students watched a series of videos that elicited laughter, and their blood pressure was taken before and after the viewings. An average decrease in blood pressure was observed, though resulting p-values attest that the results were not significant.

This selection contains factual and scientific information, is devoid of any adjectives or flowery descriptions, and is not trying to convince the reader of any particular stance. Though the audience is not directly addressed, the purpose of the passage is to present the results of an experiment to those who would be interested in the biological effects of laughter—most likely a scientific community. Thus, this passage is an example of informative writing.

Below is another passage to help identify examples of the common writing modes, taken from *The Endeavor Journal of Sir Joseph Banks*:

10th May 1769 – THE ENGLISH CREW GET TAHITIAN NAMES

We have now got the Indian name of the Island, Otahite, so therefore for the future I shall call it. As for our own names the Indians find so much dificulty in pronouncing them that we are forcd to indulge them in calling us what they please, or rather what they say when they attempt to pronounce them. I give here the List: Captn Cooke *Toote*, Dr Solander *Torano*, Mr Hicks *Hete*, Mr Gore *Toárro*, Mr Molineux *Boba* from his Christian name Robert, Mr Monkhouse *Mato*, and myself *Tapáne*. In this manner they have names for almost every man in the ship.

This extract contains no elements of an informative or persuasive intent and does not seem to follow any particular line of narrative. The passage gives a list of the different names that the Indians have given the crew members, as well as the name of an island. Although there is no context for the selection, through the descriptions, it is clear that the author and his comrades are on an island trying to communicate with the native inhabitants. Hence, this passage is a journal that reflects the descriptive mode.

These are only a few of the many examples that can be found in the four primary modes of writing.

Determining the Appropriate Mode of Writing

The author's *primary purpose* is defined as the reason an author chooses to write a selection, and it is often dependent on their *audience*. A biologist writing a textbook, for example, does so to communicate scientific knowledge to an audience of people who want to study biology. An audience can be as broad as the entire global population or as specific as women fighting for equal rights in the bicycle repair industry. Whatever the audience, it is important that the author considers its demographics—age, gender, culture, language, education level, etc.

If the author's purpose is to persuade or inform, he or she will consider how much the intended audience knows about the subject. For example, if an author is writing on the importance of recycling to anyone who will listen, he or she will use the informative mode—including background information on recycling—and the argumentative mode—evidence for why it works, while also using simple diction so that it is easy for everyone to understand. If, on the other hand, the writer is proposing new methods for recycling using solar energy, the audience is probably already familiar with standard recycling processes and will require less background information, as well as more technical language inherent to the scientific community.

If the author's purpose is to entertain through a story or a poem, he or she will need to consider whom he/she is trying to entertain. If an author is writing a script for a children's cartoon, the plot, language, conflict, characters, and humor would align with the interests of the age demographic of that audience. On the other hand, if an author is trying to entertain adults, he or she may write content not suitable for children. The author's purpose and audience are generally interdependent.

Understanding the Task, Purpose, and Audience

Identifying the Task, Purpose, and Intended Audience

An author's *writing style*—the way in which words, grammar, punctuation, and sentence fluidity are used—is the most influential element in a piece of writing, and it is dependent on the purpose and the audience for whom it is intended. Together, a writing style and mode of writing form the foundation of a written work, and a good writer will choose the most effective mode and style to convey a message to readers.

Writers should first determine what they are trying to say and then choose the most effective mode of writing to communicate that message. Different writing modes and *word choices* will affect the tone of a piece—that is, its underlying attitude, emotion, or character. The argumentative mode may utilize words that are earnest, angry, passionate, or excited whereas an informative piece may have a sterile, germane, or enthusiastic tone. The tones found in narratives vary greatly, depending on the purpose of the writing. *Tone* will also be affected by the audience—teaching science to children or those who may be uninterested would be most effective with enthusiastic language and exclamation points whereas

20

teaching science to college students may take on a more serious and professional tone, with fewer charged words and punctuation choices that are inherent to academia.

Sentence fluidity—whether sentences are long and rhythmic or short and succinct—also affects a piece of writing as it determines the way in which a piece is read. Children or audiences unfamiliar with a subject do better with short, succinct sentence structures as these break difficult concepts up into shorter points. A period, question mark, or exclamation point is literally a signal for the reader to stop and takes more time to process. Thus, longer, more complex sentences are more appropriate for adults or educated audiences as they can fit more information in between processing time.

The amount of *supporting detail* provided is also tailored to the audience. A text that introduces a new subject to its readers will focus more on broad ideas without going into greater detail whereas a text that focuses on a more specific subject is likely to provide greater detail about the ideas discussed.

Writing styles, like modes, are most effective when tailored to their audiences. Having awareness of an audience's demographic is one of the most crucial aspects of properly communicating an argument, a story, or a set of information.

Choosing the Most Appropriate Type of Writing

Before beginning any writing, it is imperative that a writer have a firm grasp on the message he or she wishes to convey and how he or she wants readers to be affected by the writing. For example, does the author want readers to be more informed about the subject? Does the writer want readers to agree with their opinion? Does the writer want readers to get caught up in an exciting narrative? The following steps are a guide to determining the appropriate type of writing for a task, purpose, and audience:

1. Identifying the purpose for writing the piece
2. Determining the audience
3. Adapting the writing mode, word choices, tone, and style to fit the audience and the purpose

It is important to distinguish between a work's purpose and its main idea. The essential difference between the two is that the *main idea* is what the author wants to communicate about the topic at hand whereas the *primary purpose* is why the author is writing in the first place. The primary purpose is what will determine the type of writing an author will choose to utilize, not the main idea, though the two are related. For example, if an author writes an article on the mistreatment of animals in factory farms and, at the end, suggests that people should convert to vegetarianism, the main idea is that vegetarianism would reduce the poor treatment of animals. The primary purpose is to convince the reader to stop eating animals. Since the primary purpose is to galvanize an audience into action, the author would choose the argumentative writing mode.

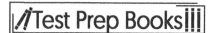
The next step is to consider to whom the author is appealing as this will determine the type of details to be included, the diction to be used, the tone to be employed, and the sentence structure to be used. An audience can be identified by considering the following questions:

- What is the purpose for writing the piece?
- To whom is it being written?
- What is their age range?
- Are they familiar with the material being presented, or are they just being newly introduced to it?
- Where are they from?
- Is the task at hand in a professional or casual setting?
- Is the task at hand for monetary gain?

These are just a few of the numerous considerations to keep in mind, but the main idea is to become as familiar with the audience as possible. Once the audience has been understood, the author can then adapt the writing style to align with the readers' education and interests. The audience is what determines the *rhetorical appeal* the author will use—ethos, pathos, or logos. *Ethos* is a rhetorical appeal to an audience's ethics and/or morals. Ethos is most often used in argumentative and informative writing modes. *Pathos* is an appeal to the audience's emotions and sympathies, and it is found in argumentative, descriptive, and narrative writing modes. *Logos* is an appeal to the audience's logic and reason and is used primarily in informative texts as well as in supporting details for argumentative pieces. Rhetorical appeals are discussed in depth in the informational texts and rhetoric section of the test.

If the author is trying to encourage global conversion to vegetarianism, he or she may choose to use all three rhetorical appeals to reach varying personality types. Those who are less interested in the welfare of animals but are interested in facts and science would relate more to logos. Animal lovers would relate better to an emotional appeal. In general, the most effective works utilize all three appeals.

Finally, after determining the writing mode and rhetorical appeal, the author will consider word choice, sentence structure, and tone, depending on the purpose and audience. The author may choose words that convey sadness or anger when speaking about animal welfare if writing to persuade, or he or she will stick to dispassionate and matter-of-fact tones, if informing the public on the treatment of animals in factory farms. If the author is writing to a younger or less-educated audience, he or she may choose to shorten and simplify sentence structures and word choice. If appealing to an audience with more expert knowledge on a particular subject, writers will more likely employ a style of longer sentences and more complex vocabulary.

Depending on the task, the author may choose to use a first person, second person, or third person point of view. First person and second person perspectives are inherently more casual in tone, including the author and the reader in the rhetoric, while third person perspectives are often seen in more professional settings.

Evaluating the Effectiveness of a Piece of Writing

An effective and engaging piece of writing will cause the reader to forget about the author entirely. Readers will become so engrossed in the subject, argument, or story at hand that they will almost identify with it, readily adopting beliefs proposed by the author or accepting all elements of the story as believable. On the contrary, poorly written works will cause the reader to be hyperaware of the author,

doubting the writer's knowledge of a subject or questioning the validity of a narrative. Persuasive or expository works that are poorly researched will have this effect, as well as poorly planned stories with significant plot holes. An author must consider the task, purpose, and audience to sculpt a piece of writing effectively.

When evaluating the effectiveness of a piece, the most important thing to consider is how well the purpose is conveyed to the audience through the mode, use of rhetoric, and writing style.

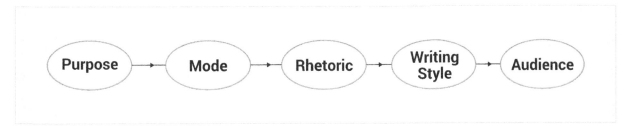

The purpose must pass through these three aspects for effective delivery to the audience. If any elements are not properly considered, the reader will be overly aware of the author, and the message will be lost. The following is a checklist for evaluating the effectiveness of a piece:

- Does the writer choose the appropriate writing mode—argumentative, narrative, descriptive, informative—for their purpose?

- Does the writing mode employed contain characteristics inherent to that mode?

- Does the writer consider the personalities/interests/demographics of the intended audience when choosing rhetorical appeals?

- Does the writer use appropriate vocabulary, sentence structure, voice, and tone for the audience demographic?

- Does the author properly establish himself/herself as having authority on the subject, if applicable?

- Does the piece make sense?

Another thing to consider is the medium in which the piece was written. If the medium is a blog, diary, or personal letter, the author may adopt a more casual stance towards the audience. If the piece of writing is a story in a book, a business letter or report, or a published article in a journal or if the task is to gain money or support or to get published, the author may adopt a more formal stance. Ultimately, the writer will want to be very careful in how he or she addresses the reader.

Finally, the effectiveness of a piece can be evaluated by asking how well the purpose was achieved. For example, if students are assigned to read a persuasive essay, instructors can ask whether the author influences students' opinions. Students may be assigned two differing persuasive texts with opposing perspectives and be asked which writer was more convincing. Students can then evaluate what factors contributed to this—for example, whether one author uses more credible supporting facts, appeals more effectively to readers' emotions, presents more believable personal anecdotes, or offers stronger counterargument refutation. Students can then use these evaluations to strengthen their own writing skills.

Inferences in a Text

Readers should be able to make *inferences*. Making an inference requires the reader to read between the lines and look for what is implied rather than what is explicitly stated. That is, using information that is known from the text, the reader is able to make a logical assumption about information that is not explicitly stated but is probably true. Read the following passage:

"Hey, do you wanna meet my new puppy?" Jonathan asked.

"Oh, I'm sorry but please don't—" Jacinta began to protest, but before she could finish, Jonathan had already opened the passenger side door of his car and a perfect white ball of fur came bouncing towards Jacinta.

"Isn't he the cutest?" beamed Jonathan.

"Yes—achoo!—he's pretty—aaaachooo!!—adora—aaa—aaaachoo!" Jacinta managed to say in between sneezes. "But if you don't mind, I—I—achoo!—need to go inside."

Which of the following can be inferred from Jacinta's reaction to the puppy?
  a. She hates animals.
  b. She is allergic to dogs.
  c. She prefers cats to dogs.
  d. She is angry at Jonathan.

An inference requires the reader to consider the information presented and then form their own idea about what is probably true. Based on the details in the passage, what is the best answer to the question? Important details to pay attention to include the tone of Jacinta's dialogue, which is overall polite and apologetic, as well as her reaction itself, which is a long string of sneezes. Answer choices (a) and (d) both express strong emotions ("hates" and "angry") that are not evident in Jacinta's speech or actions. Answer choice (c) mentions cats, but there is nothing in the passage to indicate Jacinta's feelings about cats. Answer choice (b), "she is allergic to dogs," is the most logical choice. Based on the fact that she began sneezing as soon as a fluffy dog approached her, it makes sense to guess that Jacinta might be allergic to dogs. Using the clues in the passage, it is reasonable to guess that this is true even though Jacinta never directly states, "Sorry, I'm allergic to dogs!"

Making inferences is crucial for readers of literature because literary texts often avoid presenting complete and direct information to readers about characters' thoughts or feelings, or they present this information in an unclear way, leaving it up to the reader to interpret clues given in the text. In order to make inferences while reading, readers should ask themselves:

- What details are being presented in the text?
- Is there any important information that seems to be missing?
- Based on the information that the author *does* include, what else is probably true?
- Is this inference reasonable based on what is already known?

Apply Information

A natural extension of being able to make an inference from a given set of information is also being able to apply that information to a new context. This is especially useful in non-fiction or informative writing. Considering the facts and details presented in the text, readers should consider how the same

24

information might be relevant in a different situation. The following is an example of applying an inferential conclusion to a different context:

> Often, individuals behave differently in large groups than they do as individuals. One example of this is the psychological phenomenon known as the bystander effect. According to the bystander effect, the more people who witness an accident or crime occur, the less likely each individual bystander is to respond or offer assistance to the victim. A classic example of this is the murder of Kitty Genovese in New York City in the 1960s. Although there were over thirty witnesses to her killing by a stabber, none of them intervened to help Kitty or contact the police.

Considering the phenomenon of the bystander effect, what would probably happen if somebody tripped on the stairs in a crowded subway station?
 a. Everybody would stop to help the person who tripped
 b. Bystanders would point and laugh at the person who tripped
 c. Someone would call the police after walking away from the station
 d. Few if any bystanders would offer assistance to the person who tripped

This question asks readers to apply the information they learned from the passage, which is an informative paragraph about the bystander effect. According to the passage, this is a concept in psychology that describes the way people in groups respond to an accident—the more people are present, the less likely any one person is to intervene. While the passage illustrates this effect with the example of a woman's murder, the question asks readers to apply it to a different context—in this case, someone falling down the stairs in front of many subway passengers. Although this specific situation is not discussed in the passage, readers should be able to apply the general concepts described in the paragraph. The definition of the bystander effect includes any instance of an accident or crime in front of a large group of people. The question asks about a situation that falls within the same definition, so the general concept should still hold true: in the midst of a large crowd, few individuals are likely to actually respond to an accident. In this case, answer choice (d) is the best response.

Identifying the Position and Purpose

Readers should always identify the author's position or stance in a text. No matter how objective a piece may seem, assume the author has preconceived beliefs. Reduce the likelihood of accepting an invalid argument by looking for multiple articles on the topic, including those with varying opinions. If several opinions point in the same direction, and are backed by reputable peer-reviewed sources, it's more likely the author has a valid argument. Positions that run contrary to widely held beliefs and existing data should invite scrutiny. There are exceptions to the rule, so be a careful consumer of information.

Though themes, symbols, and motifs are buried deep within the text and can sometimes be difficult to infer, an author's purpose is usually obvious from the beginning. There are four purposes of writing: to inform, to persuade, to describe, and to entertain. Informative writings present facts in an accessible way. Persuasive writing appeals to emotions and logic to inspire the reader to adopt a specific stance. Be wary of this type of writing, as it often lacks objectivity. Descriptive writing is designed to paint a picture in the reader's mind, while texts that entertain are often narratives designed to engage and delight the reader.

The various writing styles are usually blended, with one purpose dominating the rest. For example, a persuasive piece might begin with a humorous tale to make readers more receptive to the persuasive message, or a recipe in a cookbook designed to inform might be preceded by an entertaining anecdote that makes the recipe more appealing.

Writing Devices

Authors use a variety of writing devices throughout texts. Below is a list of some writing devices authors use in their writing.

- Comparison and Contrast
- Cause and Effect
- Analogy
- Point of View
- Transitional Words and Phrases

Let's look at each device individually.

Comparison and Contrast

One writing device authors use is comparison and contrast. Comparison is when authors take objects and show how they are the same. Contrast is when authors take objects and show how they differ. Comparison and contrast essays are mostly written in nonfiction form. There are common words used when authors compare or contrast. The list below will show you some of these words:

Comparison Words:

- Similar to
- Alike
- As well as
- Both

Contrast Words:

- Although
- On the other hand
- Different from
- However
- As opposed to
- More than
- Less than
- On the contrary

Cause and Effect

Cause and effect is a common writing device. A cause is why something happens. An effect is something that happens because of the cause. Many times, authors use key words to show cause and effect, such as *because, so, therefore, without, now, then,* and *since.* For example: "Because of the sun shower, a rainbow appeared." In this sentence, due to the sun shower (the cause), a rainbow appeared (the effect).

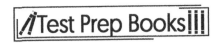

Analogy

An analogy is a comparison between two things. Sometimes the two things are very different from one another. Authors often use analogies to add meaning and make ideas relatable in texts. There are two types of analogies: metaphors and similes. Metaphors compare two things that are not similar. Similes also compare two unlike things but use the words *like* or *as*. For example, "In the library, students are asked to be as quiet as a mouse." Clearly, students and mice are very different. However, when students are asked to be as quiet as a mouse, readers understand that they are being asked to be absolutely silent.

Point of View

Point of view is the viewpoint in which authors tell stories. Authors usually tell stories in either the first or third person. If an author writes in the first person, they are a character within a story telling about their own experiences. The pronouns *I* and *we* are used when writing in the first person. If an author writes in the third person, the narrator is telling the story from an outside perspective. The author is not a character in the story, but rather tells about the characters' actions and dialogues. Pronouns such as *he, she, it,* and *they* are used in texts written in the third person. Point of view will be addressed in more detail in a subsequent section.

Transitional Words and Phrases

There are approximately 200 transitional words and phrases that are commonly used in the English language. Below are lists of common transition words and phrases.

Time	Example	Compare	Contrast	Addition	Logical Relationships	Steps
After	for example	likewise	however	and	if	first
before	in fact	also	yet	also	then	second
during	for instance		but	furthermore	therefore	last
in the middle				moreover	as a result	
					since	

Transitional words and phrases are important writing devices. They connect sentences and paragraphs. Transitional words and phrases help writing to make more sense. They provide clearer meaning to readers.

Understanding the Effect of Word Choice

An author's choice of words—also referred to as *diction*—helps to convey their meaning in a particular way. Through diction, an author can convey a particular tone—e.g., a humorous tone, a serious tone—in order to support the thesis in a meaningful way to the reader.

Connotation and Denotation

Connotation is when an author chooses words or phrases that invoke ideas or feelings other than their literal meaning. An example of the use of connotation is the word *cheap*, which suggests something is poor in value or negatively describes a person as reluctant to spend money. When something or someone is described this way, the reader is more inclined to have a particular image or feeling about it or him/her. Thus, connotation can be a very effective language tool in creating emotion and swaying opinion. However, connotations are sometimes hard to pin down because varying emotions can be

27

associated with a word. Generally, though, connotative meanings tend to be fairly consistent within a specific cultural group.

Denotation refers to An author's use of words or phrases to mean exactly what they say. It is helpful when a writer wants to present hard facts or vocabulary terms with which readers may be unfamiliar. Some examples of denotation are the words *inexpensive* and *frugal*. *Inexpensive* refers to the cost of something, not its value, and *frugal* indicates that a person is conscientiously watching their spending. These terms do not elicit the same emotions that *cheap* does. Authors sometimes choose to use both, but what they choose and when they use it is what critical readers need to differentiate. One method isn't inherently better than the other; however, one may create a better effect, depending upon an author's intent. If, for example, an author's purpose is to inform, to instruct, and to familiarize readers with a difficult subject, their use of connotation may be helpful. However, it may also undermine credibility and confuse readers. An author who wants to create a credible, scholarly effect in their text would most likely use denotation, which emphasizes literal, factual meaning and examples.

Technical Language

Test takers and critical readers alike should be very aware of technical language used within informational text. *Technical language* refers to terminology that is specific to a particular industry and is best understood by those specializing in that industry. This language is fairly easy to differentiate, since it will most likely be unfamiliar to readers. It's critical to be able to define technical language either by the author's written definition, through the use of an included glossary—if offered—or through context clues that help readers clarify word meaning.

Identifying Rhetorical Strategies

Rhetoric refers to an author's use of particular strategies, appeals, and devices to persuade an intended audience. The more effective the use of rhetoric, the more likely the audience will be persuaded.

Determining an Author's Point of View

A *rhetorical strategy*—also referred to as a *rhetorical mode*—is the structural way an author chooses to present their argument. Though the terms noted below are similar to the organizational structures noted earlier, these strategies do not imply that the entire text follows the approach. For example, a cause and effect organizational structure is solely that, nothing more. A persuasive text may use cause and effect as a strategy to convey a singular point. Thus, an argument may include several of the strategies as the author strives to convince their audience to take action or accept a different point of view. It's important that readers are able to identify an author's thesis and position on the topic in order to be able to identify the careful construction through which the author speaks to the reader. The following are some of the more common rhetorical strategies:

- *Cause and effect*—establishing a logical correlation or causation between two ideas

- *Classification/division*—the grouping of similar items together or division of something into parts

- *Comparison/contrast*—the distinguishing of similarities/differences to expand on an idea

- *Definition*—used to clarify abstract ideas, unfamiliar concepts, or to distinguish one idea from another

28

- *Description*—use of vivid imagery, active verbs, and clear adjectives to explain ideas

- *Exemplification*—the use of examples to explain an idea

- *Narration*—anecdotes or personal experience to present or expand on a concept

- *Problem/Solution*—presentation of a problem or problems, followed by proposed solution(s)

Rhetorical Strategies and Devices

A *rhetorical device* is the phrasing and presentation of an idea that reinforces and emphasizes a point in an argument. A rhetorical device is often quite memorable. One of the more famous uses of a rhetorical device is in John F. Kennedy's 1961 inaugural address: "Ask not what your country can do for you, ask what you can do for your country." The contrast of ideas presented in the phrasing is an example of the rhetorical device of antimetabole. Some other common examples are provided below, but test takers should be aware that this is not a complete list.

Device	Definition	Example
Allusion	A reference to a famous person, event, or significant literary text as a form of significant comparison	"We are apt to shut our eyes against a painful truth, and listen to the song of that siren till she transforms us into beasts." Patrick Henry
Anaphora	The repetition of the same words at the beginning of successive words, phrases, or clauses, designed to emphasize an idea	"We shall not flag or fail. We shall go on to the end. We shall fight in France, we shall fight on the seas and oceans, we shall fight with growing confidence ... we shall fight in the fields and in the streets, we shall fight in the hills. We shall never surrender." Winston Churchill
Understatement	A statement meant to portray a situation as less important than it actually is to create an ironic effect	"The war in the Pacific has not necessarily developed in Japan's favor." Emperor Hirohito, surrendering Japan in World War II
Parallelism	A syntactical similarity in a structure or series of structures used for impact of an idea, making it memorable	"A penny saved is a penny earned." Ben Franklin

Device	Definition	Example
Rhetorical question	A question posed that is not answered by the writer though there is a desired response, most often designed to emphasize a point	"Can anyone look at our reduced standing in the world today and say, 'Let's have four more years of this?'" Ronald Reagan

Understanding Methods Used to Appeal to a Specific Audience

Rhetorical Appeals

In an argument or persuasive text, an author will strive to sway readers to an opinion or conclusion. To be effective, an author must consider their intended audience. Although an author may write text for a general audience, he or she will use methods of appeal or persuasion to convince that audience. Aristotle asserted that there were three methods or modes by which a person could be persuaded. These are referred to as *rhetorical appeals*.

The three main types of rhetorical appeals are shown in the following graphic.

Ethos, also referred to as an *ethical appeal*, is an appeal to the audience's perception of the writer as credible (or not), based on their examination of their ethics and who the writer is, their experience or incorporation of relevant information, or their argument. For example, authors may present testimonials to bolster their arguments. The reader who critically examines the veracity of the testimonials and the credibility of those giving the testimony will be able to determine if the author's use of testimony is valid to their argument. In turn, this will help the reader determine if the author's thesis is valid. An author's careful and appropriate use of technical language can create an overall knowledgeable effect and, in turn, act as a convincing vehicle when it comes to credibility. Overuse of technical language, however, may create confusion in readers and obscure an author's overall intent.

Pathos, also referred to as a *pathetic* or *emotional appeal*, is an appeal to the audience's sense of identity, self-interest, or emotions. A critical reader will notice when the author is appealing to pathos through anecdotes and descriptions that elicit an emotion such as anger or pity. Readers should also beware of factual information that uses generalization to appeal to the emotions. While it's tempting to believe an author is the source of truth in their text, an author who presents factual information as universally true, consistent throughout time, and common to all groups is using *generalization*. Authors who exclusively use generalizations without specific facts and credible sourcing are attempting to sway readers solely through emotion.

Logos, also referred to as a *logical appeal*, is an appeal to the audience's ability to see and understand the logic in a claim offered by the writer. A critical reader has to be able to evaluate an author's arguments for validity of reasoning and for sufficiency when it comes to argument.

Counterarguments and Evaluating Arguments

If an author presents a differing opinion or a counterargument in order to refute it, the reader should consider how and why the information is being presented. It is meant to strengthen the original argument and shouldn't be confused with the author's intended conclusion, but it should also be considered in the reader's final evaluation.

Authors can also use bias if they ignore the opposing viewpoint or present their side in an unbalanced way. A strong argument considers the opposition and finds a way to refute it. Critical readers should look for an unfair or one-sided presentation of the argument and be skeptical, as a bias may be present. Even if this bias is unintentional, if it exists in the writing, the reader should be wary of the validity of the argument. Readers should also look for the use of stereotypes, which refer to specific groups. Stereotypes are often negative connotations about a person or place, and should always be avoided. When a critical reader finds stereotypes in a piece of writing, they should be critical of the argument, and consider the validity of anything the author presents. Stereotypes reveal a flaw in the writer's thinking and may suggest a lack of knowledge or understanding about the subject.

In general, readers should always heed attention to whether an author's ideas or stated facts are relevant to the argument or counterargument posed in the reading. Those that are irrelevant can cloud the argument or weaken it. In much the same way, critical readers are able to identify whether statements in a reading strengthen or weaken the author's argument.

Authors want you to accept their assertions and arguments as true but critical readers evaluate the strength of the argument instead of simply taking it at face value and accepting it as the truth or only point of view. All arguments need two parts: the claim and the supporting evidence or rationale. The claim *is* the argument. It asserts an opinion, idea, point of view, or conclusion. The supporting evidence is the rationale, assumptions, beliefs, as well as the factual evidence in support of the stated claim. The supporting evidence is what gives readers the information necessary to accept or reject the stated claim. Critical readers should assess the argument in its entirety by evaluating the claims and conclusions themselves, the process of reasoning, and the accuracy of the evidence. For example, arguments are weaker and should be skeptically considered when the supporting evidence is highly opinionated, biased, or derived from sources that are not credible. Authors should cite where statistics and other stated facts were found. Lastly, the support for a claim should be pertinent to it and consistent with the other statements and evidence.

31

Opinions, Facts, and Fallacies

As mentioned previously, authors write with a purpose. They adjust their writing for an intended audience. It is the readers' responsibility to comprehend the writing style or purpose of the author. When readers understand a writer's purpose, they can then form their own thoughts about the text(s) regardless of whether their thoughts are the same as or different from the author's. The following section will examine different writing tactics that authors use, such as facts versus opinions, bias and stereotypes, appealing to the readers' emotions, and fallacies (including false analogies, circular reasoning, false dichotomy, and overgeneralization).

Facts Versus Opinions

Readers need to be aware of the writer's purpose to help discern facts and opinions within texts. A *fact* is a piece of information that is true. It can either prove or disprove claims or arguments presented in texts. Facts cannot be changed or altered. For example, the statement: *Abraham Lincoln was assassinated on April 15, 1865*, is a fact. The date and related events cannot be altered.

Authors not only present facts in their writing to support or disprove their claim(s), but they may also express their opinions. Authors may use facts to support their own opinions, especially in a persuasive text; however, that does not make their opinions facts. An *opinion* is a belief or view formed about something that is not necessarily based on the truth. Opinions often express authors' personal feelings about a subject and use words like *believe, think,* or *feel.* For example, the statement: *Abraham Lincoln was the best president who has ever lived*, expresses the writer's opinion. Not all writers or readers agree or disagree with the statement. Therefore, the statement can be altered or adjusted to express opposing or supporting beliefs, such as "Abraham Lincoln was the worst president who has ever lived" or "I also think Abraham Lincoln was a great president."

When authors include facts and opinions in their writing, readers may be less influenced by the text(s). Readers need to be conscious of the distinction between facts and opinions while going through texts. Not only should the intended audience be vigilant in following authors' thoughts versus valid information, readers need to check the source of the facts presented. Facts should have reliable sources derived from credible outlets like almanacs, encyclopedias, medical journals, and so on.

Bias and Stereotypes

Not only can authors state facts or opinions in their writing, they sometimes intentionally or unintentionally show bias or portray a stereotype. A *bias* is when someone demonstrates a prejudice in favor of or against something or someone in an unfair manner. When an author is biased in their writing, readers should be skeptical despite the fact that the author's bias may be correct. For example, two athletes competed for the same position. One athlete is related to the coach and is a mediocre athlete, while the other player excels and deserves the position. The coach chose the less talented player who is related to him for the position. This is a biased decision because it favors someone in an unfair way.

Similar to a bias, a *stereotype* shows favoritism or opposition but toward a specific group or place. Stereotypes create an oversimplified or overgeneralized idea about a certain group, person, or place. For example,

Women are horrible drivers.

This statement basically labels *all* women as horrible drivers. While there may be some terrible female drivers, the stereotype implies that *all* women are bad drivers when, in fact, not *all* women are. While many readers are aware of several vile ethnic, religious, and cultural stereotypes, audiences should be cautious of authors' flawed assumptions because they can be less obvious than the despicable examples that are unfortunately pervasive in society.

Appealing to the Readers' Emotions

Authors write to captivate the attention of their readers. Oftentimes, authors will appeal to their readers' emotions to convince or persuade their audience, especially in when trying to win weak arguments that lack factual evidence. Authors may tell sob stories or use bandwagon approaches in their writing to tap into the readers' emotions. For example, "Everyone is voting yes" or "He only has two months to live" are statements that can tug at the heartstrings of readers. Authors may use other tactics, such as name-calling or advertising, to lead their readers into believing something is true or false. These emotional pleas are clear signs that the authors do not have a favorable point and that they are trying to distract the readers from the fact that their argument is factually weak.

Fallacies

A fallacy is a mistaken belief or faulty reasoning, otherwise known as a *logical fallacy.* It is important for readers to recognize logical fallacies because they discredit the author's message. Readers should continuously self-question as they go through a text to identify logical fallacies. Readers cannot simply complacently take information at face value. There are six common types of logical *fallacies:*

1. False analogy
2. Circular reasoning
3. False dichotomy
4. Overgeneralization
5. Slippery slope
6. Hasty generalization

Each of the six logical fallacies are reviewed individually.

False Analogy

A *false analogy* is when the author assumes two objects or events are alike in all aspects despite the fact that they may be vastly different. Authors intend on making unfamiliar objects relatable to convince readers of something. For example, the letters *A* and *E* are both vowels; therefore, *A* = *E*. Readers cannot assume that because *A* and *E* are both vowels that they perform the same function in words or independently. If authors tell readers, *A* = *E*, then that is a false analogy. While this is a simple example, other false analogies may be less obvious.

Circular reasoning

Circular reasoning is when the reasoning is decided based upon the outcome or conclusion and then vice versa. Basically, those who use circular reasoning start out with the argument and then use false logic to try to prove it, and then, in turn, the reasoning supports the conclusion in one big circular pattern. For example, consider the two thoughts, "I don't have time to get organized" and "My disorganization is costing me time." Which is the argument? What is the conclusion? If there is not time to get organized, will more time be spent later trying to find whatever is needed? In turn, if so much

time is spent looking for things, there is not time to get organized. The cycle keeps going in an endless series. One problem affects the other; therefore, there is a circular pattern of reasoning.

False dichotomy

A *false dichotomy,* also known as a false dilemma, is when the author tries to make readers believe that there are only two options to choose from when, in fact, there are more. The author creates a false sense of the situation because he or she wants the readers to believe that their claim is the most logical choice. If the author does not present the readers with options, then the author is purposefully limiting what readers may believe. In turn, the author hopes that readers will believe that their point of view is the most sensible choice. For example, in the statement: *you either love running, or you are lazy*, the fallacy lies in the options of loving to run or being lazy. Even though both statements do not necessarily have to be true, the author tries to make one option seem more appealing than the other.

Overgeneralization

An *overgeneralization* is a logical fallacy that occurs when authors write something so extreme that it cannot be proved or disproved. Words like *all, never, most,* and *few* are commonly used when an overgeneralization is being made. For example,

> All kids are crazy when they eat sugar; therefore, my son will not have a cupcake at the birthday party.

Not *all* kids are crazy when they eat sugar, but the extreme statement can influence the readers' points of view on the subject. Readers need to be wary of overgeneralizations in texts because authors may try to sneak them in to sway the readers' opinions.

Slippery slope

A *slippery slope* is when an author implies that something will inevitably happen as a result of another action. A slippery slope may or may not be true, even though the order of events or gradations may seem logical. For example, in the children's book *If You Give a Mouse a Cookie*, the author goes off on tangents such as "If you give a mouse a cookie, he will ask for some milk. When you give him the milk, he'll probably ask you for a straw." The mouse in the story follows a series of logical events as a result of a previous action. The slippery slope continues on and on throughout the story. Even though the mouse made logical decisions, it very well could have made a different choice, changing the direction of the story.

Hasty generalization

A *hasty generalization* is when the reader comes to a conclusion without reviewing or analyzing all the evidence. It is never a good idea to make a decision without all the information, which is why hasty generalizations are considered fallacies. For example, if two friends go to a hairdresser and give the hairdresser a positive recommendation, that does not necessarily mean that a new client will have the same experience. Two referrals is not quite enough information to form an educated and well-formed conclusion.

Overall, readers should carefully review and analyze authors' arguments to identify logical fallacies and come to sensible conclusions.

Drawing Conclusions

When drawing conclusions about texts or passages, readers should do two main things: 1) Use the information that they already know and 2) Use the information they have learned from the text or passage. Authors write with an intended purpose, and it is the readers' responsibility to understand and form logical conclusions of authors' ideas. It is important to remember that the readers' conclusions should be supported by information directly from the text. Readers cannot simply form conclusions based off of only information they already know.

There are several ways readers can draw conclusions from authors' ideas and points to consider when doing so, such as text evidence, text credibility, and directly stated information versus implications.

Text Evidence

Text evidence is the information readers find in a text or passage that supports the main idea or point(s) in a story. In turn, text evidence can help readers draw conclusions about the text or passage. The information should be taken directly from the text or passage and placed in quotation marks. Text evidence provides readers with information to support ideas about the text or passage so that they simply do not just rely on their own thoughts. Details should be precise, descriptive, and factual. Statistics are a great piece of text evidence because it provides readers with exact numbers and not just a generalization. For example, instead of saying "Asia has a larger population than Europe," authors could provide detailed information such as "In Asia there are over 7 billion people, whereas in Europe there are a little over 750 million." More definitive information provides better evidence to readers to help support their conclusions about texts or passages.

Text Credibility

Credible sources are important when drawing conclusions because readers need to be able to trust what they are reading. Authors should always use credible sources to help gain the trust of their readers. A text is *credible* when it is believable and the author is objective and unbiased. If readers do not trust authors' words, they may simply dismiss the text completely. For example, if an author writes a persuasive essay, he or she is outwardly trying to sway readers' opinions to align with their own, providing readers with the liberty to do what they please with the text. Readers may agree or disagree with the author, which may, in turn, lead them to believe that the author is credible or not credible. Also, readers should keep in mind the source of the text. If readers review a journal about astronomy, would a more reliable source be a NASA employee or a plumber? Overall, text credibility is important when drawing conclusions because readers want reliable sources that support the decisions they have made about the author's ideas.

Directly Stated Information Versus Implications

Engaged readers should constantly self-question while reviewing texts to help them form conclusions. Self-questioning is when readers review a paragraph, page, passage, or chapter and ask themselves, "Did I understand what I read?," "What was the main event in this section?," "Where is this taking place?," and so on. Authors can provide clues or pieces of evidence throughout a text or passage to guide readers toward a conclusion. This is why active and engaged readers should read the text or passage in its entirety before forming a definitive conclusion. If readers do not gather all the necessary pieces of evidence, then they may jump to an illogical conclusion.

At times, authors directly state conclusions while others simply imply them. Of course, it is easier if authors outwardly provide conclusions to readers because this does not leave any information open to

interpretation. However, implications are things that authors do not directly state but can be assumed based off of information they provided. If authors only imply what may have happened, readers can form a menagerie of ideas for conclusions. For example, in the statement: *Once we heard the sirens, we hunkered down in the storm shelter*, the author does not directly state that there was a tornado, but clues such as "sirens" and "storm shelter" provide insight to the readers to help form that conclusion.

Style, Tone, and Mood

Style, tone, and mood are often thought to be the same thing. Though they're closely related, there are important differences to keep in mind. The easiest way to do this is to remember that style "creates and affects" tone and mood. More specifically, style is how the writer uses words to create the desired tone and mood for their writing.

Style

Style can include any number of technical writing choices. A few examples of style choices include:

- Sentence Construction: When presenting facts, does the writer use shorter sentences to create a quicker sense of the supporting evidence, or do they use longer sentences to elaborate and explain the information?

- Technical Language: Does the writer use jargon to demonstrate their expertise in the subject, or do they use ordinary language to help the reader understand things in simple terms?

- Formal Language: Does the writer refrain from using contractions such as *won't* or *can't* to create a more formal tone, or do they use a colloquial, conversational style to connect to the reader?

- Formatting: Does the writer use a series of shorter paragraphs to help the reader follow a line of argument, or do they use longer paragraphs to examine an issue in great detail and demonstrate their knowledge of the topic?

On the test, examine the writer's style and how their writing choices affect the way the text comes across.

Tone

Tone refers to the writer's attitude toward the subject matter. Tone conveys how the writer feels about characters, situations, events, ideas, etc. Nonfiction writing is sometimes thought to have no tone at all; however, this is incorrect.

A lot of nonfiction writing has a neutral tone, which is an important tone for the writer to take. A neutral tone demonstrates that the writer is presenting a topic impartially and letting the information speak for itself. On the other hand, nonfiction writing can be just as effective and appropriate if the tone isn't neutral. For instance, take this example involving seat belts:

Seat belts save more lives than any other automobile safety feature. Many studies show that airbags save lives as well; however, not all cars have airbags. For instance, some older cars don't. Furthermore, air bags aren't entirely reliable. For example, studies show that in 15% of accidents airbags don't deploy as designed, but, on the other hand, seat belt malfunctions are

36

extremely rare. The number of highway fatalities has plummeted since laws requiring seat belt usage were enacted.

In this passage, the writer mostly chooses to retain a neutral tone when presenting information. If the writer would instead include their own personal experience of losing a friend or family member in a car accident, the tone would change dramatically. The tone would no longer be neutral and would show that the writer has a personal stake in the content, allowing them to interpret the information in a different way. When analyzing tone, consider what the writer is trying to achieve in the text and how they *create* the tone using style.

Mood

Mood refers to the feelings and atmosphere that the writer's words create for the reader. Like tone, many nonfiction texts can have a neutral mood. To return to the previous example, if the writer would choose to include information about a person they know being killed in a car accident, the text would suddenly carry an emotional component that is absent in the previous example. Depending on how they present the information, the writer can create a sad, angry, or even hopeful mood. When analyzing the mood, consider what the writer wants to accomplish and whether the best choice was made to achieve that end.

Point of View

As mentioned, point of view is an important writing device to consider. In fiction writing, point of view refers to who tells the story or from whose perspective readers are observing the story. In non-fiction writing, the *point of view* refers to whether the author refers to himself/herself, their readers, or chooses not to mention either. Whether fiction or nonfiction, the author will carefully consider the impact the perspective will have on the purpose and main point of the writing.

- *First-person point of view*: The story is told from the writer's perspective. In fiction, this would mean that the main character is also the narrator. First-person point of view is easily recognized by the use of personal pronouns such as *I, me, we, us, our, my,* and *myself.*

- *Third-person point of view*: In a more formal essay, this would be an appropriate perspective because the focus should be on the subject matter, not the writer or the reader. Third-person point of view is recognized by the use of the pronouns *he, she, they,* and *it.* In fiction writing, third-person point of view has a few variations.

- *Third-person limited* point of view refers to a story told by a narrator who has access to the thoughts and feelings of just one character.

- In *third-person omniscient* point of view, the narrator has access to the thoughts and feelings of all the characters.

- In *third-person objective* point of view, the narrator is like a fly on the wall and can see and hear what the characters do and say, but does not have access to their thoughts and feelings.

- *Second-person point of view*: This point of view isn't commonly used in fiction or nonfiction writing because it directly addresses the reader using the pronouns *you, your,* and *yourself.*

Second-person perspective is more appropriate in direct communication, such as business letters or emails.

Point of View	Pronouns Used
First person	I, me, we, us, our, my, myself
Second person	You, your, yourself
Third person	He, she, it, they

Consistency

Whatever style, tone, point of view, and mood the writer uses, good writing should remain consistent throughout. If the writer chooses to include the tragic, personal experience above, it would affect the style, tone, and mood of the entire text. It would seem out of place for such an example to be used in the middle of a neutral, measured, and analytical text. To adjust the rest of the text, the writer needs to make additional choices to remain consistent. For example, the writer might decide to use the word *tragedy* in place of the more neutral *fatality*, or they could describe a series of car-related deaths as an *epidemic*. Adverbs and adjectives such as *devastating* or *horribly* could be included to maintain this consistent attitude toward the content. When analyzing writing, look for sudden shifts in style, tone, and mood, and consider whether the writer would be wiser to maintain the prevailing strategy.

Comprehension and Context

Topic Versus the Main Idea

It is very important to know the difference between the topic and the main idea of the text. Even though these two are similar because they both present the central point of a text, they have distinctive differences. A *topic* is the subject of the text; This can usually be described in a concise one- to two-word phrase. On the other hand, the *main idea* is more detailed and provides the author's central point of the text. It can be expressed through a complete sentence and is often found in the beginning, the middle, or at the end of a paragraph. In most nonfiction books, the first sentence of the passage usually (but not always) states the main idea. Review the passage below to explore the topic versus the main idea.

Cheetahs

Cheetahs are one of the fastest mammals on the land, reaching up to 70 miles an hour over short distances. Even though cheetahs can run as fast as 70 miles an hour, they usually only have to run half that speed to catch up with their choice of prey. Cheetahs cannot maintain a fast pace over long periods of time because their bodies will overheat. After a chase, cheetahs need to rest for approximately 30 minutes prior to eating or returning to any other activity.

In the example above, the topic of the passage is "Cheetahs" simply because that is the subject of the text. The main idea of the text is "Cheetahs are one of the fastest mammals on the land but can only maintain a fast pace for shorter distances." While it covers the topic, it is more detailed and refers to the text in its entirety. The text continues to provide additional details called *supporting details,* which will be discussed in the next section.

Supporting Details

Supporting details help readers better develop and understand the main idea. Supporting details answer questions like *who, what, where, when, why,* and *how*. Different types of supporting details include examples, facts and statistics, anecdotes, and sensory details.

Persuasive and informative texts often use supporting details. In persuasive texts, authors attempt to make readers agree with their points of view, and supporting details are often used as "selling points." If authors make a statement, they need to support the statement with evidence in order to adequately persuade readers. Informative texts use supporting details such as examples and facts to inform readers. Review the previous "Cheetahs" passage to find examples of supporting details.

Cheetahs

Cheetahs are one of the fastest mammals on the land, reaching up to 70 miles an hour over short distances. Even though cheetahs can run as fast as 70 miles an hour, they usually only have to run half that speed to catch up with their choice of prey. Cheetahs cannot maintain a fast pace over long periods of time because their bodies will overheat. After a chase, cheetahs need to rest for approximately 30 minutes prior to eating or returning to any other activity.

In the example, supporting details include:

1. Cheetahs reach up to 70 miles per hour over short distances.
2. They usually only have to run half that speed to catch up with their prey.
3. Cheetahs will overheat if they exert a high speed over longer distances.
4. Cheetahs need to rest for 30 minutes after a chase.

Look at the diagram below (applying the cheetah example) to help determine the hierarchy of topic, main idea, and supporting details.

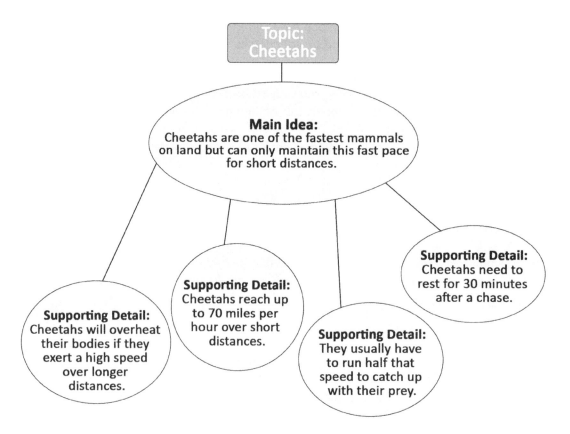

Understanding the Development of Themes

Identifying Theme or Central Message

The *theme* is the central message of a fictional work, whether that work is structured as prose, drama, or poetry. It is the heart of what an author is trying to say to readers through the writing, and theme is largely conveyed through literary elements and techniques.

In literature, a theme can often be determined by considering the over-arching narrative conflict within the work.

Though there are several types of conflicts and several potential themes within them, the following are the most common:

- *Individual against the self*—relevant to themes of self-awareness, internal struggles, pride, coming of age, facing reality, fate, free will, vanity, loss of innocence, loneliness, isolation, fulfillment, failure, and disillusionment

- *Individual against nature*— relevant to themes of knowledge vs. ignorance, nature as beauty, quest for discovery, self-preservation, chaos and order, circle of life, death, and destruction of beauty

- *Individual against society*— relevant to themes of power, beauty, good, evil, war, class struggle, totalitarianism, role of men/women, wealth, corruption, change vs. tradition, capitalism, destruction, heroism, injustice, and racism

- *Individual against another individual*— relevant to themes of hope, loss of love or hope, sacrifice, power, revenge, betrayal, and honor

For example, in Hawthorne's *The Scarlet Letter*, one possible narrative conflict could be the individual against the self, with a relevant theme of internal struggles. This theme is alluded to through characterization—Dimmesdale's moral struggle with his love for Hester and Hester's internal struggles with the truth and her daughter, Pearl. It's also alluded to through plot—Dimmesdale's suicide and Hester helping the very townspeople who initially condemned her.

Sometimes, a text can convey a *message* or *universal lesson*—a truth or insight that the reader infers from the text, based on analysis of the literary and/or poetic elements. This message is often presented as a statement. For example, a potential message in Shakespeare's *Hamlet* could be "Revenge is what ultimately drives the human soul." This message can be immediately determined through plot and characterization in numerous ways, but it can also be determined through the setting of Norway, which is bordering on war.

How Authors Develop Theme

Authors employ a variety of techniques to present a theme. They may compare or contrast characters, events, places, ideas, or historical or invented settings to speak thematically. They may use analogies, metaphors, similes, allusions, or other literary devices to convey the theme. An author's use of diction, syntax, and tone can also help convey the theme. Authors will often develop themes through the development of characters, use of the setting, repetition of ideas, use of symbols, and through contrasting value systems. Authors of both fiction and nonfiction genres will use a variety of these techniques to develop one or more themes.

Regardless of the literary genre, there are commonalities in how authors, playwrights, and poets develop themes or central ideas.

Authors often do research, the results of which contribute to theme. In prose fiction and drama, this research may include real historical information about the setting the author has chosen or include elements that make fictional characters, settings, and plots seem realistic to the reader. In nonfiction, research is critical since information contained within this literature must be accurate.

In fiction, authors present a narrative conflict that will contribute to the overall theme. This conflict may involve the storyline the storyline itself and some trouble within characters that needs resolution. In nonfiction, this conflict may be an explanation or commentary on factual people and events.

Authors will sometimes use character motivation to convey theme, such as in the example from *Hamlet* regarding revenge. In fiction, the characters an author creates will think, speak, and act in ways that effectively convey the theme to readers. In nonfiction, the characters are factual, as in a biography, but authors pay particular attention to presenting those motivations to make them clear to readers.

Authors also use literary devices as a means of conveying theme. For example, the use of moon symbolism in Mary Shelley's *Frankenstein* is significant as its phases can be compared to the phases that the Creature undergoes as he struggles with his identity.

The selected point of view can also contribute to a work's theme. The use of first-person point of view in a fiction or non-fiction work engages the reader's response differently than third person point of view. The central idea or theme from a first-person narrative may differ from a third-person limited text.

In literary nonfiction, authors usually identify the purpose of their writing, which differs from fiction, where the general purpose is to entertain. The purpose of nonfiction is usually to inform, persuade, or entertain the audience. The stated purpose of a non-fiction text will drive how the central message or theme, if applicable, is presented.

Authors identify an audience for their writing, which is critical in shaping the theme of the work. For example, the audience for J.K. Rowling's *Harry Potter* series would be different than the audience for a biography of George Washington. The audience an author chooses to address is closely tied to the purpose of the work. The choice of an audience also drives the choice of language and level of diction an author uses. Ultimately, the intended audience determines the level to which that subject matter is presented and the complexity of the theme.

Summarizing and Paraphrasing a Passage

As an aid to drawing conclusions, outlining the information contained in the passage should be a familiar skill to readers. An effective outline will reveal the structure of the passage and will lead to solid conclusions. An effective outline will have a title that refers to the basic subject of the text though the title needs not recapitulate the main idea. In most outlines, the main idea will be the first major section. Each major idea of the passage will be established as the head of a category. For instance, the most common outline format calls for the main ideas of the passage to be indicated with Roman numerals. In an effective outline of this kind, each of the main ideas will be represented by a Roman numeral and none of the Roman numerals will designate minor details or secondary ideas. Moreover, all supporting ideas and details should be placed in the appropriate place on the outline. An outline does not need to include every detail listed in the text, but the outline should feature all of those that are central to the argument or message. Each of these details should be listed under the appropriate main idea.

Ideas from a text can also be organized using graphic organizers. A graphic organizer is a way to simplify information and take key points from the text. A graphic organizer such as a timeline may have an event listed for a corresponding date on the timeline while an outline may have an event listed under a key point that occurs in the text. Each reader needs to create the type of graphic organizer that works the best for him or her in terms of being able to recall information from a story. Examples include a *spider-map,* which takes a main idea from the story and places it in a bubble with supporting points branching off the main idea. An *outline* is useful for diagramming the main and supporting points of the entire story, and a *Venn diagram* classifies information as separate or overlapping.

A helpful tool is the ability to summarize the information that you have read in a paragraph or passage format. This process is similar to creating an effective outline. First, a summary should accurately define the main idea of the passage though the summary does not need to explain this main idea in exhaustive detail. The summary should continue by laying out the most important supporting details or arguments from the passage. All of the significant supporting details should be included, and none of the details included should be irrelevant or insignificant. Also, the summary should accurately report all of these details. Too often, the desire for brevity in a summary leads to the sacrifice of clarity or accuracy. Summaries are often difficult to read because they omit all of the graceful language, digressions, and asides that distinguish great writing. However, an effective summary should contain much the same message as the original text.

Paraphrasing is another method that the reader can use to aid in comprehension. When paraphrasing, one puts what they have read into their words by rephrasing what the author has written, or one "translates" all of what the author shared into their words by including as many details as they can.

Outlining

As mentioned, an *outline* is a system used to organize writing. When reading texts, outlining is important because it helps readers organize important information in a logical pattern using Roman numerals. Usually, outlines start out with the main idea(s) and then branch out into subgroups or subsidiary thoughts or subjects. Not only do outlines provide a visual tool for readers to reflect on how events, characters, settings, or other key parts of the text or passage relate to one another, but they can also lead readers to a stronger conclusion. The sample below demonstrates what a general outline looks like.

I. Main Topic 1
   a. Subtopic 1
   b. Subtopic 2
      1. Detail 1
      2. Detail 2
II. Main Topic 2
   a. Subtopic 1
   b. Subtopic 2
      1. Detail 1
      2. Detail 2

Summarizing

At the end of a text or passage, it is important to summarize what the readers read. *Summarizing* is a strategy in which readers determine what is important throughout the text or passage, shorten those ideas, and rewrite or retell it in their own words. A summary should identify the main idea of the text or passage. Important details or supportive evidence should also be accurately reported in the summary. If writers provide irrelevant details in the summary, it may cloud the greater meaning of the text or passage. When summarizing, writers should not include their opinions, quotes, or what they thought the author should have said. A clear summary provides clarity of the text or passage to the readers.

The following checklist lists items that writers should include in a summary:

Summary Checklist

1. Title of the story
2. Someone: Who is or are the main character(s)?
3. Wanted: What did the character(s) want?
4. But: What was the problem?
5. So: How did the character(s) solve the problem?
6. Then: How did the story end? What was the resolution?

Paraphrasing

Another strategy readers can use to help them fully comprehend a text or passage is *paraphrasing*. Paraphrasing is when readers take the author's words and put them into their own words. When readers and writers paraphrase, they need to avoid copying the text—that is plagiarism. It is also important to include as many details as possible when restating the facts. Not only will this help readers and writers recall information, but by putting the information into their own words, they demonstrate if

they fully comprehend the text or passage. The example below shows an original text and how to paraphrase it.

> *Original Text*: Fenway Park is home to the beloved Boston Red Sox. The stadium opened on April 20, 1912. The stadium currently seats over 37,000 fans, many of whom travel from all over the country to experience the iconic team and nostalgia of Fenway Park.

> *Paraphrased*: On April 20, 1912, Fenway Park opened. Home to the Boston Red Sox, the stadium now seats over 37,000 fans. Many spectators travel to watch the Red Sox and experience the spirit of Fenway Park.

Paraphrasing, summarizing, and quoting can often cross paths with one another. The chart below shows the similarities and differences between the three strategies:

PARAPHRASING	SUMMARIZING	QUOTING
Uses own words	Puts main ideas into own words	Uses words that are identical to text
References original source	References original source	Requires quotation marks
Uses own sentences	Shows important ideas of source	Uses author's words and ideas

Identifying Logical Conclusions

Determining conclusions requires being an active reader, as a reader must make a prediction and analyze facts to identify a conclusion. A reader should identify key words in a passage to determine the logical conclusion or outcome that flows from the information presented. Consider the passage below:

> Lindsay, covered in flour, moved around the kitchen frantically. Her mom yelled from another room, "Lindsay, we're going to be late!"

You can conclude that Lindsay's next steps are to finish baking, clean herself up, and head off somewhere with her baked goods. Notice that the conclusion cannot be verified factually. Many conclusions are not spelled out specifically in the text; thus, they have to be identified and drawn out by the reader.

Context Clues

Context clues help readers understand unfamiliar words, and thankfully, there are many types.

Synonyms are words or phrases that have nearly, if not exactly, the same meaning as other words or phrases

> *Large* boxes are needed to pack *big* items.

Antonyms are words or phrases that have opposite definitions. Antonyms, like synonyms, can serve as context clues, although more cryptically.

44

Large boxes are not needed to pack *small* items.

Definitions are sometimes included within a sentence to define uncommon words.

They practiced the *rumba*, a *type of dance*, for hours on end.

Explanations provide context through elaboration.

Large boxes holding items weighing over 60 pounds were stacked in the corner.

Contrast provides ways in which things are different.

These *minute* creatures were much different than the *huge* mammals that the zoologist was accustomed to dealing with.

Understanding the Use of Affixes, Context, and Syntax

Affixes

Individual words are constructed from building blocks of meaning. An *affix* is an element that is added to a root or stem word that can change the word's meaning.

For example, the stem word *fix* is a verb meaning *to repair*. When the ending *–able* is added, it becomes the adjective *fixable*, meaning "capable of being repaired." Adding *un–* to the beginning changes the word to *unfixable*, meaning "incapable of being repaired." In this way, affixes attach to the word stem to create a new word and a new meaning. Knowledge of affixes can assist in deciphering the meaning of unfamiliar words.

Affixes are also related to inflection. *Inflection* is the modification of a base word to express a different grammatical or syntactical function. For example, countable nouns such as *car* and *airport* become plural with the addition of *–s* at the end: *cars* and *airports*.

Verb tense is also expressed through inflection. *Regular verbs*—those that follow a standard inflection pattern—can be changed to past tense using the affixes *–ed*, *–d*, or *–ied*, as in *cooked* and *studied*. Verbs can also be modified for continuous tenses by using *–ing*, as in *working* or *exploring*. Thus, affixes are used not only to express meaning but also to reflect a word's grammatical purpose.

A *prefix* is an affix attached to the beginning of a word. The meanings of English prefixes mainly come from Greek and Latin origins. The chart below contains a few of the most commonly used English prefixes.

Prefix	Meaning	Example
a-	Not	amoral, asymptomatic
anti-	Against	antidote, antifreeze
auto-	Self	automobile, automatic
circum-	Around	circumference, circumspect
co-, com-, con-	Together	coworker, companion
contra-	Against	contradict, contrary
de-	negation or reversal	deflate, deodorant
extra-	outside, beyond	extraterrestrial, extracurricular
in-, im-, il-, ir-	Not	impossible, irregular
inter-	Between	international, intervene
intra-	Within	intramural, intranet
mis-	Wrongly	mistake, misunderstand
mono-	One	monolith, monopoly
non-	Not	nonpartisan, nonsense
pre-	Before	preview, prediction
re-	Again	review, renew
semi-	Half	semicircle, semicolon
sub-	Under	subway, submarine
super-	Above	superhuman, superintendent
trans-	across, beyond, through	trans-Siberian, transform
un-	Not	unwelcome, unfriendly

While the addition of a prefix alters the meaning of the base word, the addition of a *suffix* may also affect a word's part of speech. For example, adding a suffix can change the noun *material* into the verb *materialize* and back to a noun again in *materialization*.

Suffix	Part of Speech	Meaning	Example
-able, -ible	adjective	having the ability to	honorable, flexible
-acy, -cy	noun	state or quality	intimacy, dependency
-al, -ical	adjective	having the quality of	historical, tribal
-en	verb	to cause to become	strengthen, embolden
-er, -ier	adjective	comparative	happier, longer
-est, -iest	adjective	superlative	sunniest, hottest
-ess	noun	female	waitress, actress
-ful	adjective	full of, characterized by	beautiful, thankful
-fy, -ify	verb	to cause, to come to be	liquefy, intensify
-ism	noun	doctrine, belief, action	Communism, Buddhism
-ive, -ative, -itive	adjective	having the quality of	creative, innovative
-ize	verb	to convert into, to subject to	Americanize, dramatize
-less	adjective	without, missing	emotionless, hopeless
-ly	adverb	in the manner of	quickly, energetically
-ness	noun	quality or state	goodness, darkness
-ous, -ious, -eous	adjective	having the quality of	spontaneous, pious
-ship	noun	status or condition	partnership, ownership
-tion	noun	action or state	renovation, promotion
-y	adjective	characterized by	smoky, dreamy

Through knowledge of prefixes and suffixes, a student's vocabulary can be instantly expanded with an understanding of *etymology*—the origin of words. This, in turn, can be used to add sentence structure variety to academic writing.

Context Clues

Familiarity with common prefixes, suffixes, and root words assists tremendously in unraveling the meaning of an unfamiliar word and making an educated guess as to its meaning. However, some words do not contain many easily-identifiable clues that point to their meaning. In this case, rather than looking at the elements within the word, it is useful to consider elements around the word—i.e., its context. *Context* refers to the other words and information within the sentence or surrounding sentences that indicate the unknown word's probable meaning. The following sentences provide context for the potentially-unfamiliar word *quixotic*:

> Rebecca had never been one to settle into a predictable, ordinary life. Her quixotic personality led her to leave behind a job with a prestigious law firm in Manhattan and move halfway around the world to pursue her dream of becoming a sushi chef in Tokyo.

A reader unfamiliar with the word *quixotic* doesn't have many clues to use in terms of affixes or root meaning. The suffix *–ic* indicates that the word is an adjective, but that is it. In this case, then, a reader would need to look at surrounding information to obtain some clues about the word. Other adjectives in the passage include *predictable* and *ordinary*, things that Rebecca was definitely not, as indicated by

47

"Rebecca had never been one to settle." Thus, a first clue might be that *quixotic* means the opposite of predictable.

The second sentence doesn't offer any other modifier of *personality* other than *quixotic*, but it does include a story that reveals further information about her personality. She had a stable, respectable job, but she decided to give it up to follow her dream. Combining these two ideas together, then—unpredictable and dream-seeking—gives the reader a general idea of what *quixotic* probably means. In fact, the root of the word is the character Don Quixote, a romantic dreamer who goes on an impulsive adventure.

While context clues are useful for making an approximate definition for newly-encountered words, these types of clues also come in handy when encountering common words that have multiple meanings. The word *reservation* is used differently in each the following sentences:

A. That restaurant is booked solid for the next month; it's impossible to make a reservation unless you know somebody.

B. The hospital plans to open a branch office inside the reservation to better serve Native American patients who cannot easily travel to the main hospital fifty miles away.

C. Janet Clark is a dependable, knowledgeable worker, and I recommend her for the position of team leader without reservation.

All three sentences use the word to express different meanings. In fact, most words in English have more than one meaning—sometimes meanings that are completely different from one another. Thus, context can provide clues as to which meaning is appropriate in a given situation. A quick search in the dictionary reveals several possible meanings for *reservation*:

1. An exception or qualification
2. A tract of public land set aside, such as for the use of American Indian tribes
3. An arrangement for accommodations, such as in a hotel, on a plane, or at a restaurant

Sentence A mentions a restaurant, making the third definition the correct one in this case. In sentence B, some context clues include Native Americans, as well as the implication that a reservation is a place—"inside the reservation," both of which indicate that the second definition should be used here. Finally, sentence C uses *without reservation* to mean "completely" or "without exception," so the first definition can be applied here.

Using context clues in this way can be especially useful for words that have multiple, widely varying meanings. If a word has more than one definition and two of those definitions are the opposite of each other, it is known as an *auto-antonym*—a word that can also be its own antonym. In the case of auto-antonyms, context clues are crucial to determine which definition to employ in a given sentence. For example, the word *sanction* can either mean "to approve or allow" or "a penalty." Approving and penalizing have opposite meanings, so *sanction* is an example of an auto-antonym.

The following sentences reflect the distinction in meaning:

A. In response to North Korea's latest nuclear weapons test, world leaders have called for harsher sanctions to punish the country for its actions.

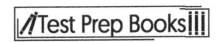

B. The general has sanctioned a withdrawal of troops from the area.

A context clue can be found in sentence A, which mentions "to punish." A punishment is similar to a penalty, so sentence A is using the word *sanction* according to this definition.

Other examples of auto-antonyms include *oversight*—"to supervise something" or "a missed detail"), *resign*—"to quit" or "to sign again, as a contract," and *screen*—"to show" or "to conceal." For these types of words, recognizing context clues is an important way to avoid misinterpreting the sentence's meaning.

Syntax

Syntax refers to the arrangement of words, phrases, and clauses to form a sentence. Knowledge of syntax can also give insight into a word's meaning. The section above considered several examples using the word *reservation* and applied context clues to determine the word's appropriate meaning in each sentence. Here is an example of how the placement of a word can impact its meaning and grammatical function:

A. The development team has reserved the conference room for today.

B. Her quiet and reserved nature is sometimes misinterpreted as unfriendliness when people first meet her.

In addition to using *reserved* to mean different things, each sentence also uses the word to serve a different grammatical function. In sentence A, *reserved* is part of the verb phrase *has reserved*, indicating the meaning "to set aside for a particular use." In sentence B, *reserved* acts as a modifier within the noun phrase "her quiet and reserved nature." Because the word is being used as an adjective to describe a personality characteristic, it calls up a different definition of the word—"restrained or lacking familiarity with others." As this example shows, the function of a word within the overall sentence structure can allude to its meaning. It is also useful to refer to the earlier chart about suffixes and parts of speech as another clue into what grammatical function a word is serving in a sentence.

Analyzing Nuances of Word Meaning and Figures of Speech

By now, it should be apparent that language is not as simple as one word directly correlated to one meaning. Rather, one word can express a vast array of diverse meanings, and similar meanings can be expressed through different words. However, there are very few words that express exactly the same meaning. For this reason, it is important to be able to pick up on the nuances of word meaning.

Many words contain two levels of meaning: connotation and denotation as discussed previously in the informational texts and rhetoric section. A word's *denotation* is its most literal meaning—the definition that can readily be found in the dictionary. A word's *connotation* includes all of its emotional and cultural associations.

In literary writing, authors rely heavily on connotative meaning to create mood and characterization. The following are two descriptions of a rainstorm:

A. The rain slammed against the windowpane, and the wind howled through the fireplace. A pair of hulking oaks next to the house cast eerie shadows as their branches trembled in the wind.

B. The rain pattered against the windowpane, and the wind whistled through the fireplace. A pair of stately oaks next to the house cast curious shadows as their branches swayed in the wind.

Description A paints a creepy picture for readers with strongly emotional words like *slammed*, connoting force and violence. *Howled* connotes pain or wildness, and *eerie* and *trembled* connote fear. Overall, the connotative language in this description serves to inspire fear and anxiety.

However, as can be seen in description B, swapping out a few key words for those with different connotations completely changes the feeling of the passage. *Slammed* is replaced with the more cheerful *pattered*, and *hulking* has been swapped out for *stately*. Both words imply something large, but *hulking* is more intimidating whereas *stately* is more respectable. *Curious* and *swayed* seem more playful than the language used in the earlier description. Although both descriptions represent roughly the same situation, the nuances of the emotional language used throughout the passages create a very different sense for readers.

Selective choice of connotative language can also be extremely impactful in other forms of writing, such as editorials or persuasive texts. Through connotative language, writers reveal their biases and opinions while trying to inspire feelings and actions in readers:

A. Parents won't stop complaining about standardized tests.

B. Parents continue to raise concerns about standardized tests.

Readers should be able to identify the nuance in meaning between these two sentences. The first one carries a more negative feeling, implying that parents are being bothersome or whiny. Readers of the second sentence, though, might come away with the feeling that parents are concerned and involved in their children's education. Again, the aggregate of even subtle cues can combine to give a specific emotional impression to readers, so from an early age, students should be aware of how language can be used to influence readers' opinions.

Another form of non-literal expression can be found in *figures of speech*. As with connotative language, figures of speech tend to be shared within a cultural group and may be difficult to pick up on for learners outside of that group. In some cases, a figure of speech may be based on the literal denotation of the words it contains, but in other cases, a figure of speech is far removed from its literal meaning. A case in point is *irony*, where what is said is the exact opposite of what is meant:

The new tax plan is poorly planned, based on faulty economic data, and unable to address the financial struggles of middle-class families. Yet legislators remain committed to passing this brilliant proposal.

When the writer refers to the proposal as brilliant, the opposite is implied—the plan is "faulty" and "poorly planned." By using irony, the writer means that the proposal is anything but brilliant by using the word in a non-literal sense.

Another figure of speech is *hyperbole*—extreme exaggeration or overstatement. Statements like "I love you to the moon and back" or "Let's be friends for a million years" utilize hyperbole to convey a greater depth of emotion, without literally committing oneself to space travel or a life of immortality.

Figures of speech may sometimes use one word in place of another. *Synecdoche*, for example, uses a part of something to refer to its whole. The expression "Don't hurt a hair on her head!" implies protecting more than just an individual hair, but rather her entire body. "The art teacher is training a class of Picassos" uses Picasso, one individual notable artist, to stand in for the entire category of talented artists. Another figure of speech using word replacement is *metonymy*, where a word is replaced with something closely associated to it. For example, news reports may use the word *Washington* to refer to the American government or *the crown* to refer to the British monarch.

Figurative Language

Literary texts also employ rhetorical devices. Figurative language like simile and metaphor is a type of rhetorical device commonly found in literature. In addition to rhetorical devices that play on the *meanings* of words, there are also rhetorical devices that use the *sounds* of words. These devices are most often found in poetry but may also be found in other types of literature and in non-fiction writing like speech texts.

Alliteration and *assonance* are both varieties of sound repetition. Other types of sound repetition include: anaphora, repetition that occurs at the beginning of the sentences; epiphora, repetition occurring at the end of phrases; antimetabole, repetition of words in reverse order; and antiphrasis, a form of denial of an assertion in a text.

Alliteration refers to the repetition of the first sound of each word. Recall Robert Burns' opening line:

> My love is like a red, red rose

This line includes two instances of alliteration: "love" and "like" (repeated *L* sound), as well as "red" and "rose" (repeated *R* sound). Next, assonance refers to the repetition of vowel sounds, and can occur anywhere within a word (not just the opening sound). Here is the opening of a poem by John Keats:

> When I have fears that I may cease to be
>
> Before my pen has glean'd my teeming brain

Assonance can be found in the words "fears," "cease," "be," "glean'd," and "teeming," all of which stress the long *E* sound. Both alliteration and assonance create a harmony that unifies the writer's language.

Another sound device is *onomatopoeia*, or words whose spelling mimics the sound they describe. Words such as "crash," "bang," and "sizzle" are all examples of onomatopoeia. Use of onomatopoetic language adds auditory imagery to the text.

Readers are probably most familiar with the technique of *pun*. A pun is a play on words, taking advantage of two words that have the same or similar pronunciation. Puns can be found throughout Shakespeare's plays, for instance:

> Now is the winter of our discontent
> Made glorious summer by this son of York

These lines from *Richard III* contain a play on words. Richard III refers to his brother, the newly crowned King Edward IV, as the "son of York," referencing their family heritage from the house of York. However, while drawing a comparison between the political climate and the weather (times of political trouble

were the "winter," but now the new king brings "glorious summer"), Richard's use of the word "son" also implies another word with the same pronunciation, "sun"—so Edward IV is also like the sun, bringing light, warmth, and hope to England. Puns are a clever way for writers to suggest two meanings at once.

Some examples of figurative language are included in the following graphic.

	Definition	Example
Simile	Compares two things using "like" or "as"	Her hair was like gold.
Metaphor	Compares two things as if they are the same	He was a giant teddy bear.
Idiom	Using words with predictable meanings to create a phrase with a different meaning	The world is your oyster.
Alliteration	Repeating the same beginning sound or letter in a phrase for emphasis	The busy baby babbled.
Personification	Attributing human characteristics to an object or an animal	The house glowered menacingly with a dark smile.
Foreshadowing	Giving an indication that something is going to happen later in the story	I wasn't aware at the time, but I would come to regret those words.
Symbolism	Using symbols to represent ideas and provide a different meaning	The ring represented the bond between us.
Onomatopoeia	Using words that imitate sound	The tire went off with a bang and a crunch.
Imagery	Appealing to the senses by using descriptive language	The sky was painted with red and pink and streaked with orange.
Hyperbole	Using exaggeration not meant to be taken literally	The girl weighed less than a feather.

Figurative language can be used to give additional insight into the theme or message of a text by moving beyond the usual and literal meaning of words and phrases. It can also be used to appeal to the senses of readers and create a more in-depth story.

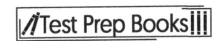

Transitional Words and Phrases

There are approximately 200 transitional words and phrases that are commonly used in the English language. Below are lists of common transition words and phrases used throughout transitions:

<u>Time</u>
After
Before
During
In the middle

<u>Example About to be Given</u>
For example
In fact
For instance

<u>Compare</u>
Likewise
Also

<u>Contrast</u>
However
Yet
But

<u>Addition</u>
And
Also
Furthermore
Moreover

<u>Logical Relationships</u>
If
Then
Therefore
As a result
Since

<u>Steps in a Process</u>
First
Second
Last

Transitional words and phrases are important writing devices because they connect sentences and paragraphs. Transitional words and phrases present logical order to writing and provide more coherent meaning to readers.

Transition words can be categorized based on the relationships they create between ideas:

- General order: signaling elaboration of an idea to emphasize a point—e.g., for example, for instance, to demonstrate, including, such as, in other words, that is, in fact, also, furthermore, likewise, and, truly, so, surely, certainly, obviously, doubtless

- Chronological order: referencing the time frame in which the main event or idea occurs—e.g., before, after, first, while, soon, shortly thereafter, meanwhile

- *Numerical order/order of importance*: indicating that related ideas, supporting details, or events will be described in a sequence, possibly in order of importance—e.g., *first, second, also, finally, another, in addition, equally important, less importantly, most significantly, the main reason, last but not least*

- *Spatial order*: referring to the space and location of something or where things are located in relation to each other—e.g., *inside, outside, above, below, within, close, under, over, far, next to, adjacent to*

- Cause and effect order: signaling a causal relationship between events or ideas—e.g., thus, therefore, since, resulted in, for this reason, as a result, consequently, hence, for, so

- Compare and contrast order: identifying the similarities and differences between two or more objects, ideas, or lines of thought—e.g., like, as, similarly, equally, just as, unlike, however, but, although, conversely, on the other hand, on the contrary

- Summary order: indicating that a particular idea is coming to a close—e.g., in conclusion, to sum up, in other words, ultimately, above all

Research and Reference Skills

Identifying Information in an Index or Table of Contents

An index is an alphabetical listing of topics, such as people, works, or concepts that appear at the end of expository materials like textbooks, cookbooks, and repair manuals. When these key words are used in paragraphs, they sometimes appear in bold writing to indicate their importance and let the reader know that they're found in the index as well.

Index listings often discard articles like *a*, *an*, and *the*. Additionally, authors will be listed by their last names, not first. Topics may be further divided into subtopics. If you start by looking for the most basic topics first, you can quickly acquire information. For example, when looking for a cookie recipe in a cookbook, first find the word *cookie* in the index and then examine the indented list of cookie-related topics located directly beneath the original heading.

Some textbooks have multiple indexes arranged by different subjects. If, for instance, you're dealing with a weighty literature textbook, you might find one index that lists authors and another devoted to concepts. The lengthier the book, the more likely you are to find this format.

While an index is typically found at the end of a book, a table of contents is found at the beginning to help readers quickly locate information. A table of contents is arranged differently, however, because it

provides a chronological listing of each chapter and a corresponding page number. Each entry may also include a description, summary statement, or objective.

When students first receive a textbook, they should take time to preview the table of contents to create a framework for mentally organizing information. By classifying the contents, the reader creates mental schemas and becomes more likely to retain the information longer.

Using Text Features

Text features are used to bring clarity or to affect the meaning of it. Sometimes a publication will follow a certain style guide/manual of style, which is a set of standards for how to write and format a publication. Some examples are APA, MLA, and the Chicago Manual of Style. If the publication is following one of those standards then the text features will be in accordance with that style guide.

Writers can come up with their own uses for text features based on what they feel is best. However, text features are generally used for a specific purpose. It's important to catch on to that purpose to maximize comprehension.

A clear layout is essential for good reader comprehension. Even with the use of many text features, the text needs to be laid out in a clear, consistent manner.

Bolding, Italics, and Underlining

Bolding, italics, and underlining are all used to make words stand out. **Bolded** words are often key concepts and can usually be found in summary statements at the end of chapters and in indexes. *Italics* can be used to identify words of another language or to add extra emphasis to a word or phrase. Writers will sometime place words in italics when the word is being referred to as the word itself. Quotation marks or italics can be used for this as well, as long as there is consistency. Italics are also used to represent a character's thoughts.

> Entering Jessica's room, Jessica's mom stepped over a pile of laundry, a stack of magazines, and a pile of dishes. *My messy daughter*, she thought, shaking her head.

Text can be underlined for a number of reasons, but generally it's to indicate a key term or important point.

Color can also be a text feature, as different color text can be used to make certain parts stand out or to indicate that a new section is beginning. Even if something is in black & white, the text may be in different shades of grey.

Formatting

In addition, formatting—such as indentation or bullet points—helps to clearly present content. Content may also be left justified, centered, or right justified:

Left Justified

Centered

Right Justified

Text is often centered to stand out and catch the reader's eye.

Analyzing Headings and Subheadings

Headings and subheadings are used in writing to organize discussions and allow the reader to find information quickly. Headings show a complete change in thought. Subheadings, which fall below headings, show different aspects of the same topic. For instance, if you saw the title *Government* and the heading *Forms of Government*, you might see the subheadings *Monarchy, Oligarchy, Democracy, Socialism*, and *Totalitarianism*.

Note the headings that got you to this point:

Reading

Research and Reference Skills

Using Text Features

Analyzing Headings and Subheadings

As well as providing organization and structure, headings and subheadings also put more white space on a page, which places less strain on the reader's eyes. It's a good idea to skim a document and get familiar with headings and subheadings. Write down the title, headings, and subheadings before you begin reading to provide structure to your notes and thoughts.

Locating Where in a Reading That Specific Information Can Be Found

Readers are often looking for specific information in a text. A student might have a question about a book. To answer the question the individual may need to locate a specific text that they have already read. Someone can also be tasked with finding a particular text in a new book that they have not read. Rather than reading the entire book, they may skim through the pages to find what they are looking for. To accomplish these objectives, the readers need to be able to locate the place where their desired information can be found, such as the chapter, paragraph, or table. In informational texts, the index is a great tool to help in this task. For narratives, the chapter titles and headings, often recorded in the table of contents, can provide helpful hints for the readers concerning the information found in each chapter.

Research studies published in journals, for example, scientific experiments, typically have a structured format. Once readers understand the structure and what sorts of information found in each section of the study, they can quickly and relatively easily hone in on the information they desire. After the title and list of authors, the study begins with an *abstract,* which is essentially a short summary of the research: the purpose and hypothesis of the study, the methodology employed, and the findings and their meanings. The abstract is usually offset from the rest of the report in a smaller font or different formatting. It is a good place to get a quick snapshot of the gist of the study.

The first section of the main part of the report is the *introduction.* The introduction identifies the problem, or the need for the research. It sometimes contains a brief literature review of prior research pertaining to the issue and what gaps or issues existed in such studies. In this way, it sets the context for the current study and the hypothesis. The *methods* section details the approach used in the study – the steps that were followed and the subjects and materials used. The data analysis procedures are also described. In the next section, *results,* the findings are summarized and often displayed in tabular and graphic form. Statistical findings and relationships between the variables and groups are reported, particularly those pertaining to the hypothesis. The final section is the *discussion.* This section reports

the results in narrative form and evaluates the significance of the findings. It often also discusses the study's strengths and weaknesses and the need for future research.

Text Structure

Depending on what the author is attempting to accomplish, certain formats or text structures work better than others. For example, a sequence structure might work for narration but not for identifying similarities and differences between concepts. Similarly, a comparison-contrast structure is not useful for narration. It's the author's job to put the right information in the correct format.

Readers should be familiar with the five main literary structures:

1. *Sequence* structure (sometimes referred to as the order structure) is when the order of events proceed in a predictable order. In many cases, this means the text goes through the plot elements: exposition, rising action, climax, falling action, and resolution. Readers are introduced to characters, setting, and conflict in the exposition. In the rising action, there's an increase in tension and suspense. The climax is the height of tension and the point of no return. Tension decreases during the falling action. In the resolution, any conflicts presented in the exposition are solved, and the story concludes. An informative text that is structured sequentially will often go in order from one step to the next.

2. In the *problem-solution* structure, authors identify a potential problem and suggest a solution. This form of writing is usually divided into two parts (the problem and the solution) and can be found in informational texts. For example, cell phone, cable, and satellite providers use this structure in manuals to help customers troubleshoot or identify problems with services or products.

3. When authors want to discuss similarities and differences between separate concepts, they arrange thoughts in a *comparison-contrast* paragraph structure. Venn diagrams are an effective graphic organizer for comparison-contrast structures because they feature two overlapping circles that can be used to organize similarities and differences. A comparison-contrast essay organizes one paragraph based on similarities and another based on differences. A comparison-contrast essay can also be arranged with the similarities and differences of individual traits addressed within individual paragraphs. Words such as *however*, *but*, and *nevertheless* help signal a contrast in ideas.

4. *Descriptive* writing structure is designed to appeal to your senses. Much like an artist who constructs a painting, good descriptive writing builds an image in the reader's mind by appealing to the five senses: sight, hearing, taste, touch, and smell. However, overly descriptive writing can become distracting; whereas sparse descriptions can make settings and characters seem flat. Good authors must strike a balance between the two and provide enough detail to enable the reader to really see and experience what is happening in the plot without distracting the reader with excessive details.

5. Passages that use the *cause and effect* structure are simply asking *why* by demonstrating some type of connection between ideas. Words such as *if, since, because, then, or consequently* indicate a cause-and-effect relationship. By switching the order of a complex sentence, the writer can rearrange the emphasis on different clauses. Saying *"If Sheryl is late, we'll miss the dance"* is different from saying *"We'll miss the dance if Sheryl is late."* One emphasizes Sheryl's tardiness while the other emphasizes missing the dance. Paragraphs can also be arranged in a cause and effect format. Cause-and-effect writing discusses the impact of decisions that have been made or could be made. Researchers often apply this paragraph structure to the scientific method.

Identifying Information from a Graph or Table

Texts may have graphic representations to help illustrate and visually support assertions made. For example, graphs can be used to express samples or segments of a population or demonstrate growth or decay. Readers should also learn to use graphs and tables to draw logical conclusions, generalizations, or identify implied relationships. Three of the most popular graph formats included in texts are line graphs, bar graphs, and pie charts.

Line graphs rely on a horizontal X-axis and a vertical Y-axis to establish baseline values. Dots are plotted where the horizontal and vertical axes intersect, and those dots are connected with lines. Compared to bar graphs or pie charts, line graphs are more useful for looking at the past and present and predicting future outcomes. For instance, a potential investor would look for stocks that demonstrated steady growth over many decades when examining the stock market. Note that severe spikes up and down indicate instability, while line graphs that display a slow but steady increase may indicate good returns.

Here's an example of a bar graph:

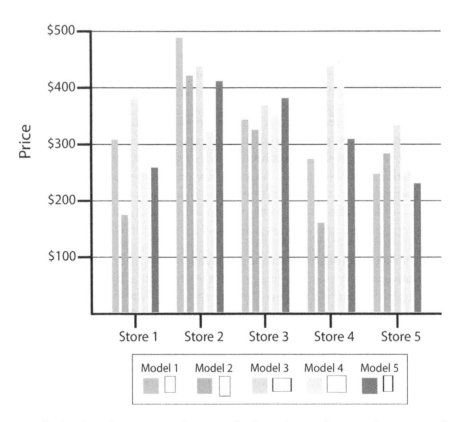

Bar graphs are usually displayed on a vertical Y-axis. The bars themselves can be two- or three-dimensional, depending on the designer's tastes. Unlike a line graph, which shows the fluctuation of only one variable, the X-axis on a bar graph is excellent for making comparisons, because it shows differences between several variables. For instance, if a consumer wanted to buy a new tablet, she could narrow the selection down to a few choices by using a bar graph to plot the prices side by side. The tallest bar would be the most expensive tablet, the shortest bar would be the cheapest.

58

A pie chart is divided into wedges that represent a numerical piece of the whole. Pie charts are useful for demonstrating how different categories add up to 100 percent. However, pie charts are not useful in comparing dissimilar items. High schools tend to use pie charts to track where students end up after graduation. Each wedge, for instance, might be labeled *vocational school*, *two-year college*, *four-year college*, *workforce*, or *unemployed*. By calculating the size of each wedge, schools can offer classes in the same ratios as where students will end up after high school. Pie charts are also useful for tracking finances. Items such as car payments, insurance, rent, credit cards, and entertainment would each get their own wedge proportional to the amount spent in a given time period. If one wedge is inordinately bigger than the rest, or if a wedge is expendable, it might be time to create a new financial strategy.

Mathematics

Estimation, Measurement, & Statistics

Measurement Systems and Standard Units of Measure

The American Measuring System

The measuring system used today in the United States developed from the British units of measurement during colonial times. The most typically used units in this customary system are those used to measure weight, liquid volume, and length, whose common units are found below. In the customary system, the basic unit for measuring weight is the ounce (oz); there are 16 ounces (oz) in 1 pound (lb) and 2000 pounds in 1 ton. The basic unit for measuring liquid volume is the ounce (oz); 1 ounce is equal to 2 tablespoons (tbsp) or 6 teaspoons (tsp), and there are 8 ounces in 1 cup, 2 cups in 1 pint (pt), 2 pints in 1 quart (qt), and 4 quarts in 1 gallon (gal). For measurements of length, the inch (in) is the base unit; 12 inches make up 1 foot (ft), 3 feet make up 1 yard (yd), and 5280 feet make up 1 mile (mi). However, as there are only a set number of units in the customary system, with extremely large or extremely small amounts of material, the numbers can become awkward and difficult to compare.

Common Customary Measurements		
Length	**Weight**	**Capacity**
1 foot = 12 inches	1 pound = 16 ounces	1 cup = 8 fluid ounces
1 yard = 3 feet	1 ton = 2,000 pounds	1 pint = 2 cups
1 yard = 36 inches		1 quart = 2 pints
1 mile = 1,760 yards		1 quart = 4 cups
1 mile = 5,280 feet		1 gallon = 4 quarts
		1 gallon = 16 cups

The Metric System

Aside from the United States, most countries in the world have adopted the metric system embodied in the International System of Units (SI). The three main SI base units used in the metric system are the meter (m), the kilogram (kg), and the liter (L); meters measure length, kilograms measure mass, and liters measure volume.

These three units can use different prefixes, which indicate larger or smaller versions of the unit by powers of ten. This can be thought of as making a new unit, which is sized by multiplying the original unit in size by a factor.

These prefixes and associated factors are:

Metric Prefixes			
Prefix	Symbol	Multiplier	Exponential
giga	G	1,000,000,000	10^9
mega	M	1,000,000	10^6
kilo	k	1,000	10^3
hecto	h	100	10^2
deca	da	10	10^1
no prefix		1	10^0
deci	d	0.1	10^{-1}
centi	c	0.01	10^{-2}
milli	m	0.001	10^{-3}
micro	μ	0.000001	10^{-6}
nano	n	0.000000001	10^{-9}

The correct prefix is then attached to the base. Some examples:

> 1 milliliter equals .001 liters.
> 1,000,000,000 nanometers equals 1 meter.
> 1 kilogram equals 1,000 grams.

Choosing the Appropriate Measuring Unit

Some units of measure are represented as square or cubic units depending on the solution. For example, perimeter is measured in linear units, area is measured in square units, and volume is measured in cubic units.

Also be sure to use the most appropriate unit for the thing being measured. A building's height might be measured in feet or meters while the length of a nail might be measured in inches or centimeters. Additionally, for SI units, the prefix should be chosen to provide the most succinct available value. For example, the mass of a bag of fruit would likely be measured in kilograms rather than grams or milligrams, and the length of a bacteria cell would likely be measured in micrometers rather than centimeters or kilometers.

Conversions

Converting measurements in different units between the two systems can be difficult because they follow different rules. The best method is to look up an English to Metric system conversion factor and then use a series of equivalent fractions to set up an equation to convert the units of one of the measurements into those of the other.

The table below lists some common conversion values that are useful for problems involving measurements with units in both systems:

English System	Metric System
1 inch	2.54 cm
1 foot	0.3048 m
1 yard	0.914 m
1 mile	1.609 km
1 ounce	28.35 g
1 pound	0.454 kg
1 fluid ounce	29.574 mL
1 quart	0.946 L
1 gallon	3.785 L

Consider the example where a scientist wants to convert 6.8 inches to centimeters. The table above is used to find that there are 2.54 centimeters in every inch, so the following equation should be set up and solved:

$$\frac{6.8 \text{ in}}{1} \times \frac{2.54 \text{ cm}}{1 \text{ in}} = 17.272 \text{ cm}$$

Notice how the inches in the numerator of the initial figure and the denominator of the conversion factor cancel out. (This equation could have been written simply as 6.8 in × 2.54 cm = 17.272 cm, but it was shown in detail to illustrate the steps). The goal in any conversion equation is to set up the fractions so that the units you are trying to convert from cancel out and the units you desire remain.

For a more complicated example, consider converting 2.15 kilograms into ounces. The first step is to convert kilograms into grams and then grams into ounces. Note that the measurement you begin with does not have to be put in a fraction.

So, in this case, 2.15 kg is by itself although it's technically the numerator of a fraction:

$$2.15 \text{ kg} \times \frac{1,000 \text{g}}{\text{kg}} = 2150 \text{ g}$$

Then, use the conversion factor from the table to convert grams to ounces:

$$2150 \text{g} \times \frac{1 \text{ oz}}{28.35 \text{g}} = 75.8 \text{ oz}$$

Perimeter and Area

Perimeter is the measurement of a distance around something or the sum of all sides of a polygon. Think of perimeter as the length of the boundary, like a fence. In contrast, **area** is the space occupied by a defined enclosure, like a field enclosed by a fence.

When thinking about perimeter, think about walking around the outside of something. When thinking about area, think about the amount of space or **surface area** something takes up.

Squares

The perimeter of a square is measured by adding together all of the sides. Since a square has four equal sides, its perimeter can be calculated by multiplying the length of one side by 4. Thus, the formula is $P = 4 \times s$, where s equals one side. For example, the following square has side lengths of 5 meters:

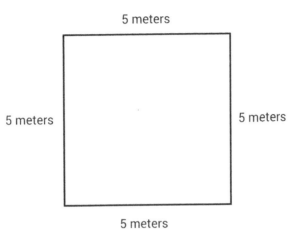

5 meters

5 meters   5 meters

5 meters

The perimeter is 20 meters because 4 times 5 is 20.

The area of a square is the length of a side squared. For example, if a side of a square is 7 centimeters, then the area is 49 square centimeters. The formula for this example is $A = s^2 = 7^2 = 49$ square centimeters. An example is if the rectangle has a length of 6 inches and a width of 7 inches, then the area is 42 square inches:

$$A = lw = 6(7) = 42 \text{ square inches}$$

Rectangles

Like a square, a rectangle's perimeter is measured by adding together all of the sides. But as the sides are unequal, the formula is different. A rectangle has equal values for its lengths (long sides) and equal values for its widths (short sides), so the perimeter formula for a rectangle is:

$$P = l + l + w + w = 2l + 2w$$

l equals length and w equals width.

The area is found by multiplying the length by the width, so the formula is $A = l \times w$.

For example, if the length of a rectangle is 10 inches and the width 8 inches, then the perimeter is 36 inches because:

$$P = 2l + 2w = 2(10) + 2(8) = 20 + 16 = 36 \text{ inches}$$

Triangles

A triangle's perimeter is measured by adding together the three sides, so the formula is $P = a + b + c$, where $a, b,$ and c are the values of the three sides. The area is the product of one-half the base and height so the formula is:

$$A = \frac{1}{2} \times b \times h$$

63

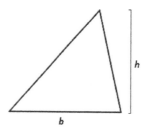
It can be simplified to:

$$A = \frac{bh}{2}$$

The base is the bottom of the triangle, and the height is the distance from the base to the peak. If a problem asks to calculate the area of a triangle, it will provide the base and height.

For example, if the base of the triangle is 2 feet and the height 4 feet, then the area is 4 square feet. The following equation shows the formula used to calculate the area of the triangle:

$$A = \frac{1}{2}bh = \frac{1}{2}(2)(4) = 4 \text{ square feet}$$

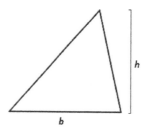

Circles

A circle's perimeter—also known as its circumference—is measured by multiplying the diameter by π.

Diameter is the straight line measured from a point on one side of the circle to a point directly across on the opposite side of the circle.

π is referred to as pi and is equal to 3.14 (with rounding).

So, the formula is $\pi \times d$.

This is sometimes expressed by the formula $C = 2 \times \pi \times r$, where r is the radius of the circle. These formulas are equivalent, as the radius equals half of the diameter.

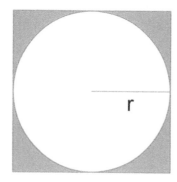

The area of a circle is calculated through the formula $A = \pi \times r^2$. The test will indicate either to leave the answer with π attached or to calculate to the nearest decimal place, which means multiplying by 3.14 for π.

Parallelograms

Similar to triangles, the height of the parallelogram is measured from one base to the other at a 90° angle (or perpendicular).

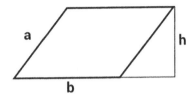

Area = bh

Perimeter = 2(a + b)

Trapezoid

The area of a trapezoid can be calculated using the formula: $A = \frac{1}{2} \times h(b_1 + b_2)$, where h is the height and b_1 and b_2 are the parallel bases of the trapezoid.

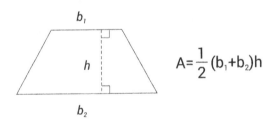

$$A = \frac{1}{2}(b_1 + b_2)h$$

Irregular Shapes

The perimeter of an irregular polygon is found by adding the lengths of all of the sides. In cases where all of the sides are given, this will be very straightforward, as it will simply involve finding the sum of the provided lengths. Other times, a side length may be missing and must be determined before the perimeter can be calculated. Consider the example below:

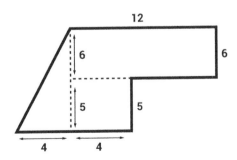

All of the side lengths are provided except for the angled side on the left. Test takers should notice that this is the hypotenuse of a right triangle. The other two sides of the triangle are provided (the base is 4 and the height is $6 + 5 = 11$). The Pythagorean Theorem can be used to find the length of the hypotenuse, remembering that $a^2 + b^2 = c^2$.

Substituting the side values provided yields:

$$(4)^2 + (11)^2 = c^2$$

Therefore:

$$c = \sqrt{16 + 121} = 11.7$$

Finally, the perimeter can be found by adding this new side length with the other provided lengths to get the total length around the figure:

$$4 + 4 + 5 + 8 + 6 + 12 + 11.7 = 50.7$$

Although units are not provided in this figure, remember that reporting units with a measurement is important.

The area of irregular polygons is found by decomposing, or breaking apart, the figure into smaller shapes. When the area of the smaller shapes is determined, the area of the smaller shapes will produce the area of the original figure when added together. Consider the earlier example:

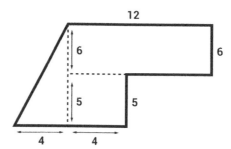

The irregular polygon is decomposed into two rectangles and a triangle. The area of the large rectangle ($A = l \times w \rightarrow A = 12 \times 6$) is 72 square units. The area of the small rectangle is 20 square units ($A = 4 \times 5$). The area of the triangle ($A = \frac{1}{2} \times b \times h \rightarrow A = \frac{1}{2} \times 4 \times 11$) is 22 square units. The sum of the areas of these figures produces the total area of the original polygon:

$$A = 72 + 20 + 22 \rightarrow A = 114 \text{ square units}$$

Here's another example:

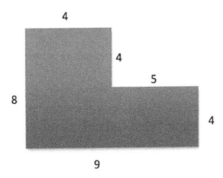

This irregular polygon is decomposed into two rectangles. The area of the large rectangle ($A = l \times w \rightarrow A = 8 \times 4$) is 32 square units. The area of the small rectangle is 20 square units ($A = 4 \times 5$). The sum of the areas of these figures produces the total area of the original polygon:

$$A = 32 + 20 \rightarrow A = 52 \text{ square units}$$

Estimating Time

Estimation is finding a value that is close to a solution but is not the exact answer. For example, if there are values in the thousands to be multiplied, then each value can be estimated to the nearest thousand and the calculation performed. This value provides an approximate solution that can be determined very quickly.

When estimating, it's often convenient to **round** a number, which means giving an approximate figure to make it easier to compare amounts or perform mental math. Round up when the digit is 5 or more. The digit used to determine the rounding, and all subsequent digits, become 0, and the selected place value is increased by 1. Here are some examples:

> 75 rounded to the nearest ten is 80
> 380 rounded to the nearest hundred is 400
> 22.697 rounded to the nearest hundredth is 22.70

Round down when rounding on any digit that is below 5. The rounded digit, and all subsequent digits, becomes 0, and the preceding digit stays the same. Here are some examples:

> 92 rounded to the nearest ten is 90
> 839 rounded to the nearest hundred is 800
> 22.643 rounded to the nearest hundredth is 22.64

The same estimation strategies and techniques used when working with standard math problems can be employed when working with real-life situations. Estimation is frequently used in calculations involving money, such as for determining if one has enough money for a purchase, how much one needs to save weekly to buy a desired product, or how much a restaurant bill will sum to.

Another equally effective application of estimation—albeit a bit more difficult and less straightforward—involves time. Many people find it helpful to estimate the length of time it will take them to complete a given task or perform some function. This enables them to budget their time and

67

energy effectively and develop a schedule or timeline by which projects and activities should be addressed. Estimating one's time is especially helpful for work-related objectives, to set reasonable expectations and meet required deadlines accordingly.

When estimating time, the same principles of rounding can be used, but now there is context behind the rounding. In other words, there is a specific meaning to what is being rounded (hours, minutes, seconds, days, etc.). This context needs to be considered when making the estimation and the rounding rules are typically not as formal and strict as those used in standard math calculations. For example, to round a number when performing regular mathematical calculations, the place value is specified. Then, as mentioned, the digit to its right is looked at. For example, if rounding to the nearest hundreds place, the digit in the tens place is used. If it is a 0, 1, 2, 3, or 4, the digit being rounded to is left alone. If it is a 5, 6, 7, 8 or 9, the digit being rounded to is increased by one.

All other digits before the decimal point are then changed to zeros, and the digits in decimal places are dropped. In contrast, there are no explicitly defined rules for rounding time. Two people may round time differently or the same person might round the same time differently depending on the situation. For example, it is 1:10pm, one person may say it is "around 1" and another might say it is "going on 1:30." Similarly, if someone is going on vacation in 24 days, he or she might say the vacation is in three weeks. If, instead, that person has been dieting for that length of time but have not seen results, he or she may say, "I've been dieting for about a month and still haven't lost a pound!" Although some of these estimations are more accurate than others, since formal rules don't exist, none are necessarily "wrong."

In general, estimating time is more complicated than estimation involved in mathematical computations because it not only involves rounding numbers and the normal mathematical techniques, but also the awareness or forethought about how long a certain task will likely take to complete. For example, if working with a team to design a new logo for a company, one has to try to imagine the realistic, but potential, factors that will affect the projected timeline (i.e., How long might meetings take with the other team members? Will a compromise or agreement be reached easily or does there tend to be a lot of stubbornness surrounding one's idea? What is the process like for logo approval?).

With that said, as one becomes more experienced in a given job position or more self-aware over time, their ability to estimate the time needed for various work-related objectives or other life functions will improve. In these cases, time estimations can be instrumental in establishing functional schedules and realistic timelines.

Estimating Prior to Calculating

Prior to performing operations and calculating the answer to a problem involving addition, subtraction, multiplication, or division, it is helpful to estimate the result. Doing so will enable the test taker to determine whether their computed answer is logical within the context of a given problem and prevent careless errors. For example, it is unfortunately common under the pressure of a testing situation for test takers to inadvertently perform the incorrect operation or make a simple calculation error on an otherwise easy math problem. By quickly estimating the answer by eyeballing the numbers, rounding if needed, and performing some simple mental math, test takers can establish an approximate expected outcome before calculating the specific answer. The derived result after computation can then be evaluated by its nearness to the expected answer. This is performed by approximating given values to perform mental math. Numbers should be rounded to the nearest value possible to check the initial results.

As mentioned, sometimes when performing operations such as multiplying numbers, the result can be estimated by rounding. For example, to estimate the value of 11.2×2.01, each number can be rounded to the nearest integer. This will yield a result of 22.

Rounding numbers helps with estimation because it changes the given number to a simpler, although less accurate, number than the exact given number. Rounding allows for easier calculations, which estimate the results of using the exact given number. The accuracy of the estimate and ease of use depends on the place value to which the number is rounded. First, the place value is specified. Then, the digit to its right is looked at. For example, if rounding to the nearest hundreds place, the digit in the tens place is used. If it is a zero, one, 2, 3, or 4, the digit being rounded to is left alone. If it is a 5, 6, 7, 8 or 9, the digit being rounded to is increased by one. All other digits before the decimal point are then changed to zeros, and the digits in decimal places are dropped. If a decimal place is being rounded to, all digits that come after are just dropped.

For example, if 845,231.45 was to be rounded to the nearest thousands place, the answer would be 845,000. The 5 would remain the same due to the 2 in the hundreds place. Also, if 4.567 were to be rounded to the nearest tenths place, the answer would be 4.6. The 5 increased to 6 due to the 6 in the hundredths place, and the rest of the decimal is dropped.

Mental math should always be considered as problems are worked through, and the ability to work through problems in one's head helps save time. If a problem is simple enough, such as $15 + 3 = 18$, it should be completed mentally. The ability to do this will increase once addition and subtraction in higher place values are grasped. Also, mental math is important in multiplication and division. The times tables multiplying all numbers from 1 to 12 should be memorized. This will allow for division within those numbers to be memorized as well. For example, we should know easily that $121 \div 11 = 11$ because it should be memorized that $11 \times 11 = 121$.

Here is the multiplication table to be memorized:

x	1	2	3	4	5	6	7	8	9	10	11	12	13	14	15
1	1	2	3	4	5	6	7	8	9	10	11	12	13	14	15
2	2	4	6	8	10	12	14	16	18	20	22	24	26	28	30
3	3	6	9	12	15	18	21	24	27	30	33	36	39	42	45
4	4	8	12	16	20	24	28	32	36	40	44	48	52	56	60
5	5	10	15	20	25	30	35	40	45	50	55	60	65	70	75
6	6	12	18	24	30	36	42	48	54	60	66	72	78	84	90
7	7	14	21	28	35	42	49	56	63	70	77	84	91	98	105
8	8	16	24	32	40	48	56	64	72	80	88	96	104	112	120
9	9	18	27	36	45	54	63	72	81	90	99	108	117	126	135
10	10	20	30	40	50	60	70	80	90	100	110	120	130	140	150
11	11	22	33	44	55	66	77	88	99	110	121	132	143	154	165
12	12	24	36	48	60	72	84	96	108	120	132	144	156	168	180
13	13	26	39	52	65	78	91	104	117	130	143	156	169	182	195
14	14	28	42	56	70	84	98	112	126	140	154	168	182	196	210
15	15	30	45	60	75	90	105	120	135	150	165	180	195	210	225

The values along the diagonal of the table consist of **perfect squares**. A perfect square is A perfect square is the product of two of the same numbers.

Estimating Absolute and Relative Error in the Numerical Answer to a Problem

Once a result is determined to be logical within the context of a given problem, the result should be evaluated by its nearness to the expected answer. This is performed by approximating given values to perform mental math. Numbers should be rounded to the nearest value possible to check the initial results.

Consider the following example: A problem states that a customer is buying a new sound system for their home. The customer purchases a stereo for $435, 2 speakers for $67 each, and the necessary cables for $12. The customer chooses an option that allows him to spread the costs over equal payments for 4 months. How much will the monthly payments be?

After making calculations for the problem, a student determines that the monthly payment will be $145.25. To check the accuracy of the results, the student rounds each cost to the nearest ten ($440 + 70 + 70 + 10$) and determines that the total is approximately $590. Dividing by 4 months gives an approximate monthly payment of $147.50. Therefore, the student can conclude that the solution of $145.25 is very close to what should be expected.

When rounding, the place-value that is used in rounding can make a difference. Suppose the student had rounded to the nearest hundred for the estimation. The result ($400 + 100 + 100 + 0 = 600; 600 \div 4 = 150$) will show that the answer is reasonable but not as close to the actual value as rounding to the nearest ten.

When considering the accuracy of estimates, the error in the estimated solution can be shown as absolute and relative. **Absolute error** tells the actual difference between the estimated value and the true, calculated value. The **relative error** tells how large the error is in relation to the true value. There may be two problems where the absolute error of the values (the estimated one and the calculated one) is 10. For one problem, this may mean the relative error in the estimate is very small because the estimated value is 15,000, and the true value is 14,990. Ten in relation to the true value of 15,000 is small: 0.06%. For the other problem, the estimated value is 50, and the true value is 40. In this case, the absolute error of 10 means a high relative error because the true value is smaller. The relative error is $\frac{10}{40} = 0.25$ or 25%.

Statistical Principles

Performing Arithmetic Operations on Basic Statistical Data

The field of statistics describes relationships between quantities that are related, but not necessarily in a deterministic manner. For example, a graduating student's salary will often be higher when the student graduates with a higher GPA, but this is not always the case. Likewise, people who smoke tobacco are more likely to develop lung cancer, but, in fact, it is possible for non-smokers to develop the disease as well. **Statistics** describes these kinds of situations, where the likelihood of some outcome depends on the starting data.

Descriptive statistics involves analyzing a collection of data to describe its broad properties such average (or mean), what percent of the data falls within a given range, and other such properties. An example of this would be taking all of the test scores from a given class and calculating the average test score. **Inferential statistics** attempts to use data about a subset of some population to make inferences about the rest of the population. An example of this would be taking a collection of students who

received tutoring and comparing their results to a collection of students who did not receive tutoring, then using that comparison to try to predict whether the tutoring program in question is beneficial.

To be sure that inferences have a high probability of being true for the whole population, the subset that is analyzed needs to resemble a miniature version of the population as closely as possible. For this reason, statisticians like to choose random samples from the population to study, rather than picking a specific group of people based on some similarity. For example, studying the incomes of people who live in Portland does not reveal anything useful about the incomes of people who live in Tallahassee.

Ratios and Proportions

A **ratio** is a comparison of two quantities in a particular order. Example: If there are 14 computers in a lab, and the class has 20 students, there is a student to computer ratio of 20 to 14, commonly written as 20:14. Ratios are normally reduced to their smallest whole number representation, so 20:14 would be reduced to 10:7 by dividing both sides by 2.

A **proportion** is a relationship between two quantities that dictates how one changes when the other changes. A direct proportion describes a relationship in which a quantity increases by a set amount for every increase in the other quantity, or decreases by that same amount for every decrease in the other quantity. Example: Assuming a constant driving speed, the time required for a car trip increases as the distance of the trip increases. The distance to be traveled and the time required to travel are directly proportional.

Inverse proportion is a relationship in which an increase in one quantity is accompanied by a decrease in the other, or vice versa. Example: the time required for a car trip decreases as the speed increases, and increases as the speed decreases, so the time required is inversely proportional to the speed of the car.

Solving for x in a Proportion

Solve for x in this proportion: $\frac{10}{15} = \frac{x}{30}$.

There are two ways to solve for x.

Method 1: Cross multiply; then, solve for x.

$$\frac{10}{15} = \frac{x}{30}$$

$$10(30) = 15(x)$$

$$300 = 15x$$

$$300 \div 15 = 15x \div 15$$

$$x = 20$$

Method 2: Notice that 30 is twice as much as 15, so x should be twice as much as 10. Therefore,

$$x = 10 \times 2 = 20$$

Mean, Median, and Mode

The **center** of a set of data (statistical values) can be represented by its mean, median, or mode. These are sometimes referred to as **measures of central tendency**.

Mean

Suppose that you have a set of data points and some description of the general properties of this data need to be found.

The first property that can be defined for this set of data is the **mean**. This is the same as the average. To find the mean, add up all the data points, then divide by the total number of data points. For example, suppose that in a class of 10 students, the scores on a test were 50, 60, 65, 65, 75, 80, 85, 85, 90, 100. Therefore, the average test score will be:

$$\frac{50 + 60 + 65 + 65 + 75 + 80 + 85 + 85 + 90 + 100}{10} = 75.5$$

The mean is a useful number if the distribution of data is normal (more on this later), which roughly means that the frequency of different outcomes has a single peak and is roughly equally distributed on both sides of that peak. However, it is less useful in some cases where the data might be split or where there are some **outliers**. Outliers are data points that are far from the rest of the data. For example, suppose there are 10 executives and 90 employees at a company. The executives make $1,000 per hour, and the employees make $10 per hour.

Therefore, the average pay rate will be:

$$\frac{\$1,000 \times 10 + \$10 \times 90}{100} = \$109 \text{ per hour}$$

In this case, this average is not very descriptive since it's not close to the actual pay of the executives or the employees.

Median

Another useful measurement is the **median**. In a data set, the median is the point in the middle. The middle refers to the point where half the data comes before it and half comes after, when the data is recorded in numerical order. For instance, these are the speeds of the fastball of a pitcher during the last inning that he pitched (in order from least to greatest):

90, 92, 93, 93, 95, 96, 97, 97, 97

There are nine total numbers, so the middle or *median* number is the 5th one, which is 95.

In cases where the number of data points is an even number, then the average of the two middle points is taken. In the previous example of test scores, the two middle points are 75 and 80. Since there is no single point, the average of these two scores needs to be found. The average is:

$$\frac{75 + 80}{2} = 77.5$$

The median is generally a good value to use if there are a few outliers in the data. It prevents those outliers from affecting the "middle" value as much as when using the mean.

Since an outlier is a data point that is far from most of the other data points in a data set, this means an outlier also is any point that is far from the median of the data set. The outliers can have a substantial effect on the mean of a data set, but they usually do not change the median or mode, or do not change them by a large quantity. For example, consider the data set (3, 5, 6, 6, 6, 8). This has a median of 6 and

72

a mode of 6, with a mean of $\frac{34}{6} \approx 5.67$. Now, suppose a new data point of 1,000 is added so that the data set is now (3, 5, 6, 6, 6, 8, 1,000). The median and mode, which are both still 6, remain unchanged. However, the average is now $\frac{1034}{7}$, which is approximately 147.7. In this case, the median and mode will be better descriptions for most of the data points.

Outliers in a given data set are sometimes the result of an error by the experimenter, but oftentimes, they are perfectly valid data points that must be taken into consideration.

Mode
One additional measure to define for X is the **mode.** This is the data point that appears most frequently. If two or more data points all tie for the most frequent appearance, then each of them is considered a mode. In the case of the test scores, where the numbers were 50, 60, 65, 65, 75, 80, 85, 85, 90, 100, there are two modes: 65 and 85.

A data set may have a single mode, multiple modes, or no mode. If different values repeat equally as often, multiple modes exist. If no value repeats, no mode exists. Consider the following data sets:

- A: 7, 9, 10, 13, 14, 14
- B: 37, 44, 33, 37, 49, 44, 51, 34, 37, 33, 44
- C: 173, 154, 151, 168, 155

Set A has a mode of 14. Set B has modes of 37 and 44. Set C has no mode.

The range of a data set is the difference between the highest and the lowest values in the set. The range can be considered the span of the data set. To determine the range, the smallest value in the set is subtracted from the largest value. The ranges for the data sets A, B, and C above are calculated as follows: A: $14 - 7 = 7$; B: $51 - 33 = 18$; C: $173 - 151 = 22$.

Changing all values of a data set in a consistent way produces predictable changes in the measures of the center and range of the set. A linear transformation changes the original value into the new value by either adding a given number to each value, multiplying each value by a given number, or both. Adding (or subtracting) a given value to each data point will increase (or decrease) the mean, median, and any modes by the same value. However, the range will remain the same due to the way that range is calculated. Multiplying (or dividing) a given value by each data point will increase (or decrease) the mean, median, and any modes, and the range by the same factor.

Consider the following data set, call it set P, representing the price of different cases of soda at a grocery store: $4.25, $4.40, $4.75, $4.95, $4.95, $5.15. The mean of set P is $4.74. The median is $4.85. The mode of the set is $4.95. The range is $0.90. Suppose the state passes a new tax of $0.25 on every case of soda sold. The new data set, set T, is calculated by adding $0.25 to each data point from set P. Therefore, set T consists of the following values: $4.50, $4.65, $5.00, $5.20, $5.20, $5.40. The mean of set T is $4.99. The median is $5.10. The mode of the set is $5.20. The range is $.90. The mean, median and mode of set T is equal to $0.25 added to the mean, median, and mode of set P. The range stays the same.

Now suppose, due to inflation, the store raises the cost of every item by 10 percent. Raising costs by 10 percent is calculated by multiplying each value by 1.1. The new data set, set I, is calculated by multiplying each data point from set T by 1.1. Therefore, set I consists of the following values: $4.95, $5.12, $5.50, $5.72, $5.72, $5.94. The mean of set I is $5.49. The median is $5.61. The mode of the set is $5.72. The range is $0.99. The mean, median, mode, and range of set I is equal to 1.1 multiplied by the mean, median, mode, and range of set T because each increased by a factor of 10 percent.

Quartiles and Percentiles

The **first quartile** of a set of data X refers to the largest value from the first $\frac{1}{4}$ of the data points. In practice, there are sometimes slightly different definitions that can be used, such as the median of the first half of the data points (excluding the median itself if there are an odd number of data points). The term also has a slightly different use: when it is said that a data point lies in the first quartile, it means it is less than or equal to the median of the first half of the data points. Conversely, if it lies *at* the first quartile, then it is equal to the first quartile.

When it is said that a data point lies in the **second quartile**, it means it is between the first quartile and the median.

The **third quartile** refers to data that lies between $\frac{1}{2}$ and $\frac{3}{4}$ of the way through the data set. Again, there are various methods for defining this precisely, but the simplest way is to include all of the data that lie between the median and the median of the top half of the data.

Data that lies in the **fourth quartile** refers to all of the data above the third quartile.

Percentiles may be defined in a similar manner to quartiles. Generally, this is defined in the following manner:

If a data point lies *in the n-th percentile*, this means it lies in the range of the first $n\%$ of the data.

If a data point lies *at* the n-th percentile, then it means that $n\%$ of the data lies below this data point.

Standard Deviation

Given a data set X consisting of data points $(x_1, x_2, x_3, \ldots x_n)$, the **variance** of X is defined to be:

$$\frac{\sum_{i=1}^{n}(x_i - \bar{X})^2}{n}$$

This means that the variance of X is the average of the squares of the differences between each data point and the mean of X. In the formula, $\bar{X}$ is the mean of the values in the data set, and x_i represents each individual value in the data set. The sigma notation indicates that the sum should be found with n being the number of values to add together. $i = 1$ means that the values should begin with the first value.

Given a data set X consisting of data points $(x_1, x_2, x_3, \ldots x_n)$, the **standard deviation** of X is defined to be:

$$s_x = \sqrt{\frac{\sum_{i=1}^{n}(x_i - \bar{X})^2}{n}}$$

74

In other words, the standard deviation is the square root of the variance.

Both the variance and the standard deviation are measures of how much the data tend to be spread out. When the standard deviation is low, the data points are mostly clustered around the mean. When the standard deviation is high, this generally indicates that the data are quite spread out, or else that there are a few substantial outliers.

As a simple example, compute the standard deviation for the data set (1, 3, 3, 5). First, compute the mean, which will be:

$$\frac{1+3+3+5}{4} = \frac{12}{4} = 3$$

Now, find the variance of X with the formula:

$$\sum_{i=1}^{4}(x_i - \bar{X})^2 = (1-3)^2 + (3-3)^2 + (3-3)^2 + (5-3)^2$$

$$-2^2 + 0^2 + 0^2 + 2^2 = 8$$

Therefore, the variance is $\frac{8}{4} = 2$. Taking the square root, the standard deviation will be $\sqrt{2}$.

Note that the standard deviation only depends upon the mean, not upon the median or mode(s). Generally, if there are multiple modes that are far apart from one another, the standard deviation will be high. A high standard deviation does not always mean there are multiple modes, however.

Choosing an Appropriate Measure of Central Tendency

Measures of central tendency, namely mean, median, and mode, describe characteristics of a set of data. Specifically, they are intended to represent a *typical* value in the set by identifying a central position of the set. Depending on the characteristics of a specific set of data, different measures of central tendency are more indicative of a typical value in the set.

When a data set is grouped closely together with a relatively small range and the data is spread out somewhat evenly, the mean is an effective indicator of a typical value in the set. Consider the following data set representing the height of sixth grade boys in inches: 61 inches, 54 inches, 58 inches, 63 inches, 58 inches. The mean of the set is 58.8 inches. The data set is grouped closely (the range is only 9 inches) and the values are spread relatively evenly (three values below the mean and two values above the mean). Therefore, the mean value of 58.8 inches is an effective measure of central tendency in this case.

When a data set contains a small number of values either extremely large or extremely small when compared to the other values, the mean is not an effective measure of central tendency. Consider the following data set representing annual incomes of homeowners on a given street: $71,000; $74,000; $75,000; $77,000; $340,000. The mean of this set is $127,400. This figure does not indicate a typical value in the set, which contains four out of five values between $71,000 and $77,000. The median is a much more effective measure of central tendency for data sets such as these. Finding the middle value diminishes the influence of outliers, or numbers that may appear out of place, like the $340,000 annual income. The median for this set is $75,000 which is much more typical of a value in the set.

The mode of a data set is a useful measure of central tendency for categorical data when each piece of data is an option from a category. Consider a survey of 31 commuters asking how they get to work with results summarized below.

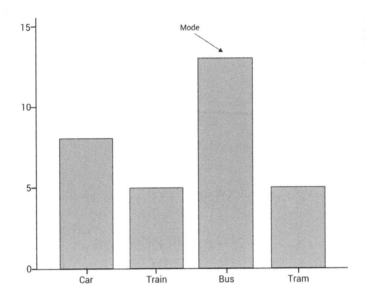

The mode for this set represents the value, or option, of the data that repeats most often. This indicates that the bus is the most popular method of transportation for the commuters.

Common Features of a Data Set

As mentioned, a set of data can be described in terms of its center, spread, shape and any unusual features. The **center** of a data set can be measured by its mean, median, or mode. The **spread** of a data set refers to how far the data points are from the center (mean or median). The spread can be measured by the range or by the quartiles and interquartile range. A data set with all its data points clustered around the center will have a small spread. A data set covering a wide range of values will have a large spread.

When a data set is displayed as a histogram or frequency distribution plot, the shape indicates if a sample is normally distributed, symmetrical, or has measures of skewness or kurtosis. When graphed, a data set with a normal distribution will resemble a bell curve.

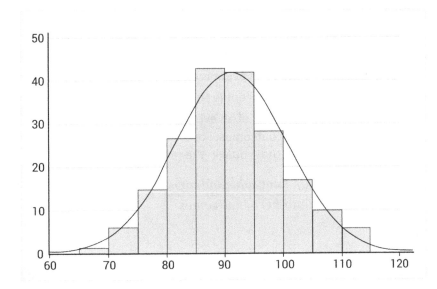

If the data set is **symmetrical**, each half of the graph when divided at the center is a mirror image of the other. If the graph has fewer data points to the right, the data is **skewed right**. If it has fewer data points to the left, the data is **skewed left**.

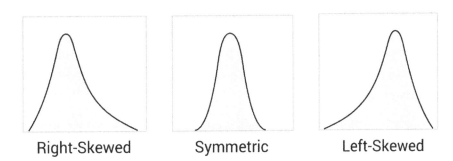

Right-Skewed   Symmetric   Left-Skewed

Kurtosis is a measure of whether the data is heavy-tailed with a high number of outliers, or light-tailed with a low number of outliers.

A description of a data set should include any unusual features such as gaps or outliers. A **gap** is a span within the range of the data set containing no data points. An **outlier** is a data point with a value either extremely large or extremely small when compared to the other values in the set.

The Basic Principles of Probability and Predicting the Likeliness of a Particular Outcome

Independent and Dependent Events

Probability is a measure of how likely an event is to occur. Probability is written as a fraction or decimal between zero and one. If an event has a probability of zero, the event will never occur. If an event has a probability of one, the event will definitely occur. If the probability of an event is closer to zero, the event is unlikely to occur. If the probability of an event is closer to one, the event is more likely to occur. For example, a probability of $\frac{1}{2}$ means that the event is equally as likely to occur as it is not to occur. An example of this is tossing a coin. The probability of an event can be calculated by dividing the number of favorable outcomes by the number of total outcomes. For example, suppose you have 2 raffle tickets out of 20 total tickets sold. The probability that you win the raffle is calculated:

$$\frac{number\ of\ favorable\ outcomes}{total\ number\ of\ outcomes} = \frac{2}{20} = \frac{1}{10}$$

Always reduce fractions.

Therefore, the probability of winning the raffle is $\frac{1}{10}$ or 0.1.

Chance is the measure of how likely an event is to occur, written as a percent. If an event will never occur, the event has a 0% chance. If an event will certainly occur, the event has a 100% chance. If an event will sometimes occur, the event has a chance somewhere between 0% and 100%. To calculate chance, probability is calculated, and the fraction is converted to a percent.

The probability of multiple events occurring can be determined by multiplying the probability of each event. For example, suppose you flip a coin with heads and tails, and roll a six-sided die numbered one through six. To find the probability that you will flip heads AND roll a two, the probability of each event is determined, and those fractions are multiplied. The probability of flipping heads is $\frac{1}{2} \left(\frac{1\ side\ with\ heads}{2\ sides\ total} \right)$, and the probability of rolling a two is:

$$\frac{1}{6} \left(\frac{1\ side\ with\ a\ 2}{6\ total\ sides} \right)$$

The probability of flipping heads AND rolling a 2 is:

$$\frac{1}{2} \times \frac{1}{6} = \frac{1}{12}$$

The above scenario with flipping a coin and rolling a die is an example of independent events. Independent events are circumstances in which the outcome of one event does not affect the outcome of the other event. Conversely, dependent events are ones in which the outcome of one event affects the outcome of the second event. Consider the following scenario: a bag contains 5 black marbles and 5 white marbles. What is the probability of picking 2 black marbles without replacing the marble after the first pick?

The probability of picking a black marble on the first pick is:

$$\frac{5}{10} = \frac{5 \text{ black marbles}}{10 \text{ total marbles}}$$

Assuming that a black marble was picked, there are now 4 black marbles and 5 white marbles for the second pick. Therefore, the probability of picking a black marble on the second pick is:

$$\frac{4}{9} = \frac{4 \text{ black marbles}}{9 \text{ total marbles}}$$

To find the probability of picking two black marbles, the probability of each is multiplied:

$$\frac{5}{10} \times \frac{4}{9} = \frac{20}{90} = \frac{2}{9}$$

Conditional Probabilities

An outcome occasionally lies within some range of possibilities B, and the probability that the outcomes also lie within some set of possibilities A needs to be figured. This is called a **conditional probability**. It is written as $P(A|B)$, which is read "the probability of A given B." The general formula for computing conditional probabilities is:

$$P(A|B) = \frac{P(A \cap B)}{P(B)}$$

However, when dealing with uniform probability distributions, simplify this a bit. Write $|A|$ to indicate the number of outcomes in A. Then, for uniform probability distributions, write $P(A|B) = \frac{|A \cap B|}{|B|}$ (recall that $A \cap B$ means "A intersect B," and consists of all of the outcomes that lie in both A and B). This means that all possible outcomes do not need to be known. To see why this formula works, suppose that the set of outcomes X is $(x_1, x_2, x_3, \ldots x_n)$, so that $|X| = n$. Then, for a uniform probability distribution, $P(A) = \frac{|A|}{n}$. However, this means:

$$(A|B) = \frac{P(A \cap B)}{P(B)} = \frac{\frac{|A \cap B|}{n}}{\frac{|B|}{n}} = \frac{|A \cap B|}{|B|}$$

Remember, the n's cancel out.

For example, suppose a die is rolled, and it is known that it will land between 1 and 4. However, how many sides the die has is unknown. Figure the probability that the die is rolled higher than 2. To figure this, $P(3)$ or $P(4)$ does not need to be determined, or any of the other probabilities, since it is known that a fair die has a uniform probability distribution. Therefore, apply the formula $\frac{|A \cap B|}{|B|}$. So, in this case B is (1, 2, 3, 4) and $A \cap B$ is (3, 4). Therefore:

$$\frac{|A \cap B|}{|B|} = \frac{2}{4} = \frac{1}{2}$$

Conditional probability is an important concept because, in many situations, the likelihood of one outcome can differ radically depending on how something else comes out. The probability of passing a

79

test given that one has studied all of the material is generally much higher than the probability of passing a test given that one has not studied at all. The probability of a person having heart trouble is much lower if that person exercises regularly. The probability that a college student will graduate is higher when their SAT scores are higher, and so on. For this reason, there are many people who are interested in conditional probabilities.

Note that in some practical situations, changing the order of the conditional probabilities can make the outcome very different. For example, the probability that a person with heart trouble has exercised regularly is quite different than the probability that a person who exercises regularly will have heart trouble. The probability of a person receiving a military-only award, given that he or she is or was a soldier, is generally not very high, but the probability that a person being or having been a soldier, given that he or she received a military-only award, is 1.

However, in some cases, the outcomes do not influence one another this way. If the probability of A is the same regardless of whether B is given; that is, if $P(A|B) = P(A)$, then A and B are considered **independent**. In this case:

$$P(A|B) = \frac{P(A \cap B)}{P(B)} = P(A)$$

Which means,

$$P(A \cap B) = P(A)P(B)$$

In fact, if $P(A \cap B) = P(A)P(B)$, it can be determined that $P(A|B) = P(A)$ and $P(A|B) = P(B)$ by working backward. Therefore, B is also independent of A.

An example of something being independent can be seen in rolling dice. In this case, consider a red die and a green die. It is expected that when the dice are rolled, the outcome of the green die should not depend in any way on the outcome of the red die. Or, to take another example, if the same die is rolled repeatedly, then the next number rolled should not depend on which numbers have been rolled previously. Similarly, if a coin is flipped, then the next flip's outcome does not depend on the outcomes of previous flips.

This can sometimes be counterintuitive, since when rolling a die or flipping a coin, there can be a streak of surprising results. If, however, it is known that the die or coin is fair, then these results are just the result of the fact that over long periods of time, it is very likely that some unlikely streaks of outcomes will occur. Therefore, avoid making the mistake of thinking that when considering a series of independent outcomes, a particular outcome is "due to happen" simply because a surprising series of outcomes has already been seen.

There is a second type of common mistake that people tend to make when reasoning about statistical outcomes: the idea that when something of low probability happens, the outcome is surprising. It would be surprising that something with low probability happened after just one attempt. However, with so much happening all at once, it is easy to see at least something happen in a way that seems to have a very low probability. In fact, a lottery is a good example. The odds of winning a lottery are very small, but the odds that somebody wins the lottery each week are actually fairly high. Therefore, no one should be surprised when some low probability things happen.

Addition Rule

The **addition rule** for probabilities states that the probability of A or B happening is:

$$P(A \cup B) = P(A) + P(B) - P(A \cap B)$$

Note that the subtraction of $P(A \cap B)$ must be performed, or else it would result in double counting any outcomes that lie in both A and in B.

For example, suppose that a 20-sided die is being rolled. Fred bets that the outcome will be greater than 10, while Helen bets that it will be greater than 4 but less than 15. What is the probability that at least one of them is correct?

We apply the rule $P(A \cup B) = P(A) + P(B) - P(A \cap B)$, where A is that outcome x is in the range $x > 10$, and B is that outcome x is in the range $4 < x < 15$. Probability A has 10 possibilities and probability B also has 10 possibilities. Multiply the possibilities by $\frac{1}{20}$ ($\frac{\text{One die side}}{\text{Total die sides}}$).

$$P(A) = 10 \times \frac{1}{20} = \frac{1}{2}$$

$$P(B) = 10 \times \frac{1}{20} = \frac{1}{2}$$

$P(A \cap B)$ can be computed by noting that $A \cap B$ means the outcome x is in the range $10 < x < 15$. $P(A \cap B)$ has 4 possibilities. So,

$$P(A \cap B) = 4 \times \frac{1}{20} = \frac{1}{5}$$

Therefore:

$$P(A \cup B) = P(A) + P(B) - P(A \cap B)$$

$$\frac{1}{2} + \frac{1}{2} - \frac{1}{5} = \frac{4}{5}$$

Note that in this particular example, we could also have directly reasoned about the set of possible outcomes $A \cup B$, by noting that this would mean that x must be in the range $5 \leq x$. However, this is not always the case, depending on the given information.

Multiplication Rule

The **multiplication rule** for probabilities states the probability of A and B both happening is:

$$P(A \cap B) = P(A) \times P(B|A)$$

As an example, suppose that when Jamie wears black pants, there is a ½ probability that she wears a black shirt as well, and that she wears black pants ¾ of the time. What is the probability that she is wearing both a black shirt and black pants?

To figure this, use the above formula, where *A* will be "Jamie is wearing black pants," while *B* will be "Jamie is wearing a black shirt." It is known that $P(A)$ is $\frac{3}{4}$. It is also known that $P(B|A) = \frac{1}{2}$. Multiplying the two, the probability that she is wearing both black pants and a black shirt is:

$$P(A)P(B|A) = \frac{3}{4} \times \frac{1}{2} = \frac{3}{8}$$

Counting Techniques

There are many counting techniques that can help solve problems involving counting possibilities; the Addition Principle and Multiplication Principle just described are two examples. Counting techniques also involve permutations. A **permutation** is an arrangement of elements in a set for which order must be considered. For example, if three letters from the alphabet are chosen, ABC and BAC are two different permutations. The multiplication rule can be used to determine the total number of possibilities. If each letter can't be selected twice, the total number of possibilities is:

$$26 \times 25 \times 24 = 15,600$$

A formula can also be used to calculate this total. In general, the notation $P(n, r)$ represents the number of ways to arrange r objects from a set of n and, the formula is:

$$P(n, r) = \frac{n!}{(n - r)!}$$

In the previous example:

$$P(26, 3) = \frac{26!}{23!} = 15,600$$

Contrasting permutations, a **combination** is an arrangement of elements in which order doesn't matter. In this case, ABC and BAC are the same combination. In the previous scenario, there are six permutations that represent each single combination. Therefore, the total number of possible combinations is $15,600 \div 6 = 2,600$. In general, $C(n, r)$ represents the total number of combinations of n items selected r at a time where order doesn't matter. Another way to represent the combinations of r items selected out of a set of n items is $\binom{n}{r}$. The formula for select combinations of items is:

$$\binom{n}{r} = C(n, r) = \frac{n!}{(n - r)!\, r!}$$

Therefore, the following relationship exists between permutations and combinations:

$$C(n, r) = \frac{P(n, r)}{r!} = \frac{P(n, r)}{P(r, r)}$$

Probability for an event is equal to the number of outcomes in that event divided by the total number of outcomes in the sample space. For example, consider rolling a 6-sided die. The probability of rolling an odd number is $\frac{3}{6}$, or $\frac{1}{2}$, because there are 3 odd numbers on the die.

The **fundamental counting principle** states that if there are m potential ways an event can occur, and n potential ways a second event can occur, then there are $m \times n$ potential ways both events can occur. For example, there are two events that can occur after flipping a coin and six events that can occur after rolling a die, so there are $2 \times 6 = 12$ total possible event scenarios if both are done simultaneously. This principle can be used to find probabilities involving finite sample spaces and independent trials because it calculates the total number of possible outcomes. For this principle to work, the events must be independent of each other.

Using Normal, Binomial, and Exponential Distributions

A **normal distribution** of data follows the shape of a bell curve and the data set's median, mean, and mode are equal. Therefore, 50 percent of its values are less than the mean and 50 percent are greater than the mean. Data sets that follow this shape can be generalized using normal distributions. Normal distributions are described as **frequency distributions** in which the data set is plotted as percentages rather than true data points. A **relative frequency distribution** is one where the y-axis is between zero and 1, which is the same as 0% to 100%.

Within a standard deviation, 68 percent of the values are within 1 standard deviation of the mean, 95 percent of the values are within 2 standard deviations of the mean, and 99.7 percent of the values are within 3 standard deviations of the mean. The number of standard deviations that a data point falls from the mean is called the **z-score.** The formula for the z-score is $Z = \frac{x-\mu}{\sigma}$, where μ is the mean, σ is the standard deviation, and x is the data point. This formula is used to fit any data set that resembles a normal distribution to a standard normal distribution in a process known as **standardizing**.

Here is a normal distribution with labeled z-scores:

Normal Distribution with Labelled Z-Scores

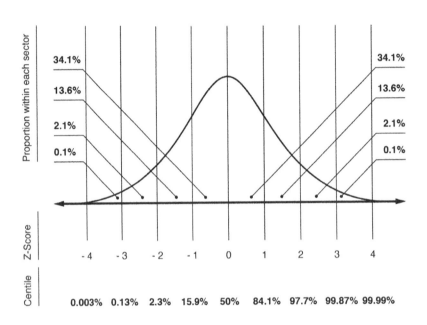

Population percentages can be estimated using normal distributions. For example, the probability that a data point will be less than the mean, or that the z-score will be less than 0, is 50%. Similarly, the probability that a data point will be within 1 standard deviation of the mean, or that the z-score will be between −1 and 1, is about 68.2%. When using a z-table, the left column states how many standard deviations (to one decimal place) away from the mean the point is, and the row heading states the second decimal place. The entries in the table corresponding to each column and row give the probability, which is equal to the area.

In statistics, a **binomial experiment** is an experiment that has the following properties. The experiment consists of n repeated trial that can each have only one of two outcomes. It can be either a success or a failure. The probability of success, p, is the same in every trial. Each trial is also independent of all other trials. An example of a binomial experiment is rolling a die 10 times with the goal of rolling a 5. Rolling a 5 is a success while any other value is a failure. In this experiment, the probability of rolling a 5 is $\frac{1}{6}$. In any binomial experiment, x is the number of resulting successes, n is the number of trials, p is the probability of success in each trial, and $q = 1 - p$ is the probability of failure within each trial.

84

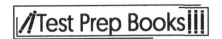

The probability of obtaining x successes within n trials is:

$$P(X = x) = \frac{n!}{x!\,(n-x)!}p^x(1-p)^{n-x}$$

With the following being the **binomial coefficient**:

$$\binom{n}{x} = \frac{n!}{x!\,(n-x)!}$$

Within this calculation, $n!$ is n factorial that's defined as:

$$n \times (n-1) \times (n-2)\ldots 1$$

Let's look at the probability of obtaining 2 rolls of a 5 out of the 10 rolls.

Start with $P(X = 2)$, where 2 is the number of successes. Then fill in the rest of the formula with what is known, n=10, x=2, p=1/6, q=5/6:

$$P(X = 2) = \left(\frac{10!}{2!\,(10-2)!}\right)\left(\frac{1}{6}\right)^2\left(1-\frac{1}{6}\right)^{10-2}$$

Which simplifies to:

$$P(X = 2) = \left(\frac{10!}{2!\,8!}\right)\left(\frac{1}{6}\right)^2\left(\frac{5}{6}\right)^8$$

Then solve to get:

$$P(X = 2) = \left(\frac{3628800}{80640}\right)(.0277)(.2325) = .2898$$

A continuous random variable x is said to have an exponential distribution if it has probability density function $f(x) = \frac{1}{\beta}e^{-(x-\mu)/\beta}, x \geq \mu;\ \beta > 0$.

The value μ is known as the **location parameter**, and β is the **scale parameter**. Oftentimes, the scale parameter is referred to as λ and is equal to $1/\beta$. λ is also referred to as the scale parameter. When $\mu =$

0 and $\beta = 1$, this function is known as the **standard exponential distribution**, and $f(x) = e^{-x}$ for $x \geq$ 0. Here is the plot of the exponential probability distribution function:

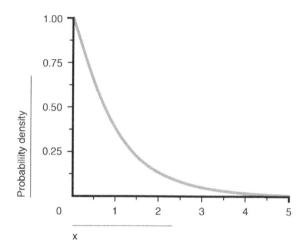

Similarly, the formula for the cumulative distribution function of the exponential function is $F(x) = 1 - e^{-x/\beta}$ for $x \geq 0, \beta > 0$, and here is its plot:

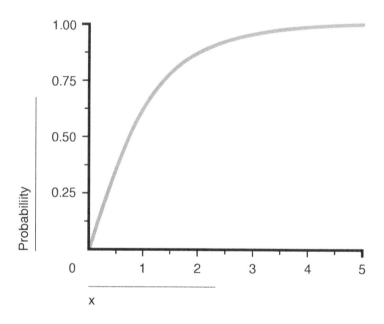

In probability and statistics, exponential distributions are used when the time between events that occur continuously and independently is a constant, average rate. The mean of an exponential distribution is $\beta = \frac{1}{\lambda}$, and its variance is $\beta^2 = \frac{1}{\lambda^2}$. Therefore, if the square root of the variance is taken, it is equal to the mean. Therefore, the standard deviation is equal to the mean.

Consider a rental car counter in which customers arrive at the rate of 20 per hour. The cumulative exponential distribution can be used to find the probability in which the arrival time between

consecutive customers is less than 2 minutes. The mean number of customers per hour is 20, and therefore this is the rate of the function, so $\lambda = 20$. Two minutes represents 0.033 hour. Therefore:

$$P(\text{arrival time less than 2 minutes}) = 1 - e^{-(20)(0.033)} = 0.483$$

Therefore, there is a 48.3% chance that the arrival time between consecutive customers is less than 2 minutes.

Calculating Expected Values

The **expected value** of a random variable represents the mean value in either a large sample size or after a large number of trials. According to the law of large numbers, after a large number of trials, the actual mean (and that of the probability distribution) is approximately equal to the expected value. The expected value is a weighted average and is calculated as $E(X) = \sum x_i p_i$, where x_i represents the value of each outcome and p_i represents the probability of each outcome. If all probabilities are equal, the expected value is:

$$E(X) = \frac{x_1 + x_2 + \cdots + x_n}{n}$$

Expected value is often called the **mean of the random variable** and is also a measure of central tendency.

Consider the following situation: A landscaper bids on jobs where she can make a $2,000 profit. The probabilities of getting 1, 2, or 3 jobs per month are shown below in the probability distribution:

Number of Jobs	1	2	3
Probability	0.4	0.5	0.1

Her expected profit per month can be calculated by using the expected value formula. Multiply each probability times the profit in each instance, and sum up those values. This results in the following:

$$E(x) = 2,000 \times 0.4 + 4,000 \times 0.5 + 6,000 \times 0.1$$

$$800 + 2,000 + 600 = 3400$$

Therefore, she expects to make, on average, $3,400 per month.

Given a statistical experiment, a theoretical probability distribution can be calculated if the theoretical probabilities are known. The theoretical probabilities are plugged into the formula for both the binomial probability and the expected value. An example of this is any scenario involving rolls of a die or flips of a coin. The theoretical probabilities are known without any observed experiments. Another example of this is finding the theoretical probability distribution for the number of correct answers obtained by guessing a specific number of multiple choice questions on a class exam.

Empirical data is defined as real data. If real data is known, approximations concerning samples and populations can be obtained by working backwards. This scenario is the case where theoretical probabilities are unknown, and experimental data must be used to make decisions. The sample data (including actual probabilities) must be plugged into the formulas for both binomial probability and the expected value. The actual probabilities are obtained using observation and can be seen in a probability distribution. An example of this scenario is determining a probability distribution for the number of

televisions per household in the United States, and determining the expected number of televisions per household as well.

Calculating if it's worth it to play a game or make a decision is a critical part of probability theory. Expected values can be calculated in terms of payoff values and deciding whether to make a decision or play a game can be done based on the actual expected value. Applying this theory to gambling and card games is fairly typical. The payoff values in these instances are the actual monetary totals.

Understanding Standardized Test Scores

Students will undoubtedly take several standardized tests throughout their academic career, and it is important for educators to be able to interpret results from these types of exams. Educators should be able to understand an individual student's score relative to the performance of their peer group, other students, or the aggregate of all test takers. Moreover, it is helpful to be able to explain this relative evaluation to inquisitive students, parents, and also school administrators. Many schools use their students' standardized test scores as a benchmark of performance for the school's curriculum and instruction in that content area. Additionally, with the importance of standardized test scores in competitive college admissions, many students and parents will likely have questions about scores that educators should be able to answer.

Standardized tests often make use of stanines, percentiles, or "grade-level equivalents" as means to compare an individual student's scores with the other students who attempted the exam. **Stanine** is a portmanteau for "standard nine" because the scores range from the minimum of 1 to the maximum of 9. This number range is further divided into three categories, which qualify an individual's performance relative to group at large. A stanine score of 1, 2, or 3 indicates that the student's raw score was "below average." Obtaining a stanine score of 4, 5, or 6 lands one in the "average" group, and scores of 7, 8, or 9 indicate an "above average" performance. Below average scores may indicate the need for further instruction and practice, and average scores mean that the student is at the same level as the majority of their peers.

Percentile scores delve into score comparisons with finer detail than stanine scores because instead of working on gross scale of 1–9, percentile scores range from 1 to 99. This multiplicative delineation of one's relative score allows for a significantly more precise performance comparison. A student's percentile score indicates the percentage of total test takers that student outperformed. For example, a student who scored in the 77th percentile achieved a score that is higher than 77% of the rest of the test cohort. A student's percentile score is different than the percentage of correct responses obtained on the test. Percentile score simply compares one student's score with the scores of all of the other students who took the test. Students whose percentile scores fall below the 50th percentile can be considered below average, as more than half of the other test takers outperformed their test attempt.

Lastly, **grade-level equivalents** are sometimes used in situations where an exam is designed to be at the complexity or competency expected of a certain grade level but is taken by students in other grades. Because students at higher and lower grades than the test's intended grade attempt the exam, it can be challenging to interpret grade-level equivalents. Grade-level equivalents fall along a continuum and are often decimal results. The number to the right of the decimal approximates the number of months into that grade level (to the left of the decimal) for which a student's performance is on par. The school year is assumed to be ten months. For example, a score of 5.2 achieved by a fourth-grade student indicates that their raw score was that which a typical fifth grade student would receive two months into the school year.

Computation & Problem Solving

Basic Addition, Subtraction, Multiplication, and Division

Gaining more of something related to addition, while taking something away relates to subtraction. Vocabulary words such as *total, more, less, left,* and *remain* are common when working with these problems. The $+$ sign means plus. This shows that addition is happening. The $-$ sign means minus. This shows that subtraction is happening. The symbols will be important when you write out equations.

Addition

Addition can also be defined in equation form. For example, $4 + 5 = 9$ shows that $4 + 5$ is the same as 9. Therefore, $9 = 9$, and "four plus five equals nine." When two quantities are being added together, the result is called the **sum**. Therefore, the sum of 4 and 5 is 9. The numbers being added, such as 4 and 5, are known as the *addends.*

Subtraction

Subtraction can also be in equation form. For example, $9 - 5 = 4$ shows that $9 - 5$ is the same as 4 and that "9 minus 5 is 4." The result of subtraction is known as a **difference.** The difference of $9 - 5$ is 4. 4 represents the amount that is left once the subtraction is done. The order in which subtraction is completed does matter. For example, $9 - 5$ and $5 - 9$ do not result in the same answer. $5 - 9$ results in a negative number. So, subtraction does not adhere to the commutative or associative property. The order in which subtraction is completed is important.

Multiplication

Multiplication is when we add equal amounts. The answer to a multiplication problem is called a **product**. Products stand for the total number of items within different groups. The symbol for multiplication is $\times$ or $\cdot$. We say 2×3 or $2 \cdot 3$ means "2 times 3."

As an example, there are three sets of four apples. The goal is to know how many apples there are in total. Three sets of four apples gives $4 + 4 + 4 = 12$. Also, three times four apples gives $3 \times 4 = 12$. Therefore, for any whole numbers a and b, where a is not equal to zero, $a \times b = b + b + \cdots b$, where b is added a times. Also, $a \times b$ can be thought of as the number of units in a rectangular block consisting of a rows and b columns. For example, 3×7 is equal to the number of squares in the following rectangle:

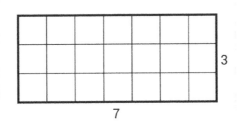

The answer is 21, and there are 21 squares in the rectangle.

With any number times one (for example, $8 \times 1 = 8$) the original amount does not change. Therefore, one is the **multiplicative identity**. For any whole number a, $1 \times a = a$. Also, any number multiplied times zero results in zero. Therefore, for any whole number a, $0 \times a = 0$.

Another method of multiplication can be done with the use of an **area model**. An area model is a rectangle that is divided into rows and columns that match up to the number of place values within each number. Take the example 29×65. These two numbers can be split into simpler numbers: $29 = 25 + 4$ and $65 = 60 + 5$. The products of those 4 numbers are found within the rectangle and then summed up to get the answer. The entire process is:

$$(60 \times 25) + (5 \times 25) + (60 \times 4) + (5 \times 4)$$

$$1,500 + 240 + 125 + 20 = 1,885$$

Here is the actual area model:

	25	**4**
60	60x25 1,500	60x4 240
5	5x25 125	5x4 20

```
    1 , 5 0 0
        2 4 0
        1 2 5
+         2 0
    1 , 8 8 5
```

Division

Division is based on dividing a given number into parts. The simplest problem involves dividing a number into equal parts. For example, a pack of 20 pencils is to be divided among 10 children. You would have to divide 20 by 10. In this example, each child would receive 2 pencils.

The symbol for division is $\div$ or $/$. The equation above is written as $20 \div 10 = 2$, or $20 / 10 = 2$. This means "20 divided by 10 is equal to 2." Division can be explained as the following: for any whole numbers a and b, where b is not equal to zero, $a \div b = c$ if and only if $a = b \times c$. This means, division can be thought of as a multiplication problem with a missing part. For instance, calculating $20 \div 10$ is the same as asking the following: "If there are 20 items in total with 10 in each group, how many are in each group?" Therefore, 20 is equal to ten times what value? This question is the same as asking, "If there are 20 items in total with 2 in each group, how many groups are there?" The answer to each question is 2.

In a division problem, a is known as the **dividend,** b is the **divisor**, and c is the **quotient**. Zero cannot be divided into parts. Therefore, for any nonzero whole number $a, 0 \div a = 0$. Also, division by zero is undefined. Dividing an amount into zero parts is not possible.

Harder division involves dividing a number into equal parts, but having some left over. An example is dividing a pack of 20 pencils among 8 friends so that each friend receives the same number of pencils. In this setting, each friend receives 2 pencils. There are 4 pencils leftover. 20 is the dividend, 8 is the divisor, 2 is the quotient, and 4 is known as the **remainder**. Within this type of division problem, for whole numbers a, b, c, and d, $a \div b = c$ with a remainder of d. This is true if and only if $a = (b \times c) + d$. When calculating $a \div b$, if there is no remainder, a is said to be *divisible* by b. **Even numbers** are all divisible by the number 2. **Odd numbers** are not divisible by 2. An odd number of items cannot be paired up into groups of 2 without having one item leftover.

Dividing a number by a single digit or two digits can be turned into repeated subtraction problems. An area model can be used throughout the problem that represents multiples of the divisor. For example, the answer to $8580 \div 55$ can be found by subtracting 55 from 8580 one at a time and counting the total number of subtractions necessary.

However, a simpler process involves using larger multiples of 55. First, $100 \times 55 = 5,500$ is subtracted from 8,580, and 3,080 is leftover. Next, $50 \times 55 = 2,750$ is subtracted from 3,080 to obtain 380. $5 \times 55 = 275$ is subtracted from 330 to obtain 55, and finally, $1 \times 55 = 55$ is subtracted from 55 to obtain zero. Therefore, there is no remainder, and the answer is $100 + 50 + 5 + 1 = 156$. Here is a picture of the area model and the repeated subtraction process:

$$8580 \div 55$$

	55
100	5500
50	2750
5	275
1	55

```
    55 ⟌ 8580
        -5500   (100 x 55)
         3080
        -2750   (50 x 55)
          330
         -275   (5 x 55)
           55
          -55   (1 x 55)
            0
```

If you want to check the answer of a division problem, multiply the answer times the divisor. This will help you check to see if the dividend is obtained. If there is a remainder, the same process is done, but the remainder is added on at the end to try to match the dividend. In the previous example, $156 \times 55 = 8580$ would be the checking procedure. Dividing decimals involves the same repeated subtraction

process. The only difference would be that the subtractions would involve numbers that include values in the decimal places. Lining up decimal places is crucial in this type of problem.

Using Operations in Math and Real-World Problems

Addition and subtraction are "inverse operations." Adding a number and then subtracting the same number will cancel each other out. This results in the original number, and vice versa. For example, $8 + 7 - 7 = 8$ and $137 - 100 + 100 = 137$.

Multiplication and division are also inverse operations. So, multiplying by a number and then dividing by the same number results in the original number. For example, $8 \times 2 \div 2 = 8$ and $12 \div 4 \times 4 = 12$. Inverse operations are used to work backwards to solve problems. In the case that 7 and a number add to 18, the inverse operation of subtraction is used to find the unknown value ($18 - 7 = 11$). If a school's entire 4th grade was divided evenly into 3 classes each with 22 students, the inverse operation of multiplication is used to determine the total students in the grade ($22 \times 3 = 66$). More scenarios involving inverse operations are listed in the tables below.

Word problems take concepts that are learned in the classroom and turn them into real-life situations. Some parts of the problem are known and at least one part is unknown. There are three types of instances in which something can be unknown: the starting point, the change, or the final result. These can all be missing from the information that is given.

For an addition problem, the change is the quantity of a new amount added to the starting point.

For a subtraction problem, the change is the quantity taken away from the starting point.

Regarding addition, the given equation is $3 + 7 = 10$.

The number 3 is the starting point. 7 is the change, and 10 is the result from adding a new amount to the starting point. Different word problems can arise from this same equation, depending on which value is the unknown. For example, here are three problems:

- If a boy had 3 pencils and was given 7 more, how many would he have in total?

- If a boy had 3 pencils and a girl gave him more so that he had 10 in total, how many were given to him?

- A boy was given 7 pencils so that he had 10 in total. How many did he start with?

All three problems involve the same equation. Finding out which part of the equation is missing is the key to solving each word problem. The missing answers would be 10, 7, and 3.

In terms of subtraction, the same three scenarios can occur. The given equation is $6 - 2 = 4$.

The number 6 is the starting point. 2 is the change, and 4 is the new amount that is the result from taking away an amount from the starting point. Again, different types of word problems can arise from this equation. For example, here are three possible problems:

- If a girl had 6 quarters and 2 were taken away, how many would be left over?

- If a girl had 6 quarters, purchased a pencil, and had 2 quarters left over, how many did she pay with?

- If a girl paid for a pencil with 4 quarters and had 2 quarters left over, how many did she have to start with?

The three question types follow the structure of the addition word problems. Finding out whether the starting point, the change, or the final result is missing is the goal in solving the problem. The missing answers would be 2, 4, and 6.

The three addition problems and the three subtraction word problems can be solved by using a picture, a number line, or an algebraic equation. If an equation is used, a question mark can be used to show the number we don't know. For example, $6 - 4 = ?$ can be written to show that the missing value is the result. Using equation form shows us what part of the addition or subtraction problem is missing.

Key words within a multiplication problem involve *times, product, doubled,* and *tripled.* Key words within a division problem involve *split, quotient, divided, shared, groups,* and *half.* Like addition and subtraction, multiplication and division problems also have three different types of missing values.

Multiplication consists of a certain number of groups, with the same number of items within each group, and the total amount within all groups. Therefore, each one of these amounts can be the missing value.

For example, the given equation is $5 \times 3 = 15$.

5 and 3 are interchangeable, so either amount can be the number of groups or the number of items within each group. 15 is the total number of items. Again, different types of word problems can arise from this equation. For example, here are three problems:

- If a classroom is serving 5 different types of apples for lunch and has 3 apples of each type, how many total apples are there to give to the students?

- If a classroom has 15 apples with 5 different types, how many of each type are there?

- If a classroom has 15 apples with 3 of each type, how many types are there to choose from?

Each question involves using the same equation to solve. It is important to decide which part of the equation is the missing value. The answers to the problems are 15, 3, and 5.

Similar to multiplication, division problems involve a total amount, a number of groups having the same amount, and a number of items within each group. The difference between multiplication and division is that the starting point is the total amount. It then gets divided into equal amounts.

For example, the equation is $15 \div 5 = 3$.

15 is the total number of items, which is being divided into 5 different groups. In order to do so, 3 items go into each group. Also, 5 and 3 are interchangeable. So, the 15 items could be divided into 3 groups of 5 items each. Therefore, different types of word problems can arise from this equation. For example, here are three types of problems:

- A boy needs 48 pieces of chalk. If there are 8 pieces in each box, how many boxes should he buy?

- A boy has 48 pieces of chalk. If each box has 6 pieces in it, how many boxes did he buy?

- A boy has partitioned all of his chalk into 8 piles, with 6 pieces in each pile. How many pieces does he have in total?

Each one of these questions involves the same equation. The third question can easily utilize the multiplication equation $8 \times 6 = ?$ instead of division. The answers are 6, 8, and 48.

Adding and Subtracting Positive and Negative Numbers

Some problems require adding positive and negative numbers or subtracting positive and negative numbers. Adding a negative number to a positive one can be thought of a reducing or subtracting from the positive number, and the result should be less than the positive number. For example, adding 8 and −3 is the same is subtracting 3 from 8; the result is 5. This can be visualized by imagining that the positive number (8) represents 8 apples that a student has in her basket. The negative number (−3) indicates the number of apples she is in debt or owes to her friend. In order to pay off her debt and "settle the score," she essentially is in possession of three fewer apples than in her basket (8 − 3 = 5), so she actually has five apples that are hers to keep.

Should the negative addend be of higher magnitude than the positive addend (for example −9 + 3), the result will be negative, but "less negative" or closer to zero than the large negative number. This is because adding a positive value, even if relatively smaller, to a negative value, reduces the magnitude of the negative in the total. Considering the apple example again, if the girl owed 9 apples to her friend (−9) but she picked 3 (+3) off a tree and gave them to her friend, she now would only owe him six apples (−6), which reduced her debt burden (her negative number of apples) by three.

Subtracting positive and negative numbers works the same way with one key distinction: subtracting a negative number from a negative number yields a "less negative" or more positive result because again, this can be considered as removing or alleviating some debt. For example, if the student with the apples owed 5 apples to her friend, she essentially has −5 applies. If her mom gives that friend 10 apples on behalf of the girl, she now has removed the need to pay back the 5 apples and surpassed neutral (no net apples owed) and now her friend owes *her* five apples (+5).

Stated mathematically: $-5 - (-10) = -5 + 10 = +5$.

Operations with Fractions, Decimals, and Percentages

Fractions

Fractions are a vital part of mathematics, and their understanding tends to be extremely challenging for students. Too often, steps are learned without understanding why they are being performed. It is important for teachers to make the concept of fractions less abstract and more tangible by providing

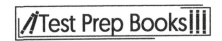

concrete examples in the classroom. With this solid foundation and a lot of practice, learning will be easier, and success with fractions in later math classes will occur.

A **fraction** is a part of something that is whole. Items such as apples can be cut into parts to help visualize fractions. If an apple is cut into 2 equal parts, each part represents ½ of the apple. If each half is cut into two parts, the apple now is cut into quarters. Each piece now represents ¼ of the apple. In this example, each part is equal because they all have the same size. Geometric shapes, such as circles and squares, can also be utilized in the classroom to help visualize the idea of fractions. For example, a circle can be drawn on the board and divided into 6 equal parts:

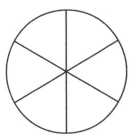

Shading can be used to represent parts of the circle that can be translated into fractions. The top of the fraction, the **numerator,** can represent how many segments are shaded. The bottom of the fraction, the **denominator,** can represent the number of segments that the circle is broken into. A pie is a good analogy to use in this example. If one piece of the circle is shaded, or one piece of pie is cut out, $^1/_6$ of the object is being referred to. An apple, a pie, or a circle can be utilized in order to compare simple fractions. For example, showing that ½ is larger than ¼ and that ¼ is smaller than $^1/_3$ can be accomplished through shading. A **unit fraction** is a fraction in which the numerator is 1, and the denominator is a positive whole number. It represents one part of a whole—one piece of pie.

Imagine that an apple pie has been baked for a holiday party, and the full pie has eight slices. After the party, there are five slices left. How could the amount of the pie that remains be expressed as a fraction? The numerator is 5 since there are 5 pieces left, and the denominator is 8 since there were eight total slices in the whole pie. Thus, expressed as a fraction, the leftover pie totals $\frac{5}{8}$ of the original amount.

Fractions come in three different varieties: proper fractions, improper fractions, and mixed numbers. **Proper fractions** have a numerator less than the denominator, such as $\frac{3}{8}$, but **improper fractions** have a numerator greater than the denominator, such as $\frac{15}{8}$. **Mixed numbers** combine a whole number with a proper fraction, such as $3\frac{1}{2}$. Any mixed number can be written as an improper fraction by multiplying the integer by the denominator, adding the product to the value of the numerator, and dividing the sum by the original denominator. For example:

$$3\frac{1}{2} = \frac{3 \times 2 + 1}{2} = \frac{7}{2}$$

Whole numbers can also be converted into fractions by placing the whole number as the numerator and making the denominator 1. For example, $3 = \frac{3}{1}$.

The bar in a fraction represents division. Therefore $\frac{6}{5}$ is the same as $6 \div 5$. In order to rewrite it as a mixed number, division is performed to obtain $6 \div 5 = 1\ R1$. The remainder is then converted into fraction form. The actual remainder becomes the numerator of a fraction, and the divisor becomes the denominator. Therefore $1\ R1$ is written as $1\frac{1}{5}$, a mixed number. A mixed number can also decompose into the addition of a whole number and a fraction. For example,

$$1\frac{1}{5} = 1 + \frac{1}{5} \text{ and } 4\frac{5}{6} = 4 + \frac{1}{6} + \frac{1}{6} + \frac{1}{6} + \frac{1}{6} + \frac{1}{6}$$

Every fraction can be built from a combination of unit fractions.

One of the most fundamental concepts of fractions is their ability to be manipulated by multiplication or division. This is possible since $\frac{n}{n} = 1$ for any non-zero integer. As a result, multiplying or dividing by $\frac{n}{n}$ will not alter the original fraction since any number multiplied or divided by 1 doesn't change the value of that number. Fractions of the same value are known as equivalent fractions. For example, $\frac{2}{8}, \frac{25}{100}$, and $\frac{40}{160}$ are equivalent, as they all equal $\frac{1}{4}$.

Like fractions, or **equivalent fractions**, are the terms used to describe these fractions that are made up of different numbers but represent the same quantity. For example, the given fractions are $^4/_8$ and $^3/_6$. If a pie was cut into 8 pieces and 4 pieces were removed, half of the pie would remain. Also, if a pie was split into 6 pieces and 3 pieces were eaten, half of the pie would also remain. Therefore, both of the fractions represent half of a pie. These two fractions are referred to as like fractions. **Unlike fractions** are fractions that are different and cannot be thought of as representing equal quantities. When working with fractions in mathematical expressions, like fractions should be simplified. Both $^4/_8$ and $^3/_6$ can be simplified into $^1/_2$.

Comparing fractions can be completed through the use of a number line. For example, if $^3/_5$ and $^6/_{10}$ need to be compared, each fraction should be plotted on a number line. To plot $^3/_5$, the area from 0 to 1 should be broken into 5 equal segments, and the fraction represents 3 of them. To plot $^6/_{10}$, the area from 0 to 1 should be broken into 10 equal segments, and the fraction represents 6 of them.

It can be seen that $\frac{3}{5} = \frac{6}{10}$

Like fractions are plotted at the same point on a number line. Unit fractions can also be used to compare fractions. For example, if it is known that

$$\frac{4}{5} > \frac{1}{2}$$

and

$$\frac{1}{2} > \frac{4}{10}$$

then it is also known that

$$\frac{4}{5} > \frac{4}{10}$$

Also, converting improper fractions to mixed numbers can be helpful in comparing fractions because the whole number portion of the number is more visible.

Adding and subtracting mixed numbers and fractions can be completed by decomposing fractions into a sum of whole numbers and unit fractions. For example, the given problem is

$$5\frac{3}{7} + 2\frac{1}{7}$$

Decomposing into

$$5 + \frac{1}{7} + \frac{1}{7} + \frac{1}{7} + 2 + \frac{1}{7}$$

This shows that the whole numbers can be added separately from the unit fractions. The answer is:

$$5 + 2 + \frac{1}{7} + \frac{1}{7} + \frac{1}{7} + \frac{1}{7} = 7 + \frac{4}{7} = 7\frac{4}{7}$$

Although many equivalent fractions exist, they are easier to compare and interpret when reduced or simplified. The numerator and denominator of a simple fraction will have no factors in common other than 1. When reducing or simplifying fractions, divide the numerator and denominator by the greatest common factor. A simple strategy is to divide the numerator and denominator by low numbers, like 2, 3, or 5 until arriving at a simple fraction, but the same thing could be achieved by determining the greatest common factor for both the numerator and denominator and dividing each by it. Using the first method is preferable when both the numerator and denominator are even, end in 5, or are obviously a multiple of another number. However, if no numbers seem to work, it will be necessary to factor the numerator and denominator to find the GCF. For example:

1) Simplify the fraction $\frac{6}{8}$:

Dividing the numerator and denominator by 2 results in $\frac{3}{4}$, which is a simple fraction.

2) Simplify the fraction $\frac{12}{36}$:

Dividing the numerator and denominator by 2 leaves $\frac{6}{18}$. This isn't a simple fraction, as both the numerator and denominator have factors in common. Dividing each by 3 results in $\frac{2}{6}$, but this can be further simplified by dividing by 2 to get $\frac{1}{3}$. This is the simplest fraction, as the numerator is 1. In cases like this, multiple division operations can be avoided by determining the greatest common factor between the numerator and denominator.

3) Simplify the fraction $\frac{18}{54}$ by dividing by the greatest common factor:

First, determine the factors for the numerator and denominator. The factors of 18 are 1, 2, 3, 6, 9, and 18. The factors of 54 are 1, 2, 3, 6, 9, 18, 27, and 54. Thus, the greatest common factor is 18. Dividing $\frac{18}{54}$ by 18 leaves $\frac{1}{3}$, which is the simplest fraction. This method takes slightly more work, but it definitively arrives at the simplest fraction.

Adding and Subtracting Fractions

Adding and subtracting fractions that have the same denominators involves adding or subtracting the numerators. The denominator will stay the same. Therefore, the decomposition process can be made simpler, and the fractions do not have to be broken into unit fractions.

For example, the given problem is:

$$4\frac{7}{8} - 2\frac{6}{8}$$

The answer is found by adding the answers to both

$$4 - 2 \text{ and } \frac{7}{8} - \frac{6}{8}$$

$$2 + \frac{1}{8} = 2\frac{1}{8}$$

A common mistake would be to add the denominators so that

$$\frac{1}{4} + \frac{1}{4} = \frac{1}{8} \text{ or } \frac{2}{8}$$

However, conceptually, it is known that two quarters make a half, so neither one of these are correct.

If two fractions have different denominators, equivalent fractions must be used to add or subtract them. The fractions must be converted into fractions that have common denominators. A **least common denominator** or the product of the two denominators can be used as the common denominator. For example, in the problem $\frac{5}{6} + \frac{2}{3}$, either 6, which is the least common denominator, or 18, which is the product of the denominators, can be used. In order to use 6, $\frac{2}{3}$ must be converted to sixths. A number line can be used to show the equivalent fraction is $\frac{4}{6}$. What happens is that $\frac{2}{3}$ is multiplied by a fractional form of 1 to obtain a denominator of 6. Hence:

$$\frac{2}{3} \times \frac{2}{2} = \frac{4}{6}$$

98

Therefore, the problem is now $\frac{5}{6} + \frac{4}{6} = \frac{9}{6}$, which can be simplified into $\frac{3}{2}$. In order to use 18, both fractions must be converted into having 18 as their denominator. $\frac{5}{6}$ would have to be multiplied by $\frac{3}{3}$, and $\frac{2}{3}$ would need to be multiplied by $\frac{6}{6}$. The addition problem would be $\frac{15}{18} + \frac{12}{18} = \frac{27}{18}$, which reduces into $\frac{3}{2}$.

It is always possible to find a common denominator by multiplying the denominators. However, when the denominators are large numbers, this method is unwieldy, especially if the answer must be provided in its simplest form. Thus, it's beneficial to find the least common denominator of the fractions—the least common denominator is incidentally also the least common multiple.It is always possible to find a common denominator by multiplying the denominators. However, when the denominators are large numbers, this method is unwieldy, especially if the answer must be provided in its simplest form. Thus, it's beneficial to find the **least common denominator** of the fractions—the least common denominator is incidentally also the **least common multiple**.

Once equivalent fractions have been found with common denominators, simply add or subtract the numerators to arrive at the answer:

1) $\frac{1}{2} + \frac{3}{4} = \frac{2}{4} + \frac{3}{4} = \frac{5}{4}$

2) $\frac{3}{12} + \frac{11}{20} = \frac{15}{60} + \frac{33}{60} = \frac{48}{60} = \frac{4}{5}$

3) $\frac{7}{9} - \frac{4}{15} = \frac{35}{45} - \frac{12}{45} = \frac{23}{45}$

4) $\frac{5}{6} - \frac{7}{18} = \frac{15}{18} - \frac{7}{18} = \frac{8}{18} = \frac{4}{9}$

Multiplying and Dividing Fractions

Of the four basic operations that can be performed on fractions, the one that involves the least amount of work is multiplication. To multiply two fractions, simply multiply the numerators together, multiply the denominators together, and place the products of each as a fraction. Whole numbers and mixed numbers can also be expressed as a fraction, as described above, to multiply with a fraction.

Because multiplication is commutative, multiplying a fraction times a whole number is the same as multiplying a whole number times a fraction. The problem involves adding a fraction a specific number of times. The problem $3 \times \frac{1}{4}$ can be translated into adding the unit fraction 3 times:

$$\frac{1}{4} + \frac{1}{4} + \frac{1}{4} = \frac{3}{4}$$

In the problem $4 \times \frac{2}{5}$, the fraction can be decomposed into $\frac{1}{5} + \frac{1}{5}$ and then added 4 times to obtain $\frac{8}{5}$. Also, both of these answers can be found by just multiplying the whole number times the numerator of the fraction being multiplied.

The whole numbers can be written in fraction form as:

$$\frac{3}{1} \times \frac{1}{4} = \frac{3}{4}$$

$$\frac{4}{1} \times \frac{2}{5} = \frac{8}{5}$$

Multiplying a fraction times a fraction involves multiplying the numerators together separately and the denominators together separately. For example,

$$\frac{3}{8} \times \frac{2}{3} = \frac{3 \times 2}{8 \times 3} = \frac{6}{24}$$

This can then be reduced to $\frac{1}{4}$.

Dividing a fraction by a fraction is actually a multiplication problem. It involves flipping the divisor and then multiplying normally. For example,

$$\frac{22}{5} \div \frac{1}{2} = \frac{22}{5} \times \frac{2}{1} = \frac{44}{5}$$

The same procedure can be implemented for division problems involving fractions and whole numbers. The whole number can be rewritten as a fraction over a denominator of 1, and then division can be completed.

A common denominator approach can also be used in dividing fractions. Considering the same problem, $\frac{22}{5} \div \frac{1}{2}$, a common denominator between the two fractions is 10. $\frac{22}{5}$ would be rewritten as $\frac{22}{5} \times \frac{2}{2} = \frac{44}{10}$, and $\frac{1}{2}$ would be rewritten as $\frac{1}{2} \times \frac{5}{5} = \frac{5}{10}$. Dividing both numbers straight across results in:

$$\frac{44}{10} \div \frac{5}{10} = \frac{44/5}{10/10} = \frac{44/5}{1} = 44/5$$

Many real-world problems will involve the use of fractions. Key words include actual fraction values, such as half, quarter, third, fourth, etc. The best approach to solving word problems involving fractions is to draw a picture or diagram that represents the scenario being discussed, while deciding which type of operation is necessary in order to solve the problem. A phrase such as "one fourth of 60 pounds of coal" creates a scenario in which multiplication should be used, and the mathematical form of the phrase is $\frac{1}{4} \times 60$.

Decimals

The **decimal system** is a way of writing out numbers that uses ten different numerals: 0, 1, 2, 3, 4, 5, 6, 7, 8, and 9. This is also called a "base ten" or "base 10" system. Other bases are also used. For example, computers work with a base of 2. This means they only use the numerals 0 and 1.

The **decimal place** denotes how far to the right of the decimal point a numeral is. The first digit to the right of the decimal point is in the *tenths* place. The next is the **hundredths**. The third is the **thousandths**.

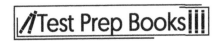

So, 3.142 has a 1 in the tenths place, a 4 in the hundredths place, and a 2 in the thousandths place.

The **decimal point** is a period used to separate the **ones** place from the **tenths** place when writing out a number as a decimal.

A **decimal number** is a number written out with a decimal point instead of as a fraction, for example, 1.25 instead of $\frac{5}{4}$. Depending on the situation, it can sometimes be easier to work with fractions and sometimes easier to work with decimal numbers.

A decimal number is terminating if it stops at some point. It is called repeating if it never stops but repeats over and over. It is important to note that every rational number can be written as a terminating decimal or as a repeating decimal.

Addition with Decimals

To add decimal numbers, each number needs to be lined up by the decimal point in vertical columns. For each number being added, the zeros to the right of the last number need to be filled in so that each of the numbers has the same number of places to the right of the decimal. Then, the columns can be added together. Here is an example of 2.45 + 1.3 + 8.891 written in column form:

$$\begin{array}{r} 2.450 \\ 1.300 \\ + \, 8.891 \end{array}$$

Zeros have been added in the columns so that each number has the same number of places to the right of the decimal.

Added together, the correct answer is 12.641:

$$\begin{array}{r} 2.450 \\ 1.300 \\ + \, 8.891 \\ \hline 12.641 \end{array}$$

Subtraction with Decimals

Subtracting decimal numbers is the same process as adding decimals. Here is 7.89 – 4.235 written in column form:

$$\begin{array}{r} 7.890 \\ - \, 4.235 \\ \hline 3.655 \end{array}$$

A zero has been added in the column so that each number has the same number of places to the right of the decimal.

Multiplication with Decimals

The simplest way to multiply decimals is to calculate the product as if the decimals are not there, then count the number of decimal places in the original problem. Use that total to place the decimal the same number of places over in your answer, counting from right to left. For example, 0.5×1.25 can be rewritten and multiplied as 5×125, which equals 625. Then the decimal is added three places from the right for .625.

The final answer will have the same number of decimal *points* as the total number of decimal *places* in the problem. The first number has one decimal place, and the second number has two decimal places. Therefore, the final answer will contain three decimal places:

$$0.5 \times 1.25 = 0.625$$

Division with Decimals
Dividing a decimal by a whole number entails using long division first by ignoring the decimal point. Then, the decimal point is moved the number of places given in the problem.

For example, $6.8 \div 4$ can be rewritten as $68 \div 4$, which is 17. There is one non-zero integer to the right of the decimal point, so the final solution would have one decimal place to the right of the solution. In this case, the solution is 1.7.

Dividing a decimal by another decimal requires changing the divisor to a whole number by moving its decimal point. The decimal place of the dividend should be moved by the same number of places as the divisor. Then, the problem is the same as dividing a decimal by a whole number.

For example, $5.72 \div 1.1$ has a divisor with one decimal point in the denominator. The expression can be rewritten as $57.2 \div 11$ by moving each number one decimal place to the right to eliminate the decimal. The long division can be completed as $572 \div 11$ with a result of 52. Since there is one non-zero integer to the right of the decimal point in the problem, the final solution is 5.2.

In another example, $8 \div 0.16$ has a divisor with two decimal points in the denominator. The expression can be rewritten as $800 \div 16$ by moving each number two decimal places to the right to eliminate the decimal in the divisor. The long division can be completed with a result of 50.

Percentages
Think of percentages as fractions with a denominator of 100. In fact, percentage means "per hundred." Problems often require converting numbers from percentages, fractions, and decimals.

The basic percent equation is the following:

$$\frac{is}{of} = \frac{\%}{100}$$

The placement of numbers in the equation depends on what the question asks.

Example 1
Find 40% of 80.

Basically, the problem is asking, "What is 40% of 80?" The 40% is the percent, and 80 is the number to find the percent "of." The equation is:

$$\frac{x}{80} = \frac{40}{100}$$

After cross-multiplying, the problem becomes $100x = 80(40)$. Solving for x produces the answer:

$$x = 32$$

Example 2
What percent of 100 is 20?

20 fills in the "is" portion, while 100 fills in the "of." The question asks for the percent, so that will be x, the unknown. The following equation is set up:

$$\frac{20}{100} = \frac{x}{100}$$

Cross-multiplying yields the equation $100x = 20(100)$. Solving for x gives the answer: 20%.

Example 3
30% of what number is 30?

The following equation uses the clues and numbers in the problem:

$$\frac{30}{x} = \frac{30}{100}$$

Cross-multiplying results in the equation $30(100) = 30x$. Solving for x gives the answer:

$$x = 100$$

Conversions
Decimals and Percentages
Since a percentage is based on "per hundred," decimals and percentages can be converted by multiplying or dividing by 100. Practically speaking, this always amounts to moving the decimal point two places to the right or left, depending on the conversion. To convert a percentage to a decimal, move the decimal point two places to the left and remove the % sign. To convert a decimal to a percentage, move the decimal point two places to the right and add a % sign. Here are some examples:

$$65\% = 0.65$$
$$0.33 = 33\%$$
$$0.215 = 21.5\%$$
$$99.99\% = 0.9999$$
$$500\% = 5.00$$
$$7.55 = 755\%$$

Fractions and Percentages
Remember that a percentage is a number per one hundred. So, a percentage can be converted to a fraction by making the number in the percentage the numerator and putting 100 as the denominator:

$$43\% = \frac{43}{100}$$

$$97\% = \frac{97}{100}$$

Note that the percent symbol (%) kind of looks like a 0, a 1, and another 0. So, think of a percentage like 54% as 54 over 100.

To convert a fraction to a percent, follow the same logic. If the fraction happens to have 100 in the denominator, you're in luck. Just take the numerator and add a percent symbol:

$$\frac{28}{100} = 28\%$$

Otherwise, divide the numerator by the denominator to get a decimal:

$$\frac{9}{12} = 0.75$$

Then convert the decimal to a percentage:

$$0.75 = 75\%$$

Another option is to make the denominator equal to 100. Be sure to multiply the numerator and the denominator by the same number. For example:

$$\frac{3}{20} \times \frac{5}{5} = \frac{15}{100}$$

$$\frac{15}{100} = 15\%$$

Changing Fractions to Decimals

To change a fraction into a decimal, divide the denominator into the numerator until there are no remainders. There may be repeating decimals, so rounding is often acceptable. A straight line above the repeating portion denotes that the decimal repeats.

Example

Express 4/5 as a decimal.

Set up the division problem.

$$5\overline{)4}$$

5 does not go into 4, so place the decimal and add a zero.

$$5\overline{)4\,.\,0}$$

5 goes into 40 eight times. There is no remainder.

$$
\begin{array}{r}
0\,.\,8 \\
5\overline{)4\,.\,0} \\
-\,4\,.\,0 \\
\hline
0
\end{array}
$$

The solution is 0.8.

Example

Express 33 1/3 as a decimal.

Since the whole portion of the number is known, set it aside to calculate the decimal from the fraction portion.

Set up the division problem.

$$3\overline{)1}$$

3 does not go into 1, so place the decimal and add zeros. 3 goes into 10 three times.

$$\begin{array}{r} 0.3 \\ 3\overline{)1.0} \end{array}$$

This will repeat with a remainder of 1.

$$\begin{array}{r} 0.333 \\ 3\overline{)1.000} \\ -9 \\ \hline 10 \\ -9 \\ \hline 10 \end{array}$$

So, we will place a line over the 3 to denote the repetition. The solution is written $33.\overline{3}$.

Changing Decimals to Fractions
To change decimals to fractions, place the decimal portion of the number, the numerator, over the respective place value, the denominator, then reduce, if possible.

Example: Express 0.25 as a fraction.

This is read as twenty-five hundredths, so put 25 over 100. Then reduce to find the solution.

$$\frac{25}{100} = \frac{1}{4}$$

Example: Express 0.455 as a fraction

This is read as four hundred fifty-five thousandths, so put 455 over 1,000. Then reduce to find the solution.

$$\frac{455}{1,000} = \frac{91}{200}$$

There are two types of problems that commonly involve percentages. The first is to calculate some percentage of a given quantity, where you convert the percentage to a decimal, and multiply the

105

quantity by that decimal. Secondly, you are given a quantity and told it is a fixed percent of an unknown quantity. In this case, convert to a decimal, then divide the given quantity by that decimal.

Example: What is 30% of 760?

Convert the percent into a useable number. "Of" means to multiply.

$$30\% = 0.30$$

Set up the problem based on the givens, and solve.

$$0.30 \times 760 = 228$$

Example: 8.4 is 20% of what number?

Convert the percent into a useable number.

$$20\% = 0.20$$

The given number is a percent of the answer needed, so divide the given number by this decimal rather than multiplying it.

$$\frac{8.4}{0.20} = 42$$

Solving Practical Math Problems

Word problems, or story problems, are math problems that have a real-world context. In word problems, multiple quantities are often provided with a request to find some kind of relation between them. This often will mean that one variable (the dependent variable whose value needs to be found) can be written as a function of another variable (the independent variable whose value can be figured from the given information). The usual procedure for solving these problems is to start by giving each quantity in the problem a variable, and then figuring the relationship between these variables.

For example, suppose a car gets 25 miles per gallon. How far will the car travel if it uses 2.4 gallons of fuel? In this case, y would be the distance the car has traveled in miles, and x would be the amount of fuel burned in gallons (2.4). Then the relationship between these variables can be written as an algebraic equation, $y = 25x$. In this case, the equation is $y = 25 \times 2.4 = 60$, so the car has traveled 60 miles.

Translating Verbal Relationships into Algebraic Equations or Expressions

When attempting to solve a math problem, it's important to apply the correct algorithm. It is much more difficult to determine what algorithm is necessary when solving word problems, because the necessary operations and equations are typically not provided. In these instances, the test taker must translate the words in the problem into true mathematical statements that can be solved. The following are examples:

Symbol	Phrase
+	Added to; increased by; sum of; more than
−	Decreased by; difference between; less than; take away
×	Multiplied by; 3(4,5...) times as large; product of
÷	Divided by; quotient of; half (third, etc.) of
=	Is; the same as; results in; as much as; equal to
x,t,n, etc.	A number; unknown quantity; value of; variable

Addition and subtraction are **inverse operations**. Adding a number and then subtracting the same number will cancel each other out, resulting in the original number, and vice versa. For example, $8 + 7 - 7 = 8$ and $137 - 100 + 100 = 137$. Similarly, multiplication and division are inverse operations. Therefore, multiplying by a number and then dividing by the same number results in the original number, and vice versa. For example, $8 \times 2 \div 2 = 8$ and $12 \div 4 \times 4 = 12$. Inverse operations are used to work backwards to solve problems. In the case that 7 and a number add to 18, the inverse operation of subtraction is used to find the unknown value ($18 - 7 = 11$). If a school's entire 4th grade was divided evenly into 3 classes each with 22 students, the inverse operation of multiplication is used to determine the total students in the grade ($22 \times 3 = 66$). Additional scenarios involving inverse operations are included in the tables below.

There are a variety of real-world situations in which one or more of the operators is used to solve a problem. The tables below display the most common scenarios.

Addition & Subtraction

	Unknown Result	Unknown Change	Unknown Start
Adding to	5 students were in class. 4 more students arrived. How many students are in class? $5 + 4 = ?$	8 students were in class. More students arrived late. There are now 18 students in class. How many students arrived late? $8 + ? = 18$ Solved by inverse operations $18 - 8 = ?$	Some students were in class early. 11 more students arrived. There are now 17 students in class. How many students were in class early? $? + 11 = 17$ Solved by inverse operations $17 - 11 = ?$
Taking from	15 students were in class. 5 students left class. How many students are in class now? $15 - 5 = ?$	12 students were in class. Some students left class. There are now 8 students in class. How many students left class? $12 - ? = 8$ Solved by inverse operations $8 + ? = 12 \rightarrow 12 - 8 = ?$	Some students were in class. 3 students left class. Then there were 13 students in class. How many students were in class before? $? - 3 = 13$ Solved by inverse operations $13 + 3 = ?$

	Unknown Total	Unknown Addends (Both)	Unknown Addends (One)
Putting together/ taking apart	The homework assignment is 10 addition problems and 8 subtraction problems. How many problems are in the homework assignment? $10 + 8 = ?$	Bobby has $9. How much can Bobby spend on candy and how much can Bobby spend on toys? $9 = ? + ?$	Bobby has 12 pairs of pants. 5 pairs of pants are shorts, and the rest are long. How many pairs of long pants does he have? $12 = 5 + ?$ Solved by inverse operations $12 - 5 = ?$

	Unknown Difference	Unknown Larger Value	Unknown Smaller Value
Comparing	Bobby has 5 toys. Tommy has 8 toys. How many more toys does Tommy have than Bobby? $$5 + ? = 8$$ Solved by inverse operations $8 - 5 = ?$ Bobby has $6. Tommy has $10. How many fewer dollars does Bobby have than Tommy? $$10 - 6 = ?$$	Tommy has 2 more toys than Bobby. Bobby has 4 toys. How many toys does Tommy have? $$2 + 4 = ?$$ Bobby has 3 fewer dollars than Tommy. Bobby has $8. How many dollars does Tommy have? $$? - 3 = 8$$ Solved by inverse operations $8 + 3 = ?$	Tommy has 6 more toys than Bobby. Tommy has 10 toys. How many toys does Bobby have? $$? + 6 = 10$$ Solved by inverse operations $10 - 6 = ?$ Bobby has $5 less than Tommy. Tommy has $9. How many dollars does Bobby have? $$9 - 5 = ?$$

Multiplication and Division

	Unknown Product	Unknown Group Size	Unknown Number of Groups
Equal groups	There are 5 students, and each student has 4 pieces of candy. How many pieces of candy are there in all? $$5 \times 4 = ?$$	14 pieces of candy are shared equally by 7 students. How many pieces of candy does each student have? $$7 \times ? = 14$$ Solved by inverse operations $14 \div 7 = ?$	If 18 pieces of candy are to be given out 3 to each student, how many students will get candy? $$? \times 3 = 18$$ Solved by inverse operations $18 \div 3 = ?$

	Unknown Product	Unknown Factor	Unknown Factor
Arrays	There are 5 rows of students with 3 students in each row. How many students are there? $$5 \times 3 = ?$$	If 16 students are arranged into 4 equal rows, how many students will be in each row? $$4 \times ? = 16$$ Solved by inverse operations $16 \div 4 = ?$	If 24 students are arranged into an array with 6 columns, how many rows are there? $$? \times 6 = 24$$ Solved by inverse operations $24 \div 6 = ?$

	Larger Unknown	Smaller Unknown	Multiplier Unknown
Comparing	A small popcorn costs $1.50. A large popcorn costs 3 times as much as a small popcorn. How much does a large popcorn cost? $1.50 \times 3 =?$	A large soda costs $6 and that is 2 times as much as a small soda costs. How much does a small soda cost? $2 \times ? = 6$ Solved by inverse operations $6 \div 2 =?$	A large pretzel costs $3 and a small pretzel costs $2. How many times as much does the large pretzel cost as the small pretzel? $? \times 2 = 3$ Solved by inverse operations $3 \div 2 =?$

Modeling and Solving Word Problems

Word problems can appear daunting, but don't let the wording intimidate you. No matter the scenario or specifics, the key to answering them is to translate the words into a math problem. Always keep in mind what the question is asking and what operations could lead to that answer.

Some word problems require more than just one simple equation to be written and solved. Consider the following situations and the linear equations used to model them.

Suppose Margaret is 2 miles to the east of John at noon. Margaret walks to the east at 3 miles per hour. How far apart will they be at 3 p.m.? To solve this, x would represent the time in hours past noon, and y would represent the distance between Margaret and John. Now, noon corresponds to the equation where x is 0, so the y intercept is going to be 2. It's also known that the slope will be the rate at which the distance is changing, which is 3 miles per hour.

This means that the slope will be 3 (be careful at this point: if units were used, other than miles and hours, for x and y variables, a conversion of the given information to the appropriate units would be required first). The simplest way to write an equation given the y-intercept, and the slope is the Slope-Intercept form, which is $y = mx + b$. Recall that m here is the slope and b is the y intercept. So, $m = 3$ and $b = 2$. Therefore, the equation will be $y = 3x + 2$. The word problem asks how far to the east Margaret will be from John at 3 p.m., which means when x is 3. So, substitute $x = 3$ into this equation to obtain:

$$y = 3 \times 3 + 2 = 9 + 2 = 11$$

Therefore, she will be 11 miles to the east of him at 3 p.m.

For another example, suppose that a box with 4 cans in it weighs 6 lbs., while a box with 8 cans in it weighs 12 lbs. Find out how much a single can weighs. To do this, let x denote the number of cans in the box, and y denote the weight of the box with the cans in lbs. This line touches two pairs: $(4, 6)$ and $(8, 12)$. A formula for this relation could be written using the two-point form, with $x_1 = 4, y_1 = 6, x_2 = 8, y_2 = 12$. This would yield $\frac{y-6}{x-4} = \frac{12-6}{8-4}$, or $\frac{y-6}{x-4} = \frac{6}{4} = \frac{3}{2}$. However, only the slope is needed to solve this problem, since the slope will be the weight of a single can. From the computation, the slope is $\frac{3}{2}$. Therefore, each can weighs $\frac{3}{2}$ lb.

Solving Simple Algebraic Problems

Linear equations and **linear inequalities** are both comparisons of two algebraic expressions. However, unlike equations in which the expressions are equal, linear inequalities compare expressions that may be unequal. Linear equations typically have one value for the variable that makes the statement true. Linear inequalities generally have an infinite number of values that make the statement true.

When solving a linear equation, the desired result requires determining a numerical value for the unknown **variable**. If given a linear equation involving addition, subtraction, multiplication, or division, working backwards isolates the variable. Addition and subtraction are inverse operations, as are multiplication and division. Therefore, they can be used to cancel each other out.

Since variables are the letters that represent an unknown number, you must solve for that unknown number in single variable problems. The main thing to remember is that you can do anything to one side of an equation as long as you do it to the other.

The first steps to solving linear equations are distributing, if necessary, and combining any like terms on the same side of the equation. Sides of an equation are separated by an **equal sign**. Next, the equation is manipulated to show the variable on one side. Again, whatever is done to one side of the equation must be done to the other side of the equation to remain equal. Inverse operations are then used to isolate the variable and undo the order of operations backwards. Addition and subtraction are undone, then multiplication and division are undone.

For example, solve $4(t - 2) + 2t - 4 = 2(9 - 2t)$

Distributing: $4t - 8 + 2t - 4 = 18 - 4t$

Combining like terms: $6t - 12 = 18 - 4t$

Adding $4t$ to each side to move the variable: $10t - 12 = 18$

Adding 12 to each side to isolate the variable: $10t = 30$

Dividing each side by 10 to isolate the variable: $t = 3$

The answer can be checked by substituting the value for the variable into the original equation, ensuring that both sides calculate to be equal.

Linear inequalities express the relationship between unequal values. More specifically, they describe in what way the values are unequal. A value can be greater than (>), less than (<), greater than or equal to (≥), or less than or equal to (≤) another value. $5x + 40 > 65$ is read as *five times a number added to forty is greater than sixty-five.*

When solving a linear inequality, the solution is the set of all numbers that make the statement true. The inequality $x + 2 \geq 6$ has a solution set of 4 and every number greater than 4 (4.01; 5; 12; 107; etc.). Adding 2 to 4 or any number greater than 4 results in a value that is greater than or equal to 6. Therefore, $x \geq 4$ is the solution set.

To algebraically solve a linear inequality, follow the same steps as those for solving a linear equation. The inequality symbol stays the same for all operations except when multiplying or dividing by a negative number. If multiplying or dividing by a negative number while solving an inequality, the

111

relationship reverses (the sign flips). In other words, > switches to < and vice versa. Multiplying or dividing by a positive number does not change the relationship, so the sign stays the same.

An example is shown below.

Solve $-2x - 8 \leq 22$ for the value of x.

Add 8 to both sides to isolate the variable:

$$-2x \leq 30$$

Divide both sides by –2 to solve for x:

$$x \geq -15$$

Although linear equations generally have one solution, this is not always the case. If there is no value for the variable that makes the statement true, there is no solution to the equation. Consider the equation:

$$x + 3 = x - 1$$

There is no value for x in which adding 3 to the value produces the same result as subtracting one from the value. Conversely, if any value for the variable makes a true statement, the equation has an infinite number of solutions. Consider the equation:

$$3x + 6 = 3(x + 2)$$

Any number substituted for x will result in a true statement (both sides of the equation are equal).

By manipulating equations like the two above, the variable of the equation will cancel out completely. If the remaining constants express a true statement (ex. $6 = 6$), then all real numbers are solutions to the equation. If the constants left express a false statement (ex. $3 = -1$), then no solution exists for the equation.

When solving radical and rational equations, extraneous solutions must be accounted for when finding the answers. For example, the equation $\frac{x}{x-5} = \frac{3x}{x+3}$ has two values that create a 0 denominator: $x \neq 5, -3$. When solving for x, these values must be considered because they cannot be solutions. In the given equation, solving for x can be done using cross-multiplication, yielding the equation:

$$x(x + 3) = 3x(x - 5)$$

Distributing results in the quadratic equation $x^2 + 3x = 3x^2 - 15x$; therefore, all terms must be moved to one side of the equals sign. This results in $2x^2 - 18x = 0$, which in factored form is $2x(x - 9) = 0$. Setting each factor equal to zero, the apparent solutions are $x = 0$ and $x = 9$. These two solutions are neither 5 nor –3, so they are viable solutions. Neither 0 nor 9 create a 0 denominator in the original equation.

A similar process exists when solving radical equations. One must check to make sure the solutions are defined in the original equations. Solving an equation containing a square root involves isolating the root and then squaring both sides of the equals sign. Solving a cube root equation involves isolating the radical and then cubing both sides. In either case, the variable can then be solved for because there are no longer radicals in the equation.

Solving a linear inequality requires all values that make the statement true to be determined. For example, solving $3x - 7 \geq -13$ produces the solution $x \geq -2$. This means that –2 and any number greater than –2 produces a true statement. Solution sets for linear inequalities will often be displayed using a number line. If a value is included in the set ($\geq$ or $\leq$), a shaded dot is placed on that value and an arrow extending in the direction of the solutions. For a variable $>$ or $\geq$ a number, the arrow will point right on a number line, the direction where the numbers increase. If a variable is $<$ or $\leq$ a number, the arrow will point left on a number line, which is the direction where the numbers decrease. If the value is not included in the set ($>$ or $<$), an open (unshaded) circle on that value is used with an arrow in the appropriate direction.

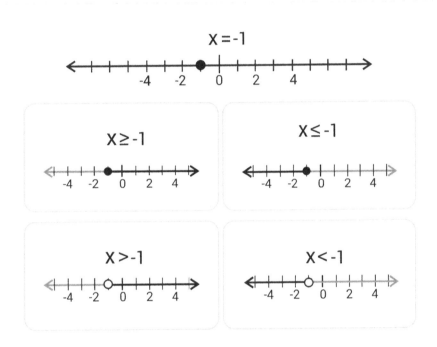

Similar to linear equations, a linear inequality may have a solution set consisting of all real numbers, or can contain no solution. When solved algebraically, a linear inequality in which the variable cancels out and results in a true statement (ex. $7 \geq 2$) has a solution set of all real numbers. A linear inequality in which the variable cancels out and results in a false statement (ex. $7 \leq 2$) has no solution.

Equations and inequalities in two variables represent a relationship. Jim owns a car wash and charges $40 per car. The rent for the facility is $350 per month. An equation can be written to relate the number of cars Jim cleans to the money he makes per month. Let x represent the number of cars and y represent the profit Jim makes each month from the car wash. The equation $y = 40x - 350$ can be used to show Jim's profit or loss. Since this equation has two variables, the coordinate plane can be used to show the relationship and predict profit or loss for Jim. The following graph shows that Jim must wash at least nine cars to pay the rent, where $x = 9$. Anything nine cars and above yield a profit shown in the value on the y-axis.

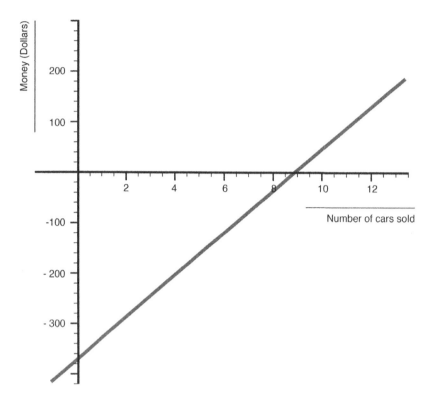

With a single equation in two variables, the solutions are limited only by the situation the equation represents. When two equations or inequalities are used, more constraints are added. For example, in a system of linear equations, there is often—although not always—only one answer. The point of intersection of two lines is the solution. For a system of inequalities, there are infinitely many answers.

The intersection of two solution sets gives the solution set of the system of inequalities. In the following graph, the darker shaded region is where two inequalities overlap. Any set of x and y found in that region satisfies both inequalities. The line with the positive slope is solid, meaning the values on that line are included in the solution. The line with the negative slope is dotted, so the coordinates on that line are not included.

Here's an example:

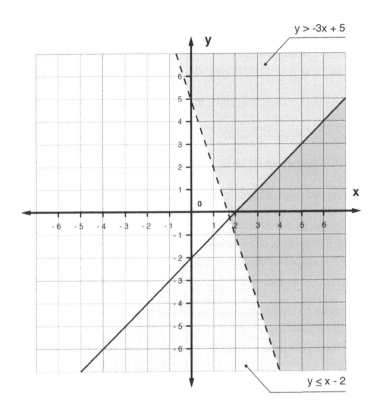

Formulas with two variables are equations used to represent a specific relationship. For example, the formula $d = rt$ represents the relationship between distance, rate, and time. If Bob travels at a rate of 35 miles per hour on his road trip from Westminster to Seneca, the formula $d = 35t$ can be used to represent his distance traveled in a specific length of time. Formulas can also be used to show different roles of the variables, transformed without any given numbers. Solving for r, the formula becomes $\frac{d}{t} = r$. The t is moved over by division so that *rate* is a function of distance and time.

The Problem-Solving Process and Determining If Enough Information Is Provided to Solve a Problem

Overall, the problem-solving process in mathematics involves a step-by-step procedure that one must follow when deciding what approach to take. First, one must understand the problem by deciding what is being sought, then if enough information is given, and what units are necessary in the solution. This is a crucial, but sometimes difficult step. It involves carefully reading the entire problem, identifying (perhaps even underlining) the facts or information that *is* known, and then deciphering the question words to determine what the problem is asking. In this way, math problems require students to be detectives, evaluating the "clues" or facts given in the problem, deciding what the problem is looking for, and evaluating whether sufficient information or "clues" are presented in the problem to solve the posed question.

In general, when solving word problems (also called story problems), it's important to understand what is being asked and to properly set up the initial equation. Always read the entire problem through, and then separate out what information is given in the statement. Decide what you are being asked to find

115

and label each quantity with a variable or constant. Then write an equation to determine the unknown variable. Remember to label answers; sometimes knowing what the answers' units can help eliminate other possible solutions.

When trying to solve any word problem, look for a series of key words indicating addition, subtraction, multiplication, or division to help you determine how to set up the problem:

Addition: add, altogether, together, plus, increased by, more than, in all, sum, and total

Subtraction: minus, less than, difference, decreased by, fewer than, remain, and take away

Multiplication: *times*, *twice*, *of*, *double*, and *triple*

Division: divided by, cut up, half, quotient of, split, and shared equally

If a question asks to give words to a mathematical expression and says "equals," then an = sign must be included in the answer. Similarly, "less than or equal to" is expressed by the inequality symbol ≤, and "greater than or equal" to is expressed as ≥. Furthermore, "less than" is represented by <, and "greater than" is expressed by >.

These strategies are applicable to other question types. For example, calculating salary after deductions, balancing a checkbook, and calculating a dinner bill are common word problems similar to business planning. Just remember to use the correct operations. When a balance is increased, use addition. When a balance is decreased, use subtraction. Common sense and organization are your greatest assets when answering word problems.

For example, suppose the following word problem is encountered:

Walter's Coffee Shop sells a variety of drinks and breakfast treats.

Price List	
Hot Coffee	$2.00
Slow-Drip Iced Coffee	$3.00
Latte	$4.00
Muffin	$2.00
Crepe	$4.00
Egg Sandwich	$5.00

Costs	
Hot Coffee	$0.25
Slow-Drip Iced Coffee	$0.75
Latte	$1.00
Muffin	$1.00
Crepe	$2.00
Egg Sandwich	$3.00

Walter's utilities, rent, and labor costs him $500 per day. Today, Walter sold 200 hot coffees, 100 slow-drip iced coffees, 50 lattes, 75 muffins, 45 crepes, and 60 egg sandwiches. What was Walter's total profit today?

First, it is necessary to establish what is known (the "facts"), what one wants to know, (the question), how to determine the answer (the process), and if there is enough information to solve (sufficient "clues"). The problem clearly asks: "what was Walter's total profit today," so to accurately answer this type of question, the total cost of making his drinks and treats must be calculated, then the total revenue he earned from selling those products must be determined. After arriving at these two totals, the profit is measured found by deducting the total cost from the total revenue.

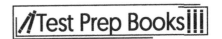

Now that the question and steps are identified, the provided facts are evaluated. Walter's costs for today:

Item	Quantity	Cost Per Unit	Total Cost
Hot Coffee	200	$0.25	$50
Slow-Drip Iced Coffee	100	$0.75	$75
Latte	50	$1.00	$50
Muffin	75	$1.00	$75
Crepe	45	$2.00	$90
Egg Sandwich	60	$3.00	$180
Utilities, rent, and labor			$500
Total Costs			$1,020

Walter's revenue for today:

Item	Quantity	Revenue Per Unit	Total Revenue
Hot Coffee	200	$2.00	$400
Slow-Drip Iced Coffee	100	$3.00	$300
Latte	50	$4.00	$200
Muffin	75	$2.00	$150
Crepe	45	$4.00	$180
Egg Sandwich	60	$5.00	$300
Total Revenue			$1,530

$$Walter's\ Profit = Revenue - Costs = \$1,530 - \$1,020 = \$510$$

In this case, enough information was given in the problem to adequately solve it. If, however, the number of sandwiches and drinks were not provided, or Walter's cost per unit sold, insufficient information would prevent one from arriving at the answer.

Alternative Methods for Solving Mathematical Problems

When solving a math problem, once the question is identified and the clues are evaluated, the plan of action must be determined. In some cases, there might be many options. Therefore, one should begin with one approach and if the strategy does not fit, he or she should move on to another. In some cases, a combination of approaches can be used. A beginning estimate is always useful for comparison once a solution is found. The answer must be reasonable and must fulfill all requirements of the problem.

Presenting students with a variety of methods to solve the same type of math problem empowers each student to select the process that works best for them personally. It can help increase motivation and confidence to tackle difficult math problems. Just as there are different types of learners (visual, kinesthetic, etc.), so too are there particular problem-solving approaches that different students prefer or grasp more easily than others. Skilled mathematicians are versed in multiple methods to tackle various problems, with each method bolstering their toolbox with a strategy that can be employed for ease and efficiency when encountering math work.

Instead of focusing on the "right" way to solve a problem, teachers should strive to present multiple methods and explain the pros, cons, and appropriate applications for each method. For example, when

117

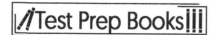

trying to find the zeros in a binomial expression, one might be able to factor the expression, complete the square, use the quadratic equation, or make a rough sketch of the graph and identify the x-intercepts. In some cases, one method may not be possible and another may be "easiest," but by providing students with the various strategies, teachers enable them to be critical thinkers and select the method they deem most appropriate.

The following two examples demonstrate how different methods can be used for the same problem:

Example:

A store is having a spring sale, where everything is 70% off. You have $45.00 to spend. A jacket is regularly priced at $80.00. Do you have enough to buy the jacket and a pair of gloves, regularly priced at $20.00?

There are two ways to approach this.

Method 1:

Set up the equations to find the sale prices: the original price minus the amount discounted.

$$\$80.00 - (\$80.00\ (0.70)) = sale\ cost\ of\ the\ jacket$$
$$\$20.00 - (\$20.00\ (0.70)) = sale\ cost\ of\ the\ gloves$$

Solve for the sale cost.

$$\$24.00 = sale\ cost\ of\ the\ jacket$$
$$\$6.00 = sale\ cost\ of\ the\ gloves$$

Determine if you have enough money for both.

$$\$24.00 + \$6.00 = total\ sale\ cost$$

$30.00 is less than $45.00, so you can afford to purchase both.

Method 2:

Determine the percent of the original price that you will pay.

$$100\% - 70\% = 30\%$$

Set up the equations to find the sale prices.

$$\$80.00\ (0.30) = cost\ of\ the\ jacket$$
$$\$20.00\ (0.30) = cost\ of\ the\ gloves$$

Solve.

$$\$24.00 = cost\ of\ the\ jacket$$
$$\$6.00 = cost\ of\ the\ gloves$$

Determine if you have enough money for both.

$$\$24.00 + \$6.00 = total\ sale\ cost$$

$30.00 is less than $45.00, so you can afford to purchase both.

118

Example:

Mary and Dottie team up to mow neighborhood lawns. If Mary mows 2 lawns per hour and the two of them can mow 17.5 lawns in 5 hours, how many lawns does Dottie mow per hour?

Given rate for Mary.

$$Mary = \frac{2 \text{ lawns}}{1 \text{ hour}}$$

Unknown rate of D for Dottie.

$$Dottie = \frac{D \text{ lawns}}{1 \text{ hour}}$$

Given rate for both.

$$Total \ mowed \ together = \frac{17.5 \text{ lawns}}{5 \text{ hours}}$$

Set up the equation for what is being asked.

$$Mary + Dottie = total \ together.$$

Fill in the givens.

$$2 + D = \frac{17.5}{5}$$

Divide.

$$2 + D = 3.5$$

Subtract 2 from both sides to isolate the variable.

$$2 - 2 + D = 3.5 - 2$$

Solve and label Dottie's mowing rate.

$$D = 1.5 \text{ lawns per hour}$$

Numerical & Graphic Relationships

Relationships in Numerical Data

In some cases, it is useful to compare numerical data and determine the relationship between values. One of the best ways to mathematically compare two values is to compute the percentage difference between the two values. For example, consider a given music shop that had a net profit of $120,000 in the first year of operation and $185,000 over the second year. Rather than simply finding the net difference between the two years (using subtraction), the business owner may want to know by what percentage his profit increased; in other words, how much his profit in the second year increased

relative to his first year. In such cases, the percentage change is desired. The following sections provide some guidance for this process.

Percent Increase/Decrease

Problems dealing with percentages may involve an original value, a change in that value, and a percentage change. A problem will provide two pieces of information and ask to find the third. To do so, this formula is used:

$$\frac{change}{original\ value} \times 100 = percent\ change$$

Here's a sample problem:

> Attendance at a baseball stadium has dropped 16% from last year. Last year's average attendance was 40,000. What is this year's average attendance?

Using the formula and information, the change is unknown (x), the original value is 40,000, and the percent change is 16%. The formula can be written as:

$$\frac{x}{40,000} \times 100 = 16$$

When solving for x, it is determined the change was 6,400. The problem asked for this year's average attendance, so to calculate, the change (6,400) is subtracted from last year's attendance (40,000) to determine this year's average attendance is 33,600.

Percent More Than/Less Than

Percentage problems may give a value and what percent that given value is more than or less than an original unknown value. Here's a sample problem:

> A store advertises that all its merchandise has been reduced by 25%. The new price of a pair of shoes is $60. What was the original price?

This problem can be solved by writing a proportion. Two ratios should be written comparing the cost and the percent of the original cost. The new cost is 75% of the original cost (100% - 25%); and the original cost is 100% of the original cost. The unknown original cost can be represented by x. The proportion would be set up as: $\frac{60}{75} = \frac{x}{100}$. Solving the proportion, it is determined the original cost was $80.

The Position of Numbers Relative to Each Other

Place Value of a Digit

Numbers count in groups of 10. That number is the same throughout the set of natural numbers and whole numbers. It is referred to as working within a base 10 numeration system. Only the numbers from zero to 9 are used to represent any number. The foundation for doing this involves **place value**. Numbers are written side by side. This is to show the amount in each place value.

For place value, let's look at how the number 10 is different from zero to 9. It has two digits instead of just one. The one is in the tens' place, and the zero is in the ones' place. Therefore, there is one group of tens and zero ones. 11 has one 10 and one 1. The introduction of numbers from 11 to 19 should be the

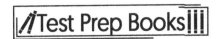

next step. Each value within this range of numbers consists of one group of 10 and a specific number of leftover ones. Counting by tens can be practiced once the tens column is understood. This process consists of increasing the number in the tens place by one. For example, counting by 10 starting at 17 would result in the next four values being 27, 37, 47, and 57.

A place value chart can be used for understanding and learning about numbers that have more digits. Here is an example of a place value chart:

	MILLIONS			THOUSANDS			ONES			.	DECIMALS		
billions	hundred millions	ten millions	millions	hundred thousands	ten thousands	thousands	hundreds	tens	ones		tenths	hundredths	thousandths

In the number 1,234, there are 4 ones and 3 tens. The 2 is in the hundreds' place, and the one is in the thousands' place. Note that each group of three digits is separated by a comma. The 2 has a value that is 10 times greater than the 3. Every place to the left has a value 10 times greater than the place to its right. Also, each group of three digits is also known as a *period*. 234 is in the ones' period.

The number 1,234 can be written out as *one-thousand, two hundred thirty-four*. The process of writing out numbers is known as the *decimal system*. It is also based on groups of 10. The place value chart is a helpful tool in using this system. In order to write out a number, it always starts with the digit(s) in the highest period. For example, in the number 23,815,467, the 23 is in highest place and is in the millions' period. The number is read *twenty-three million, eight hundred fifteen thousand, four hundred sixty-seven*. Each period is written separately through the use of commas. Also, no "ands" are used within the number. Another way to think about the number 23,815,467 is through the use of an addition problem. For example:

$$23,815,467 = 20,000,000 + 3,000,000 + 800,000 + 10,000 + 5,000 + 400 + 60 + 7$$

This expression is known as *expanded form*. The actual number 23,815,467 is known as being in *standard form*.

In order to compare whole numbers with many digits, place value can be used. In each number to be compared, it is necessary to find the highest place value in which the numbers differ and to compare the value within that place value. For example, $4,523,345 < 4,532,456$ because of the values in the ten thousands place. A similar process can be used for decimals. However, number lines can also be used. Tick marks can be placed within two whole numbers on the number line that represent tenths, hundredths, etc. Each number being compared can then be plotted. The value farthest to the right on the number line is the largest.

Comparing, Classifying, and Ordering Real Numbers

A **rational number** is any number that can be written as a fraction or ratio. Within the set of rational numbers, several subsets exist that are referenced throughout the mathematics topics. **Counting numbers** are the first numbers learned as a child. Counting numbers consist of 1,2,3,4, and so on. **Whole numbers** include all counting numbers and zero (0,1,2,3,4,...). **Integers** include counting numbers, their opposites, and zero (...,−3,−2,−1,0,1,2,3,...). **Rational numbers** are inclusive of integers, fractions, and decimals that terminate, or end (1.7, 0.04213) or repeat (0.136$\overline{5}$).

A **number line** typically consists of integers (...3,2,1,0,−1,−2,−3...), and is used to visually represent the value of a rational number. Each rational number has a distinct position on the line determined by comparing its value with the displayed values on the line. For example, if plotting −1.5 on the number line below, it is necessary to recognize that the value of −1.5 is .5 less than −1 and .5 greater than −2. Therefore, −1.5 is plotted halfway between −1 and −2.

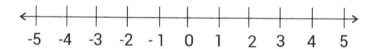

The number system that is used consists of only ten different digits or characters. However, this system is used to represent an infinite number of values. As mentioned, the **place value system** makes this infinite number of values possible. The position in which a digit is written corresponds to a given value. Starting from the decimal point (which is implied, if not physically present), each subsequent place value to the left represents a value greater than the one before it. Conversely, starting from the decimal point, each subsequent place value to the right represents a value less than the one before it.

In accordance with the **base-10 system**, the value of a digit increases by a factor of ten each place it moves to the left. For example, consider the number 7. Moving the digit one place to the left (70), increases its value by a factor of 10 ($7 \times 10 = 70$). Moving the digit two places to the left (700) increases its value by a factor of 10 twice ($7 \times 10 \times 10 = 700$). Moving the digit three places to the left (7,000) increases its value by a factor of 10 three times ($7 \times 10 \times 10 \times 10 = 7,000$), and so on.

Conversely, the value of a digit decreases by a factor of ten each place it moves to the right. (Note that multiplying by $\frac{1}{10}$ is equivalent to dividing by 10). For example, consider the number 40. Moving the digit one place to the right (4) decreases its value by a factor of 10 ($40 \div 10 = 4$). Moving the digit two places to the right (0.4), decreases its value by a factor of 10 twice ($40 \div 10 \div 10 = 0.4$) or ($40 \times \frac{1}{10} \times \frac{1}{10} = 0.4$). Moving the digit three places to the right (0.04) decreases its value by a factor of 10 three times ($40 \div 10 \div 10 \div 10 = 0.04$) or ($40 \times \frac{1}{10} \times \frac{1}{10} \times \frac{1}{10} = 0.04$), and so on.

Ordering Numbers

A common question type asks to order rational numbers from least to greatest or greatest to least. The numbers will come in a variety of formats, including decimals, percentages, roots, fractions, and whole numbers. These questions test for knowledge of different types of numbers and the ability to determine their respective values.

Before discussing ordering all numbers, let's start with decimals.

To compare decimals and order them by their value, utilize a method similar to that of ordering large numbers.

The main difference is where the comparison will start. Assuming that any numbers to left of the decimal point are equal, the next numbers to be compared are those immediately to the right of the decimal point. If those are equal, then move on to compare the values in the next decimal place to the right.

For example:

Which number is greater, 12.35 or 12.38?

Check that the values to the left of the decimal point are equal:

$$12 = 12$$

Next, compare the values of the decimal place to the right of the decimal:

$$12.3 = 12.3$$

Those are also equal in value.

Finally, compare the value of the numbers in the next decimal place to the right on both numbers:

$$12.3\mathbf{5} \text{ and } 12.3\mathbf{8}$$

Here the 5 is less than the 8, so the final way to express this inequality is:

$$12.35 < 12.38$$

Comparing decimals is regularly exemplified with money because the "cents" portion of money ends in the hundredths place. When paying for gasoline or meals in restaurants, and even in bank accounts, if enough errors are made when calculating numbers to the hundredths place, they can add up to dollars and larger amounts of money over time.

Now that decimal ordering has been explained, let's expand and consider all real numbers. Whether the question asks to order the numbers from greatest to least or least to greatest, the crux of the question is the same—convert the numbers into a common format. Generally, it's easiest to write the numbers as whole numbers and decimals so they can be placed on a number line. Follow these examples to understand this strategy.

1) Order the following rational numbers from greatest to least:

$$\sqrt{36}, 0.65, 78\%, \frac{3}{4}, 7, 90\%, \frac{5}{2}$$

Of the seven numbers, the whole number (7) and decimal (0.65) are already in an accessible form, so concentrate on the other five.

First, the square root of 36 equals 6. (If the test asks for the root of a non-perfect root, determine which two whole numbers the root lies between.) Next, convert the percentages to decimals. A percentage means "per hundred," so this conversion requires moving the decimal point two places to the left, leaving 0.78 and 0.9.

Lastly, evaluate the fractions:

$$\frac{3}{4} = \frac{75}{100} = 0.75 \ ; \frac{5}{2} = 2\frac{1}{2} = 2.5$$

Now, the only step left is to list the numbers in the request order:

$$7, \sqrt{36}, \frac{5}{2}, 90\%, 78\%, \frac{3}{4}, 0.65$$

2) Order the following rational numbers from least to greatest:

$$2.5, \sqrt{9}, -10.5, 0.853, 175\%, \sqrt{4}, \frac{4}{5}$$

$$\sqrt{9} = 3$$

$$175\% = 1.75$$

$$\sqrt{4} = 2$$

$$\frac{4}{5} = 0.8$$

From least to greatest, the answer is:

$$-10.5, \frac{4}{5}, 0.853, 175\%, \sqrt{4}, 2.5, \sqrt{9}$$

Expressing Numeric Relationships

If a question asks to give words to a mathematical expression and says "equals," then an = sign must be included in the answer. Similarly, "less than or equal to" is expressed by the inequality symbol ≤, and "greater than or equal" to is expressed as ≥. Furthermore, "less than" is represented by <, and "greater than" is expressed by >.

Equations use the equals sign because the numeric expressions on either side of the symbol (=) are equivalent. In contrast, inequalities compare values or expressions that are unequal. Although not always true, linear equations that include a variable often have just one value for the variable that makes the statement true. Linear inequalities generally have an infinite number of values that make the statement true.

Inequalities are a concise mathematical way to express the relationship between unequal values. More specifically, they describe in what way the values are unequal. A value could be greater than (>); less than (<); greater than or equal to (≥); or less than or equal to (≤) another value. The statement "five times a number added to forty is more than sixty-five" can be expressed as $5x + 40 > 65$. Common words and phrases that express inequalities are:

Symbol	Phrase
<	is under, is below, smaller than, beneath
>	is above, is over, bigger than, exceeds
≤	no more than, at most, maximum
≥	no less than, at least, minimum

Solving Linear Inequalities

When solving a linear inequality, the solution is the set of all numbers that makes the statement true. The inequality $x + 2 \geq 6$ has a solution set of 4 and every number greater than 4 (4.0001, 5, 12, 107, etc.). Adding 2 to 4 or any number greater than 4 would result in a value that is greater than or equal to 6. Therefore, $x \geq 4$ would be the solution set.

Solution sets for linear inequalities often will be displayed using a number line. If a value is included in the set ($\geq$ or $\leq$), there is a shaded dot placed on that value and an arrow extending in the direction of the solutions. For a variable $>$ or $\geq$ a number, the arrow would point right on the number line (the direction where the numbers increase); and if a variable is $<$ or $\leq$ a number, the arrow would point left (where the numbers decrease). If the value is not included in the set ($>$ or $<$), an open circle on that value would be used with an arrow in the appropriate direction.

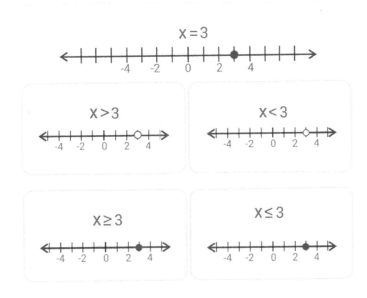

Students may be asked to write a linear inequality given a graph of its solution set. To do so, they should identify whether the value is included (shaded dot or open circle) and the direction in which the arrow is pointing.

In order to algebraically solve a linear inequality, the same steps should be followed as in solving a linear equation. The inequality symbol stays the same for all operations EXCEPT when multiplying or dividing by a negative number. If multiplying or dividing by a negative number while solving an inequality, the relationship reverses (the sign flips). Multiplying or dividing by a positive does not change the relationship, so the sign stays the same. In other words, $>$ switches to $<$ and vice versa. An example is shown below.

Solve $-2(x + 4) \leq 22$

Distribute: $-2x - 8 \leq 22$

Add 8 to both sides: $-2x \leq 30$

Divide both sides by -2: $x \geq 15$

Mathematically Equivalent Expressions

It is helpful to be skilled at identifying values that are equivalent but that are expressed in different forms, such as a fraction, decimal, and percent, because it enables one to convert the representation of a value for easier calculation in a given problem. Manipulating values is often required when working with percentages in order to carry out calculations. The word percent means "per hundred." When dealing with percentages, it may be helpful to think of the number as a value in hundredths. For example, 15% can be expressed as "fifteen hundredths" and written as $\frac{15}{100}$ or .15.

Converting from Decimals and Fractions to Percentages

To convert a decimal to a percent, a number is multiplied by 100. To write .25 as a percent, the equation $.25 \times 100$ yields 25%. To convert a fraction to a percent, the fraction is converted to a decimal and then multiplied by 100. To convert $\frac{3}{5}$ to a decimal, the numerator (3) is divided by the denominator (5). This results in .6, which is then multiplied by 100 to get 60%.

To convert a percent to a decimal, the number is divided by 100. For example, 150% is equal to 1.5 $\left(\frac{150}{100}\right)$. To convert a percent to a fraction, the percent sign is deleted, and the value is written as the numerator with a denominator of 100. For example, $2\% = \frac{2}{100}$. Fractions should be reduced:

$$\frac{2}{100} = \frac{1}{50}$$

Rounding Rules

As mentioned, rounding is an important concept dealing with place value. **Rounding** is the process of either bumping a number up or down, based on a certain place value.

Rounding numbers consists of:

- determining what place value the number is being rounded to
- examining the digit to the right of the desired place value to decide whether to round up or keep the digit, and
- replacing all digits to the right of the desired place value with zeros.

To round 746,311 to the nearest ten thousand, the digit in the ten thousands place should be located first. In this case, this digit is 4 (7<u>4</u>6,311). Then, the digit to its right is examined. If this digit is 5 or greater, the number will be rounded up by increasing the digit in the desired place by one. If the digit to the right of the place value being rounded is 4 or less, the number will be kept the same. For the given example, the digit being examined is a 6, which means that the number will be rounded up by increasing the digit to the left by one.

Therefore, the digit 4 is changed to a 5. Finally, to write the rounded number, any digits to the left of the place value being rounded remain the same and any to its right are replaced with zeros. For the given example, rounding 746,311 to the nearest ten thousand will produce 750,000. To round 746,311 to the nearest hundred, the digit to the right of the three in the hundreds place is examined to determine whether to round up or keep the same number. In this case, that digit is a 1, so the number will be kept the same and any digits to its right will be replaced with zeros. The resulting rounded number is 746,300.

Rounding place values to the right of the decimal follows the same procedure, but digits being replaced by zeros can simply be dropped. To round 3.752891 to the nearest thousandth, the desired place value is located (3.752891) and the digit to the right is examined. In this case, the digit 8 indicates that the number will be rounded up, and the 2 in the thousandths place will increase to a 3. Rounding up and replacing the digits to the right of the thousandths place produces 3.753000 which is equivalent to 3.753. Therefore, the zeros are not necessary, and the rounded number should be written as 3.753.

When rounding up, if the digit to be increased is a 9, the digit to its left is increased by 1 and the digit in the desired place value is changed to a zero. For example, the number 1,598 rounded to the nearest ten is 1,600. Another example shows the number 43.72961 rounded to the nearest thousandth is 43.730 or 43.73.

Logical Connectives and Quantifiers

Logical connectives such as *and, or if,* and *then,* are often used with deductive reasoning. This type of reasoning in math involves starting with stating a general rule, and then moving forward with logic to obtain a desired conclusion. If the original statements are true, then the conclusion is true. Most of mathematics involves deductive reasoning. For example, if $x = 2$ and $y = 4$ then $x + y = 6$. Also, if x is an even number and y is an odd number, then $x + y$ is an odd number.

Quantifiers may also be encountered in mathematical problems. The quantifier *all* means that the rule applies across the board or universally or that the entire number of something is present or true. For example, *all* pentagons have five angles. In contrast, the quantifier *none* indicates that not a single one of the items or values in the statement make the statement true or fit the criteria. For example, *none* of the angles in an equilateral triangle are obtuse. The vague quantifier *some* treads the middle ground between those two extremes, and means that an unspecified number or amount of something applies or makes the statement true. For example, the whole amount or number of." For example, *some* rectangles are squares.

Filling in Missing Values in a Data Table

Missing values in a table can be calculated by determining if there is a formula to represent the relationship among values or levels in the table or if empty cells denote subtotals. For example, if a data table presents an itemized list of the type and number of items purchased and the unit price of each item, the subtotal for the cost of each type of item can be calculated by multiplying the number of that item purchased by the unit price.

Consider the table presented earlier of Walter's expenses. This time, several of the "total cost" cells are blank:

Item	Quantity	Cost Per Unit	Total Cost
Hot Coffee	200	$0.25	$50
Slow-Drip Iced Coffee	100	$0.75	
Latte	50		$50
Muffin	75	$1.00	$75
Crepe		$2.00	$90
Egg Sandwich	60	$3.00	$180
Utilities, rent, and labor			$500
Total Costs			$1,020

The total cost for slow-drip iced coffee can be calculated by multiplying the quantity (100) by the cost per unit ($0.75):

$$100 \times \$0.75 = \$75$$

The cost per unit for a latte can be calculated by dividing the total cost ($50) by the number of lattes sold (50):

$$\$50 \div 50 = \$1.00$$

The number of crepes sold can be found in the same manner, but this time, the total cost is divided by the unit cost: $\$90 \div \$2.00 = 45$ crepes.

Using Information from Tables and Graphs to Solve Problems

Data can be represented in many ways. It is important to be able to organize the data into categories that could be represented using one of these methods. Equally important is the ability to read these types of diagrams and interpret their meaning.

Data in Tables

One of the most common ways to express data is in a table. The primary reason for plugging data into a table is to make interpretation more convenient. It's much easier to look at the table than to analyze results in a narrative paragraph. When analyzing a table, pay close attention to the title, variables, and data.

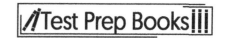

Let's analyze a theoretical antibiotic study. The study has 6 groups, named A through F, and each group receives a different dose of medicine. The results of the study are listed in the table below.

Results of Antibiotic Studies		
Group	Dosage of Antibiotics in milligrams (mg)	Efficacy (% of participants cured)
A	0 mg	20%
B	20 mg	40%
C	40 mg	75%
D	60 mg	95%
E	80 mg	100%
F	100 mg	100%

Tables generally list the title immediately above the data. The title should succinctly explain what is listed below. Here, "Results of Antibiotic Studies" informs the audience that the data pertains to the results of a scientific study on antibiotics.

Identifying the variables at play is one of the most important parts of interpreting data. Remember, the independent variable is intentionally altered, and its change is independent of the other variables. Here, the dosage of antibiotics administered to the different groups is the independent variable. The study is intentionally manipulating the strength of the medicine to study the related results. Efficacy is the dependent variable since its results *depend* on a different variable, the dose of antibiotics. Generally, the independent variable will be listed before the dependent variable in tables.

Also, pay close attention to the variables' labels. Here, the dose is expressed in milligrams (mg) and efficacy in percentages (%). Keep an eye out for questions referencing data in a different unit measurement, or questions asking for a raw number when only the percentage is listed.

Now that the nature of the study and variables at play have been identified, the data itself needs be interpreted. Group A did not receive any of the medicine. As discussed earlier, Group A is the control, as it reflects the amount of people cured in the same timeframe without medicine. It's important to see that efficacy positively correlates with the dosage of medicine. A question using this study might ask for the lowest dose of antibiotics to achieve 100% efficacy. Although Group E and Group F both achieve 100% efficacy, it's important to note that Group E reaches 100% with a lower dose.

Data is often recorded using fractions, such as half a mile, and understanding fractions is critical because of their popular use in real-world applications. Also, it is extremely important to label values with their units when using data. For example, regarding length, the number 2 is meaningless unless it is attached to a unit. Writing 2 cm shows that the number refers to the length of an object.

Data in Graphs

Graphs provide a visual representation of data. The variables are placed on the two axes. The bottom of the graph is referred to as the horizontal axis or x-axis. The left-hand side of the graph is known as the vertical axis or y-axis. Typically, the independent variable is placed on the x-axis, and the dependent variable is located on the y-axis. Sometimes the x-axis is a timeline, and the dependent variables for different trials or groups have been measured throughout points in time; time is still an independent variable but is not always immediately thought of as the independent variable being studied.

The most common types of graphs are the bar graph and the line graph.

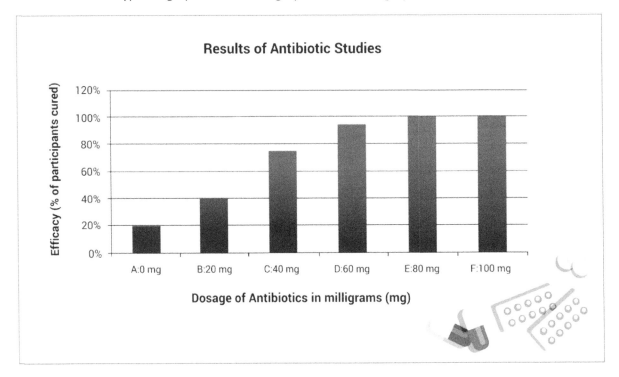

The **bar graph** above expresses the data from the table entitled "Results of Antibiotic Studies." To interpret the data for each group in the study, look at the top of their bars and read the corresponding efficacy on the Y-axis.

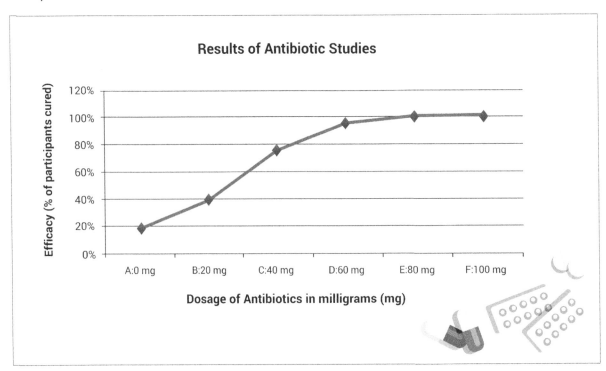

Here, the same data is expressed on a **line graph**. The points on the line correspond with each data entry. Reading the data on the line graph works like the bar graph. The data trend is measured by the slope of the line.

Data in Other Charts

Chart is a broad term that refers to a variety of ways to represent data.

To graph relations, the **Cartesian plane** is used. This means to think of the plane as being given a grid of squares, with one direction being the x-axis and the other direction the y-axis. Generally, the independent variable is placed along the horizontal axis, and the dependent variable is placed along the vertical axis. Any point on the plane can be specified by saying how far to go along the x-axis and how far along the y-axis with a pair of numbers (x, y). Specific values for these pairs can be given names such as $C = (-1, 3)$. Negative values mean to move left or down; positive values mean to move right or up. The point where the axes cross one another is called the **origin**. The origin has coordinates $(0, 0)$ and is usually called O when given a specific label.

An illustration of the Cartesian plane, along with the plotted points $(2, 1)$ and $(-1, -1)$, is below.

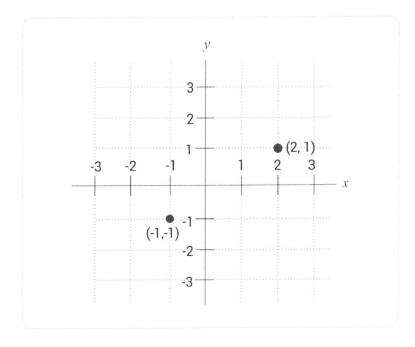

A **box plot**, also called a **box-and-whisker plot**, divides the data points into four groups and displays the five number summary for the set, as well as any outliers. The five number summary consists of:

- The lower extreme: the lowest value that is not an outlier
- The higher extreme: the highest value that is not an outlier
- The median of the set: also referred to as the second quartile or Q_2
- The first quartile or Q_1: the median of values below Q_2
- The third quartile or Q_3: the median of values above Q_2

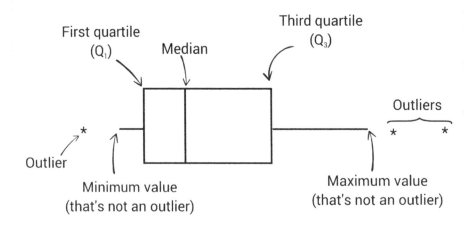

Suppose the box plot displays IQ scores for 12th grade students at a given school. The five number summary of the data consists of: lower extreme (67); upper extreme (127); Q_2 or median (100); Q_1 (91); Q_3 (108); and outliers (135 and 140). Although all data points are not known from the plot, the points are divided into four quartiles each, including 25% of the data points. Therefore, 25% of students scored between 67 and 91, 25% scored between 91 and 100, 25% scored between 100 and 108, and 25% scored between 108 and 127. These percentages include the normal values for the set and exclude the outliers. This information is useful when comparing a given score with the rest of the scores in the set.

A **line plot** is a diagram that shows quantity of data along a number line. It is a quick way to record data in a structure similar to a bar graph without needing to do the required shading of a bar graph. Here is an example of a line plot:

A **tally chart** is a diagram in which tally marks are utilized to represent data. Tally marks are a means of showing a quantity of objects within a specific classification. Here is an example of a tally chart:

Number of days with rain	Number of weeks
0			
1	ⅢⅠ
2	Ⅲ ‖‖
3	Ⅲ Ⅲ Ⅲ
4	Ⅲ
5	Ⅲ Ⅰ
6	Ⅲ
7	Ⅰ

A **picture graph** is a diagram that shows pictorial representation of data being discussed. The symbols used can represent a certain number of objects. Notice how each fruit symbol in the following graph represents a count of two fruits. One drawback of picture graphs is that they can be less accurate if each symbol represents a large number. For example, if each banana symbol represented ten bananas, and

students consumed 22 bananas, it may be challenging to draw and interpret two and one-fifth bananas as a frequency count of 22.

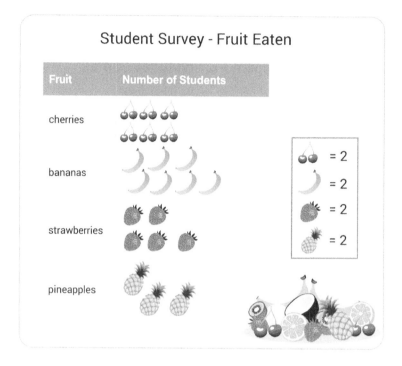

A **circle graph**, also called a **pie chart**, shows categorical data with each category representing a percentage of the whole data set. To make a circle graph, the percent of the data set for each category must be determined. To do so, the frequency of the category is divided by the total number of data points and converted to a percent. For example, if 80 people were asked what their favorite sport is and 20 responded basketball, basketball makes up 25% of the data ($\frac{20}{80} = 0.25 = 25\%$). Each category in a data set is represented by a *slice* of the circle proportionate to its percentage of the whole.

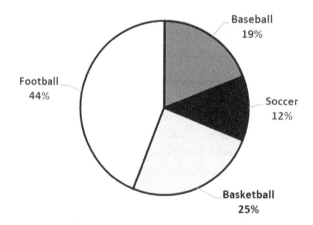

134

A **scatterplot** displays the relationship between two variables. Values for the independent variable, typically denoted by x, are paired with values for the dependent variable, typically denoted by y. Each set of corresponding values are written as an ordered pair (x, y). To construct the graph, a coordinate grid is labeled with the x-axis representing the independent variable and the y-axis representing the dependent variable. Each ordered pair is graphed.

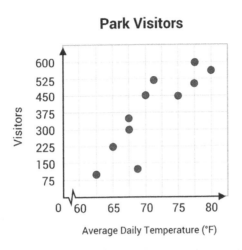

Park Visitors

Like a scatter plot, a **line graph** compares two variables that change continuously, typically over time. Paired data values (ordered pair) are plotted on a coordinate grid with the x- and y-axis representing the two variables. A line is drawn from each point to the next, going from left to right. A double line graph simply displays two sets of data that contain values for the same two variables. The double line graph below displays the profit for given years (two variables) for Company A and Company B (two data sets).

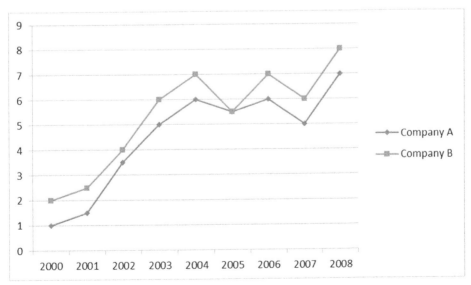

Scatter plots and line graphs can be used to display data consisting of two variables. Examples include height and weight, or distance and time. A correlation between the variables is determined by

examining the points on the graph. Line graphs are used if each value for one variable pairs with a distinct value for the other variable. Line graphs show relationships between variables.

Choosing the appropriate graph to display a data set depends on what type of data is included in the set and what information must be shown. Histograms and box plots can be used for data sets consisting of individual values across a wide range. Examples include test scores and incomes. Histograms and box plots will indicate the center, spread, range, and outliers of a data set. A histogram will show the shape of the data set, while a box plot will divide the set into quartiles (25% increments), allowing for comparison between a given value and the entire set.

Scatter plots and line graphs can be used to display data consisting of two variables. Examples include height and weight, or distance and time. A correlation between the variables is determined by examining the points on the graph. Line graphs are used if each value for one variable pairs with a distinct value for the other variable. Line graphs show relationships between variables.

Drawing Conclusions Based on Graphical Displays

Comparing data sets within statistics can mean many things. The first way to compare data sets is by looking at the center and spread of each set. The **center of a data** set can mean two things: median or mean. The **median** is the value that's halfway into each data set, and it splits the data into two intervals. The **mean** is the average value of the data within a set. It's calculated by adding up all of the data in the set and dividing the total by the number of data points. Outliers can significantly impact the mean. Additionally, two completely different data sets can have the same mean. For example, a data set with values ranging from 0 to 100 and a data set with values ranging from 44 to 56 can both have means of 50. The first data set has a much wider range, which is known as the **spread** of the data. This measures how varied the data is within each set.

In an experiment, variables are the key to analyzing data, especially when data is in a graph or table. Variables can represent anything, including objects, conditions, events, and amounts of time.

Covariance is a general term referring to how two variables move in relation to each other. Take for example an employee that gets paid by the hour. For them, hours worked and total pay have a positive covariance. As hours worked increases, so does pay.

Constant variables remain unchanged by the scientist across all trials. Because they are held constant for all groups in an experiment, they aren't being measured in the experiment, and they are usually ignored. Constants can either be controlled by the scientist directly like the nutrition, water, and sunlight given to plants, or they can be selected by the scientist specifically for an experiment like using a certain animal species or choosing to investigate only people of a certain age group.

Independent variables are also controlled by the scientist, but they are the same only for each group or trial in the experiment. Each group might be composed of students that all have the same color of car or each trial may be run on different soda brands. The independent variable of an experiment is what is being indirectly tested because it causes change in the dependent variables.

Dependent variables experience change caused by the independent variable and are what is being measured or observed. For example, college acceptance rates could be a dependent variable of an experiment that sorted a large sample of high school students by an independent variable such as test scores. In this experiment, the scientist groups the high school students by the independent variable (test scores) to see how it affects the dependent variable (their college acceptance rates).

Note that most variables can be held constant in one experiment, but also serve as the independent variable or a dependent variable in another. For example, when testing how well a fertilizer aids plant growth, its amount of sunlight should be held constant for each group of plants, but if the experiment is being done to determine the proper amount of sunlight a plant should have, the amount of sunlight is an independent variable because it is necessarily changed for each group of plants.

An **X-Y diagram**, also known as a **scatter diagram**, visually displays the relationship between two variables. The independent variable is placed on the *x-axis*, or horizontal axis, and the dependent variable is placed on the *y-axis*, or vertical axis.

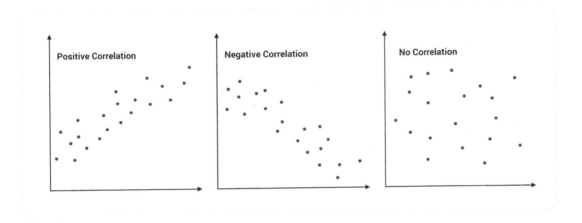

As shown in the figures above, an *X-Y* diagram may result in positive, negative, or no correlation between the two variables. In the first scatter plot, as the *Y* factor increases, the *X* factor increases as well. The opposite is true as well: as the *X* factor increases the *Y* factor also increases. Thus, there is a positive correlation because one factor appears to positively affect the other factor

It's important to note, however, that finding a significant relationship between the dependent variable and the independent variable does not necessarily imply that there is a causal relationship between the two variables. It only means that once the independent variable is known, a fairly accurate prediction of the dependent variable can be made. This is often expressed with the phrase *correlation does not imply causation*. In other words, just because there is a relationship between two variables does not mean that one is the cause of the other. There could be other factors involved that are the real cause. For example, a positive correlation between labor hours and units produced may not equate to a cause-and-effect relationship between the two. Any instance of correlation only indicates how likely the presence of one variable is in the instance of another. The variables should be further analyzed to determine which, if any, other variables (i.e., quality of employee work) may contribute to the positive correlation.

As another example of the phenomenon that correlation does not imply causation, consider an experiment where the independent variable is the value of a person's house, and the dependent variable is their income. Although people in more expensive houses are expected to make more money, it is clear that their expensive houses are not the cause of them making more money. This illustrates one example of why it is important for experimenters to be careful when drawing conclusions about causation from their data.

Linear Data Fitting

The simplest type of correlation between two variables is a **linear correlation**. If the independent variable is x and the dependent variable is y, then a linear correlation means $y = mx + b$. If m is positive, then y will increase as x increases. While if m is negative, then y decreases while x increases. The variable b represents the value of y when x is 0.

As one example of such a correlation, consider a manufacturing plant. Suppose x is the number of units produced by the plant, and y is the cost to the company. In this example, b will be the cost of the plant itself. The plant will cost money even if it is never used, just by buying the machinery. For each unit produced, there will be a cost for the labor and the material. Let m represent this cost to produce one unit of the product.

For a more concrete example, suppose a computer factory costs \$100,000. It requires \$100 of parts and \$50 of labor to make one computer. How much will it cost for a company to make 1,000 computers? To figure this, let y be the amount of money the company spends, and let x be the number of computers. The cost of the factory is \$100,000, so $b = 100,000$. On the other hand, the cost of producing a computer is the parts plus labor, or \$150, so $m = 150$. Therefore, $y = 150x + 100,000$. Substitute 1,000 for x and get $y = 150 \times 1,000 + 100,000 = 150,000 + 100,000 = 250,000$. It will cost the company \$250,000 to make 1,000 computers.

Interpreting Competing Data

Be careful of questions with competing studies. These questions will ask the student to interpret which of two studies shows the greater amount or the higher rate of change between two results.

Here's an example. A research facility runs studies on two different antibiotics: Drug A and Drug B. The Drug A study includes 1,000 participants and cures 600 people. The Drug B study includes 200 participants and cures 150 people. Which drug is more successful?

The first step is to determine the percentage of each drug's rate of success. Drug A was successful in curing 60% of participants, while Drug B achieved a 75% success rate. Thus, Drug B is more successful based on these studies, even though it cured fewer people.

Sample size and experiment consistency should also be considered when answering questions based on competing studies. Is one study significantly larger than the other? In the antibiotics example, the Drug A study is five times larger than Drug B. Thus, Drug B's higher efficacy (desired result) could be a result of the smaller sample size, rather than the quality of drug.

Consistency between studies is directly related to sample size. Let's say the research facility elects to conduct more studies on Drug B. In the next study, there are 400 participants, and 200 are cured. The success rate of the second study is 50%. The results are clearly inconsistent with the first study, which means more testing is needed to determine the drug's efficacy. A hallmark of mathematical or scientific research is repeatability. Studies should be consistent and repeatable, with an appropriately large sample size, before drawing extensive conclusions.

Writing

POWER Strategy for Writing

The POWER strategy helps all writers focus and do well during the writing process.

The POWER strategy stands for the following:

- Prewriting or Planning
- Organizing
- Writing a first draft
- Evaluating the writing
- Revising and rewriting

Prewriting and Planning
During the prewriting and planning phase, writers learn to think about their audience and purpose for the writing assignment. Then they gather information they wish to include in the writing. They do this from their background knowledge or new sources.

Organizing
Next, writers decide on the organization of their writing project. There are many types of organizational structures, but the common ones are: story/narrative, informative, opinion, persuasive, compare and contrast, explanatory, and problem/solution formats.

Writing
In this step, the writers write a first draft of their project.

Evaluating
In this stage, writers reread the writing and note the sections that are strong or that need improvement.

Revising and Rewriting
Finally, the writer incorporates any changes they wish to make based on what they've read. Then writers rewrite the piece into a final draft.

Introducing, Developing, and Concluding a Text Effectively

Almost all coherent written works contain three primary parts: a beginning, middle, and end. The organizational arrangements differ widely across distinct writing modes. Persuasive and expository texts utilize an introduction, body, and conclusion whereas narrative works use an orientation, series of events/conflict, and a resolution.

Every element within a written piece relates back to the main idea, and the beginning of a persuasive or expository text generally conveys the main idea or the purpose. For a narrative piece, the beginning is the section that acquaints the reader with the characters and setting, directing them to the purpose of the writing. The main idea in narrative may be implied or addressed at the end of the piece.

Depending on the primary purpose, the arrangement of the middle will adhere to one of the basic organizational structures described in the information texts and rhetoric section. They are cause and

139

effect, problem and solution, compare and contrast, description/spatial, sequence, and order of importance.

The ending of a text is the metaphorical wrap-up of the writing. A solid ending is crucial for effective writing as it ties together loose ends, resolves the action, highlights the main points, or repeats the central idea. A conclusion ensures that readers come away from a text understanding the author's main idea. The table below highlights the important characteristics of each part of a piece of writing.

Structure	Argumentative/Informative	Narrative
Beginning	Introduction *Purpose, main idea*	Orientation *Introduces characters, setting, necessary background*
Middle	Body *Supporting details, reasons and evidence*	Events/Conflict *Story's events that revolve around a central conflict*
End	Conclusion *Highlights main points, summarizes and paraphrases ideas, reiterates the main idea*	Resolution *The solving of the central conflict*

Elements of Effective Writing

The following are characteristics that make writing readable and effective:

- Ideas
- Organization
- Voice
- Word choice
- Sentence fluency
- Proper Writing Conventions
- Presentation

Ideas

This refers to the content of the writing. Writers should focus on the topic shown in the picture or prompt. They should narrow down and focus their idea, remembering that they only have fifteen minutes to plan and write! Then they learn to develop the idea and choose the details that best shows the idea to others.

Organization

Many writers are inclined to jump into their writing without a clear direction for where it is going. Organization helps plan out the writing so that it's successful. Your writing should have an introduction, a body, and a conclusion.

Introduction (beginning): Writers should invite the reader into their work with a good introduction. They should restate the prompt in their own words so that readers know what they are going to read about.

Body (middle): The body is where the main thoughts and ideas are put together. Thoughtful transitions between ideas and key points help keep readers interested. Writers should create logical and purposeful sequences of ideas.

Conclusion (end): Writers should include a powerful conclusion to their piece that summarizes the information but leaves the reader with something to think about.

Voice
Voice is how the writer uses words and how they use sentence structure to sound like themselves! It shows that the writing is meaningful and that the author cares about it. It is what makes the writing uniquely the author's own. It is how the reader begins to know the author and what they "sound like."

Word Choice
The right word choice helps the author connect with their audience. If the work is narrative, the words tell a story. If the work is descriptive, the words can almost make you taste, touch, and feel what you are reading! If the work is an opinion, the words give new ideas and invite thought. Writers should choose detailed vocabulary and language that is clear and lively.

Sentence Fluency
When sentences are built to fit together and move with one another to create writing that is easy to read aloud, the author has written with fluency. Sentences and paragraphs start and stop in just the right places so that the writing moves well. Sentences should have a lot of different of structures and lengths.

Proper Writing Conventions
Writers should make their writing clear and understandable through the use of proper grammar, spelling, capitalization, and punctuation.

Presentation
Writers should try to make their work inviting to the reader. Writers show they care about their writing when it is neat and readable.

Tips for the Writing Section

1. Don't panic! This section isn't scored. It is just a great way to show teachers how smart you are and how well you can tell a story and write. You can do it!

2. Use your time well. Fifteen minutes is quick! It is shorter than almost every TV show. Don't spend too much time doing any one thing. Try to brainstorm briefly and then get writing. Leave a few minutes to read it over and correct any spelling mistakes or confusing parts.

3. Be yourself! You are smart and interesting and teachers want to get to know you and your unique ideas. Don't feel pressured to use big vocabulary words if you aren't positive what they mean. You will be more understandable if you use the right word, not the fanciest word.

Conventions of Standard English Grammar, Punctuation, and Spelling

Conventions of Standard English

Educators must first be masters of the English language in order to teach it. Teachers serve several key roles in the classroom that all require that they know the conventions of grammar, punctuation, and spelling. Teachers are communicators. They must know how to structure their own language for clarity. They must also be able to interpret what the students are saying to accurately either affirm or revise it for correctness. Teachers are educators of language. They are the agents of change from poor-quality conventions to mastery of the concepts. Teachers are responsible for differentiating instruction so that students at all levels and aptitudes can succeed with language learning. Teachers need to be able to isolate gaps in skill sets and decide which skills need intervention in the classroom. Teachers are evaluators. They are responsible for making key decisions about a student's educational trajectory based on their assessment of the student's capabilities.

Teachers also have great impact on how students view themselves as learners. Teachers are models. They must be superb examples of educated individuals. Just like with any other subject, people need a strong grasp of the basics of language. They will not be able to learn these things unless the teachers themselves have mastered it. Teachers foster socialization; socialization to cultural norms and to the everyday practices of the community in which they live is of utmost importance to students' lives. These processes begin at home but continue early in a child's life at school. Teachers play a key role in guiding and scaffolding students' socialization skills. If teachers are to excel in this role, they need to be adept with the use of the English language.

Understanding the Conventions of Standard English

Parts of Speech
The English language has eight parts of speech, each serving a different grammatical function.

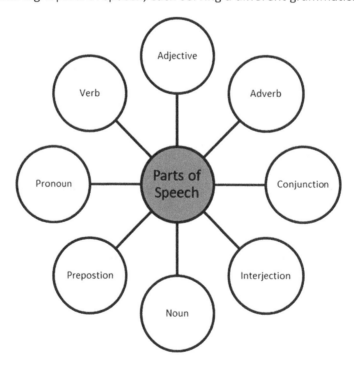

Verb

Verbs describe an action—e.g., *run, play, eat*—or a state of being—e.g., *is, are, was.* It is impossible to make a grammatically-complete sentence without a verb.

He *runs* to the store.

She *is* eight years old.

Noun

Nouns can be a person, place, or thing. They can refer to concrete objects—e.g., chair, apple, house—or abstract things—love, knowledge, friendliness.

Look at the *dog*!

Where are my *keys*?

Some nouns are *countable*, meaning they can be counted as separate entities—one chair, two chairs, three chairs. They can be either singular or plural. Other nouns, usually substances or concepts, are *uncountable*—e.g., air, information, wealth—and some nouns can be both countable and uncountable depending on how they are used.

I bought three *dresses.*

Respect is important to me.

I ate way too much *food* last night.

At the international festival, you can sample *foods* from around the world.

Proper nouns are the specific names of people, places, or things and are almost always capitalized.

Marie Curie studied at the Flying University in Warsaw, Poland.

Pronoun

Pronouns function as substitutes for nouns or noun phrases. Pronouns are often used to avoid constant repetition of a noun or to simplify sentences. *Personal pronouns* are used for people. Some pronouns are *subject pronouns*; they are used to replace the subject in a sentence—I, we, he, she, they.

Is *he* your friend?

We work together.

Object pronouns can function as the object of a sentence—me, us, him, her, them.

Give the documents to *her.*

Did you call *him* back yet?

Some pronouns can function as either the subject or the object—e.g., you, it. The subject of a sentence is the noun of the sentence that is doing or being something.

> *You* should try it.

> *It* tastes great.

Possessive pronouns indicate ownership. They can be used alone—mine, yours, his, hers, theirs, ours—or with a noun—my, your, his, her, their, ours. In the latter case, they function as a determiner, which is described in detail in the below section on adjectives.

> This table is *ours*.

> I can't find *my* phone!

Reflexive pronouns refer back to the person being spoken or written about. These pronouns end in -*self/-selves*.

> I've heard that New York City is gorgeous in the autumn, but I've never seen it for *myself*.

> After moving away from home, young people have to take care of *themselves*.

Indefinite pronouns are used for things that are unknown or unspecified. Some examples are *anybody, something,* and *everything*.

> I'm looking for *someone* who knows how to fix computers.

> I wanted to buy some shoes today, but I couldn't find *any* that I liked.

Adjective

An adjective modifies a noun, making it more precise or giving more information about it. Adjectives answer these questions: What kind? Which one?

> I just bought a *red* car.

> I don't like *cold* weather.

One special type of word that modifies a noun is a *determiner.* In fact, some grammarians classify determiners as a separate part of speech because whereas adjectives simply describe additional qualities of a noun, a determiner is often a necessary part of a noun phrase, without which the phrase is grammatically incomplete. A determiner indicates whether a noun is definite or indefinite and can identify which noun is being discussed. It also introduces context to the noun in terms of quantity and possession. The most commonly-used determiners are articles—a, an, the.

> I ordered *a* pizza.

> She lives in *the* city.

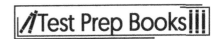

Possessive pronouns discussed above, such as *my*, *your*, and *our*, are also determiners, along with *demonstratives*—this, that—and *quantifiers*—much, many, some. These determiners can take the place of an article.

> Are you using *this* chair?

> I need *some* coffee!

Adverb
Adverbs modify verbs, adjectives, and other adverbs. Words that end in –ly are usually adverbs. Adverbs answer these questions: When? Where? In what manner? To what degree?

> She talks *quickly*.

> The mountains are *incredibly* beautiful!

> The students arrived *early*.

> Please take your phone call *outside*.

Preposition
Prepositions show the relationship between different elements in a phrase or sentence and connect nouns or pronouns to other words in the sentence. Some examples of prepositions are words such as *after*, *at*, *behind*, *by*, *during*, *from*, *in*, *on*, *to*, and *with*.

> Let's go *to* class.

> Starry Night was painted *by* Vincent van Gogh *in* 1889.

Conjunction
Conjunctions join words, phrases, clauses, or sentences together, indicating the type of connection between these elements.

> I like pizza, *and* I enjoy spaghetti.

> I like to play baseball, *but* I'm allergic to mitts.

Some conjunctions are *coordinating*, meaning they give equal emphasis to two main clauses. Coordinating conjunctions are short, simple words that can be remembered using the mnemonic FANBOYS: for, and, nor, but, or, yet, so. Other conjunctions are *subordinating*. Subordinating conjunctions introduce dependent clauses and include words such as *because*, *since*, *before*, *after*, *if*, and *while*.

Interjection
An *interjection* is a short word that shows greeting or emotion. Examples of interjections include *wow*, *ouch*, *hey*, *oops*, *alas*, and *hey*.

> *Wow*! Look at that sunset!

> Was it your birthday yesterday? *Oops*! I forgot.

145

Errors in Standard English Grammar, Usage, Syntax, and Mechanics

Sentence Fragments

A complete sentence requires a verb and a subject, and it must express a complete thought. Sometimes, the subject is omitted in the case of the implied *you*, used in sentences that are the command or imperative form—e.g., "Look!" or "Give me that." It is understood that the subject of the command is *you*, the listener or reader, so it is possible to have a structure without an explicit subject. Without these elements, though, the sentence is incomplete—it is a *sentence fragment.* While sentence fragments often occur in conversational English or creative writing, they are generally not appropriate in academic writing. Sentence fragments often occur when dependent clauses are not joined to an independent clause:

> *Sentence fragment*: Because the airline overbooked the flight.

The sentence above is a dependent clause that does not express a complete thought. What happened as a result of this cause? With the addition of an independent clause, this now becomes a complete sentence:

> *Complete sentence*: Because the airline overbooked the flight, several passengers were unable to board.

Sentences fragments may also occur through improper use of conjunctions:

> I'm going to the Bahamas for spring break. And to New York City for New Year's Eve.

While the first sentence above is a complete sentence, the second one is not because it is a prepositional phrase that lacks a subject [I] and a verb [am going]. Joining the two together with the coordinating conjunction forms one grammatically-correct sentence:

> I'm going to the Bahamas for spring break and to New York City for New Year's Eve.

Run-ons

A *run-on* is a sentence with too many independent clauses that are improperly connected to each other:

> This winter has been very cold some farmers have suffered damage to their crops.

The sentence above has two subject-verb combinations. The first is "this winter has been"; the second is "some farmers have suffered." However, they are simply stuck next to each other without any punctuation or conjunction. Therefore, the sentence is a run-on.

Another type of run-on occurs when writers use inappropriate punctuation:

> This winter has been very cold, some farmers have suffered damage to their crops.

Though a comma has been added, this sentence is still not correct. When a comma alone is used to join two independent clauses, it is known as a **comma splice**. Without an appropriate conjunction, a comma cannot join two independent clauses by itself.

Run-on sentences can be corrected by either dividing the independent clauses into two or more separate sentences or inserting appropriate conjunctions and/or punctuation. The run-on sentence can be amended by separating each subject-verb pair into its own sentence:

> This winter has been very cold. Some farmers have suffered damage to their crops.

The run-on can also be fixed by adding a comma and conjunction to join the two independent clauses with each other:

> This winter has been very cold, so some farmers have suffered damage to their crops.

Parallelism

Parallel structure occurs when phrases or clauses within a sentence contain the same structure. Parallelism increases readability and comprehensibility because it is easy to tell which sentence elements are paired with each other in meaning.

> Jennifer enjoys cooking, knitting, and to spend time with her cat.

This sentence is not parallel because the items in the list appear in two different forms. Some are *gerunds*, which is the verb + ing: *cooking, knitting*. The other item uses the *infinitive* form, which is to + verb: *to spend*. To create parallelism, all items in the list may reflect the same form:

> Jennifer enjoys cooking, knitting, and spending time with her cat.

All of the items in the list are now in gerund forms, so this sentence exhibits parallel structure. Here's another example:

> The company is looking for employees who are responsible and with a lot of experience.

Again, the items that are listed in this sentence are not parallel. "Responsible" is an adjective, yet "with a lot of experience" is a prepositional phrase. The sentence elements do not utilize parallel parts of speech.

> The company is looking for employees who are responsible and experienced.

"Responsible" and "experienced" are both adjectives, so this sentence now has parallel structure.

Dangling and Misplaced Modifiers

Modifiers enhance meaning by clarifying or giving greater detail about another part of a sentence. However, incorrectly-placed modifiers have the opposite effect and can cause confusion. A *misplaced modifier* is a modifier that is not located appropriately in relation to the word or phrase that it modifies:

> Because he was one of the greatest thinkers of Renaissance Italy, John idolized Leonardo da Vinci.

In this sentence, the modifier is "because he was one of the greatest thinkers of Renaissance Italy," and the noun it is intended to modify is "Leonardo da Vinci." However, due to the placement of the modifier next to the subject, John, it seems as if the sentence is stating that John was a Renaissance genius, not Da Vinci.

> John idolized Leonard da Vinci because he was one of the greatest thinkers of Renaissance Italy.

The modifier is now adjacent to the appropriate noun, clarifying which of the two men in this sentence is the greatest thinker.

Dangling modifiers modify a word or phrase that is not readily apparent in the sentence. That is, they "dangle" because they are not clearly attached to anything:

> After getting accepted to college, Amir's parents were proud.

The modifier here, "after getting accepted to college," should modify who got accepted. The noun immediately following the modifier is "Amir's parents"—but they are probably not the ones who are going to college.

> After getting accepted to college, Amir made his parents proud.

The subject of the sentence has been changed to Amir himself, and now the subject and its modifier are appropriately matched.

Inconsistent Verb Tense

Verb tense reflects when an action occurred or a state existed. For example, the tense known as *simple present* expresses something that is happening right now or that happens regularly:

> She *works* in a hospital.

Present continuous tense expresses something in progress. It is formed by to be + verb + -ing.

> Sorry, I can't go out right now. I *am doing* my homework.

Past tense is used to describe events that previously occurred. However, in conversational English, speakers often use present tense or a mix of past and present tense when relating past events because it gives the narrative a sense of immediacy. In formal written English, though, consistency in verb tense is necessary to avoid reader confusion.

> I traveled to Europe last summer. As soon as I stepped off the plane, I feel like I'm in a movie! I'm surrounded by quaint cafes and impressive architecture.

The passage above abruptly switches from past tense—*traveled, stepped*—to present tense—*feel, am surrounded*.

> I *traveled* to Europe last summer. As soon as I *stepped* off the plane, I *felt* like I was in a movie! I *was surrounded* by quaint cafes and impressive architecture.

All verbs are in past tense, so this passage now has consistent verb tense.

Split Infinitives

The *infinitive form* of a verb consists of "to + base verb"—e.g., to walk, to sleep, to approve. A *split infinitive* occurs when another word, usually an adverb, is placed between *to* and the verb:

> I decided *to simply walk* to work to get more exercise every day.

The infinitive *to walk* is split by the adverb *simply*.

> It was a mistake *to hastily approve* the project before conducting further preliminary research.

The infinitive *to approve* is split by *hastily*.

Although some grammarians still advise against split infinitives, this syntactic structure is common in both spoken and written English and is widely accepted in standard usage.

Subject-Verb Agreement

In English, verbs must agree with the subject. The form of a verb may change depending on whether the subject is singular or plural, or whether it is first, second, or third person. For example, the verb *to be* has various forms:

> I <u>am </u>a student.

> You <u>are</u> a student.

> She <u>is</u> a student.

> We <u>are</u> students.

> They <u>are</u> students.

Errors occur when a verb does not agree with its subject. Sometimes, the error is readily apparent:

> We is hungry.

Is is not the appropriate form of *to be* when used with the third person plural *we*.

> We are hungry.

This sentence now has correct subject-verb agreement.

However, some cases are trickier, particularly when the subject consists of a lengthy noun phrase with many modifiers:

> Students who are hoping to accompany the anthropology department on its annual summer trip to Ecuador needs to sign up by March 31st.

The verb in this sentence is *needs*. However, its subject is not the noun adjacent to it—Ecuador. The subject is the noun at the beginning of the sentence—students. Because *students* is plural, *needs* is the incorrect verb form.

> *Students* who are hoping to accompany the anthropology department on its annual summer trip to Ecuador *need* to sign up by March 31st.

This sentence now uses correct agreement between *students* and *need*.

Another case to be aware of is a *collective noun*. A collective noun refers to a group of many things or people but can be singular in itself—e.g., family, committee, army, pair team, council, jury. Whether or

not a collective noun uses a singular or plural verb depends on how the noun is being used. If the noun refers to the group performing a collective action as one unit, it should use a singular verb conjugation:

> The family is moving to a new neighborhood.

The whole family is moving together in unison, so the singular verb form *is* is appropriate here.

> The committee has made its decision.

The verb *has* and the possessive pronoun *its* both reflect the word *committee* as a singular noun in the sentence above; however, when a collective noun refers to the group as individuals, it can take a plural verb:

> The newlywed pair spend every moment together.

This sentence emphasizes the love between two people in a pair, so it can use the plural verb *spend*.

> The council are all newly elected members.

The sentence refers to the council in terms of its individual members and uses the plural verb *are*.

Overall, though, American English is more likely to pair a collective noun with a singular verb, while British English is more likely to pair a collective noun with a plural verb.

Grammar, Usage, Syntax, and Mechanics Choices

Colons and Semicolons

In a sentence, *colons* are used before a list, a summary or elaboration, or an explanation related to the preceding information in the sentence:

> There are two ways to reserve tickets for the performance: by phone or in person.

> One thing is clear: students are spending more on tuition than ever before.

As these examples show, a colon must be preceded by an independent clause. However, the information after the colon may be in the form of an independent clause or in the form of a list.

Semicolons can be used in two different ways—to join ideas or to separate them. In some cases, semicolons can be used to connect what would otherwise be stand-alone sentences. Each part of the sentence joined by a semicolon must be an independent clause. The use of a semicolon indicates that these two independent clauses are closely related to each other:

> The rising cost of childcare is one major stressor for parents; healthcare expenses are another source of anxiety.

> Classes have been canceled due to the snowstorm; check the school website for updates.

Semicolons can also be used to divide elements of a sentence in a more distinct way than simply using a comma. This usage is particularly useful when the items in a list are especially long and complex and contain other internal punctuation.

> Retirees have many modes of income: some survive solely off their retirement checks; others supplement their income through part time jobs, like working in a supermarket or substitute

150

teaching; and others are financially dependent on the support of family members, friends, and spouses.

Its and It's

These pronouns are some of the most confused in the English language as most possessives contain the suffix –'s. However, for *it*, it is the opposite. *Its* is a possessive pronoun:

The government is reassessing *its* spending plan.

It's is a contraction of the words *it is*:

It's snowing outside.

Saw and Seen

Saw and *seen* are both conjugations of the verb *to see*, but they express different verb tenses. *Saw* is used in the simple past tense. *Seen* is the past participle form of *to see* and can be used in all perfect tenses.

I seen her yesterday.

This sentence is incorrect. Because it expresses a completed event from a specified point in time in the past, it should use simple past tense:

I *saw* her yesterday.

This sentence uses the correct verb tense. Here's how the past participle is used correctly:

I *have seen* her before.

The meaning in this sentence is slightly changed to indicate an event from an unspecific time in the past. In this case, present perfect is the appropriate verb tense to indicate an unspecified past experience. Present perfect conjugation is created by combining *to have* + past participle.

Then and Than

Then is generally used as an adverb indicating something that happened next in a sequence or as the result of a conditional situation:

We parked the car and *then* walked to the restaurant.

If enough people register for the event, *then* we can begin planning.

Than is a conjunction indicating comparison:

This watch is more expensive *than* that one.

The bus departed later *than* I expected.

They're, Their, and There

They're is a contraction of the words *they are*:

They're moving to Ohio next week.

Their is a possessive pronoun:

> The baseball players are training for *their* upcoming season.

There can function as multiple parts of speech, but it is most commonly used as an adverb indicating a location:

> Let's go to the concert! Some great bands are playing *there*.

Insure and Ensure

These terms are both verbs. *Insure* means to guarantee something against loss, harm, or damage, usually through an insurance policy that offers monetary compensation:

> The robbers made off with her prized diamond necklace, but luckily it was *insured* for one million dollars.

Ensure means to make sure, to confirm, or to be certain:

> *Ensure* that you have your passport before entering the security checkpoint.

Accept and Except

Accept is a verb meaning to take or agree to something:

> I would like to *accept* your offer of employment.

Except is a preposition that indicates exclusion:

> I've been to every state in America *except* Hawaii.

Affect and Effect

Affect is a verb meaning to influence or to have an impact on something:

> The amount of rainfall during the growing season *affects* the flavor of wine produced from these grapes.

Effect can be used as either a noun or a verb. As a noun, *effect* is synonymous with a result:

> If we implement the changes, what will the *effect* be on our profits?

As a verb, *effect* means to bring about or to make happen:

> In just a few short months, the healthy committee has *effected* real change in school nutrition.

Components of Sentences

Clauses

Clauses contain a subject and a verb. An *independent clause* can function as a complete sentence on its own, but it might also be one component of a longer sentence. *Dependent clauses* cannot stand alone as complete sentences. They rely on independent clauses to complete their meaning. Dependent clauses usually begin with a subordinating conjunction. Independent and dependent clauses are sometimes also referred to as *main clauses* and *subordinate clauses*, respectively. The following structure highlights the differences:

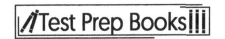

Apiculturists raise honeybees because they love insects.

Apiculturists raise honeybees is an independent or main clause. The subject is *apiculturists*, and the verb is *raise*. It expresses a complete thought and could be a standalone sentence.

Because they love insects is a dependent or subordinate clause. If it were not attached to the independent clause, it would be a sentence fragment. While it contains a subject and verb—*they love*—this clause is dependent because it begins with the subordinate conjunction *because*. Thus, it does not express a complete thought on its own.

Another type of clause is a *relative clause*, and it is sometimes referred to as an *adjective clause* because it gives further description about the noun. A relative clause begins with a *relative pronoun*: *that*, *which*, *who*, *whom*, *whichever*, *whomever*, or *whoever*. It may also begin with a *relative adverb*: *where*, *why*, or *when*. Here's an example of a relative clause, functioning as an adjective:

The strawberries that I bought yesterday are already beginning to spoil.

Here, the relative clause is *that I bought yesterday*; the relative pronoun is *that*. The subject is *I*, and the verb is *bought*. The clause modifies the subject *strawberries* by answering the question, "Which strawberries?" Here's an example of a relative clause with an adverb:

The tutoring center is a place where students can get help with homework.

The relative clause is *where students can get help with homework*, and it gives more information about a place by describing what kind of place it is. It begins with the relative adverb *where* and contains the noun *students* along with its verb phrase *can get*.

Relative clauses may be further divided into two types: essential or nonessential. *Essential clauses* contain identifying information without which the sentence would lose significant meaning or not make sense. These are also sometimes referred to as *restrictive clauses*. The sentence above contains an example of an essential relative clause. Here is what happens when the clause is removed:

The tutoring center is a place where students can get help with homework.

The tutoring center is a place.

Without the relative clause, the sentence loses the majority of its meaning; thus, the clause is essential or restrictive.

Nonessential clauses—also referred to as *non-restrictive clauses*—offer additional information about a noun in the sentence, but they do not significantly control the overall meaning of the sentence. The following example indicates a nonessential clause:

New York City, which is located in the northeastern part of the country, is the most populated city in America.

New York City is the most populated city in America.

Even without the relative clause, the sentence is still understandable and continues to communicate its central message about New York City. Thus, it is a nonessential clause.

Punctuation differs between essential and nonessential relative clauses, too. Nonessential clauses are set apart from the sentence using commas whereas essential clauses are not separated with commas. Also, the relative pronoun *that* is generally used for essential clauses, while *which* is used for nonessential clauses. The following examples clarify this distinction:

> *Romeo and Juliet* is my favorite play *that Shakespeare wrote*.

The relative clause *that Shakespeare wrote* contains essential, controlling information about the noun *play*, limiting it to those plays by Shakespeare. Without it, it would seem that *Romeo and Juliet* is the speaker's favorite play out of every play ever written, not simply from Shakespeare's repertoire.

> *Romeo and Juliet*, *which Shakespeare wrote*, is my favorite play.

Here, the nonessential relative clause—"which Shakespeare wrote"—modifies *Romeo and Juliet*. It doesn't provide controlling information about the play, but simply offers further background details. Thus, commas are needed.

Phrases

Phrases are groups of words that do not contain the subject-verb combination required for clauses. Phrases are classified by the part of speech that begins or controls the phrase.

A *noun phrase* consists of a noun and all its modifiers—adjectives, adverbs, and determiners. Noun phrases can serve many functions in a sentence, acting as subjects, objects, and object complements:

> *The shallow yellow bowl* sits on the top shelf.

> Nina just bought *some incredibly fresh organic produce*.

Prepositional phrases are made up of a preposition and its object. The object of a preposition might be a noun, noun phrase, pronoun, or gerund. Prepositional phrases may function as either an adjective or an adverb:

> Jack picked up the book *in front of him*.

The prepositional phrase *in front of him* acts as an adjective indicating which book Jack picked up.

> The dog ran into the back yard.

The phrase *into the backyard* describes where the dog ran, so it acts as an adverb.

Verb phrases include all of the words in a verb group, even if they are not directly adjacent to each other:

> I *should have woken up* earlier this morning.

> The company **is** now *offering* membership discounts for new enrollers.

This sentence's verb phrase is *is offering*. Even though they are separated by the word *now*, they function together as a single verb phrase.

Structures of Sentences

All sentences contain the same basic elements: a subject and a verb. The *subject* is who or what the sentence is about; the *verb* describes the subject's action or condition. However, these elements, subjects and verbs, can be combined in different ways. The following graphic describes the different types of sentence structures.

Sentence Structure	Independent Clauses	Dependent Clauses
Simple	1	0
Compound	2 or more	0
Complex	1	1 or more
Compound-Complex	2 or more	1 or more

A *simple sentence* expresses a complete thought and consists of one subject and verb combination:

> The children ate pizza.

The subject is *children*. The verb is *ate*.

Either the subject or the verb may be *compound*—that is, it could have more than one element:

> *The children and their parents* ate pizza.

> The children *ate pizza and watched a movie*.

All of these are still simple sentences. Despite having either compound subjects or compound verbs, each sentence still has only one subject and verb combination.

Compound sentences combine two or more simple sentences to form one sentence that has multiple subject-verb combinations:

> *The children ate pizza,* and *their parents watched a movie.*

This structure is comprised of two independent clauses: (1) *the children ate pizza* and (2) *their parents watched a movie*. Compound sentences join different subject-verb combinations using a comma and a coordinating conjunction.

> I called my mom, *but* she didn't answer the phone.

> The weather was stormy, *so* we canceled our trip to the beach.

A *complex sentence* consists of an independent clause and one or more dependent clauses. Dependent clauses join a sentence using *subordinating conjunctions*. Some examples of subordinating conjunctions are *although*, *unless*, *as soon as*, *since*, *while*, *when*, *because*, *if*, and *before*.

> I missed class yesterday *because* my mother was ill.

> *Before* traveling to a new country, you need to exchange your money to the local currency.

The order of clauses determines their punctuation. If the dependent clause comes first, it should be separated from the independent clause with a comma. However, if the complex sentence consists of an independent clause followed by a dependent clause, then a comma is not always necessary.

155

A *compound-complex sentence* can be created by joining two or more independent clauses with at least one dependent clause:

> After the earthquake struck, thousands of homes were destroyed, and many families were left without a place to live.

The first independent clause in the compound structure includes a dependent clause—*after the earthquake struck*. Thus, the structure is both complex and compound.

CBEST Practice Test #1

Reading

Questions 1–3 refer to the following paragraph.

The Brookside area is an older part of Kansas City, developed mainly in the 1920s and '30s, and is considered one of the nation's first "planned" communities with shops, restaurants, parks, and churches all within a quick walk. A stroll down any street reveals charming two-story Tudor and Colonial homes with smaller bungalows sprinkled throughout the beautiful tree-lined streets. It is common to see lemonade stands on the corners and baseball games in the numerous "pocket" parks tucked neatly behind rows of well-manicured houses. The Brookside shops on 63rd street between Wornall Road and Oak Street are a hub of commerce and entertainment where residents freely shop and dine with their pets (and children) in tow. This is also a common "hangout" spot for younger teenagers because it is easily accessible by bike for most. In short, it is an idyllic neighborhood just minutes from downtown Kansas City.

1. Which of the following states the main idea of this paragraph?
   a. The Brookside shops are a popular hangout for teenagers.
   b. There are a number of pocket parks in the Brookside neighborhood.
   c. Brookside is a great place to live.
   d. Brookside has a high crime rate.
   e. Everyone should move to Brookside.

2. In what kind of publication might you read the above paragraph?
   a. Fictional novel
   b. Literary journal
   c. Newspaper article
   d. Movie review
   e. Community profile

3. According to this paragraph, which of the following is unique to this neighborhood?
   a. It is old.
   b. It is in Kansas City.
   c. It has shopping.
   d. It is one of the nation's first planned communities.
   e. It has both Tudor and Colonial homes.

Questions 4–6 refer to the following excerpt from a government publication table of contents.

Contents

From http://purl.fdlp.gov/GPO/gpo66588

4. In which chapter would you find information for a research paper about the problem of child neglect in disproportionately affected communities?
   a. Chapter 3
   b. Chapter 4
   c. Chapter 5
   d. Chapter 6
   e. Chapter 7

5. On which page would you find information about the needs of the American Indian child?
   a. 52
   b. 60
   c. 86
   d. 106
   e. 120

6. According to the table of contents, Chapter 1 is titled "Confronting the Tragedy of Child Abuse and Neglect Fatalities." Based on the chapter title and sections, which of the following is a good summary of this chapter?
   a. Children's lives today are valuable and worth saving, and the children of the future are just as important.
   b. The outlining of a plan to solve the problem of child neglect in disproportionately affected communities is one of the main goals here.
   c. Child abuse and neglect is alive and rampant in our communities, and this chapter outlines those who are in dire need of our attention.
   d. This chapter outlines resources for families who are affected by child abuse and neglect.
   e. Provides quantitative facts in order to help make sense of the issue of child abuse.

Questions 7–9 refer to the following excerpt taken from Walt Whitman's "Letters from a Traveling Bachelor," published in the New York Sunday Dispatch *on 14 October 1849.*

> At its easternmost part, Long Island opens like the upper and under jaws of some prodigious alligator; the upper and larger one terminating in Montauk Point. The bay that lies in here, and part of which forms the splendid harbor of Greenport, where the Long Island Railroad ends, is called Peconic Bay; and a beautiful and varied water is it, fertile in fish and feathered game. I, who am by no means a skillful fisherman, go down for an hour of a morning on one of the docks, or almost anywhere along shore, and catch a mess of black-fish, which you couldn't buy in New York for a dollar—large fat fellows, with meat on their bones that it takes a pretty long fork to stick through. They have a way here of splitting these fat black-fish and poggies, and broiling them on the coals, beef-steak-fashion, which I recommend your Broadway cooks to copy.

7. Whitman's comparison of the easternmost part of Long Island to an alligator is an example of which literary device?
   a. Hyperbole
   b. Metaphor
   c. Personification
   d. Alliteration
   e. Simile

8. Which of the following is the best summary of this passage?
   a. Walt Whitman was impressed with the quantity and quality of fish he found in Peconic Bay.
   b. Walt Whitman preferred the fish found in restaurants in New York.
   c. Walt Whitman was a Broadway chef.
   d. Walt Whitman was frustrated because he was not a very skilled fisherman.
   e. Long Island reminded Walt Whitman of an alligator.

9. Using the context clues in the passage, what is the meaning of the word *prodigious* in the first line?
   a. Out of place
   b. Great in extent, size, or degree
   c. Mean-spirited
   d. Extremely intelligent
   e. Of a somber disposition

10. Which of the following would be a good topic sentence if you were writing a paragraph about the effects of education on crime rates?
   a. Crime statistics are difficult to verify for a number of reasons.
   b. Educated people do not commit crimes.
   c. Education is an important factor in lowering crime rates.
   d. Education has been proven to lower crime rates by as much as 20% in some urban areas.
   e. It is untrue that areas that have higher education are higher in crime rates.

11. Which of the following is not an example of a good thesis statement for an essay?
   a. Animals in danger of becoming extinct come from a wide range of countries.
   b. Effective leadership requires specific qualities that anyone can develop.
   c. Cashew milk is perfect for bakers who want to use dairy-free alternatives.
   d. In order to fully explore the wreck of the Titanic, scientists must address several problems.
   e. Industrial waste poured into Lake Michigan has killed 27 percent of marine life in the past decade.

Questions 12–15 refer to the following passage, titled "Education is Essential to Civilization."

Early in my career, a master teacher shared this thought with me: "Education is the last bastion of civility." While I did not completely understand the scope of those words at the time, I have since come to realize the depth, breadth, truth, and significance of what he said. Education provides society with a vehicle for raising its children to be civil, decent human beings with something valuable to contribute to the world. It is really what makes us human and what distinguishes us as civilized creatures.

Being "civilized" humans means being "whole" humans. Education must address the minds, bodies, and souls of students. It would be detrimental to society if our schools were myopic in their focus, only meeting the needs of the mind. As humans, we are multidimensional, multifaceted beings who need more than head knowledge to survive. The human heart and psyche have to be fed in order for the mind to develop properly, and the body must be maintained and exercised to help fuel the working of the brain.

Education is a basic human right, and it allows us to sustain a democratic society in which participation is fundamental to its success. It should inspire students to seek better solutions to world problems and to dream of a more equitable society. Education should never discriminate on any basis, and it should create individuals who are self-sufficient, patriotic, and tolerant of others' ideas.

All children can learn, although not all children learn in the same manner. All children learn best, however, when their basic physical needs are met, and they feel safe, secure, and loved. Students are much more responsive to a teacher who values them and shows them respect as individual people. Teachers must model at all times the way they

160

expect students to treat them and their peers. If teachers set high expectations for their students, the students will rise to that high level. Teachers must make the well-being of their students their primary focus and must not be afraid to let their students learn from their own mistakes.

In the modern age of technology, a teacher's focus is no longer the "what" of the content, but more importantly, the "why." Students are bombarded with information and have access to any information they need right at their fingertips. Teachers have to work harder than ever before to help students identify salient information and to think critically about the information they encounter. Students have to read between the lines, identify bias, and determine who they can trust in the milieu of ads, data, and texts presented to them.

Schools must work in concert with families in this important mission. While children spend most of their time in school, they are dramatically and indelibly shaped by the influences of their family and culture. Teachers must not only respect this fact but must strive to include parents in the education of their children and must work to keep parents informed of progress and problems. Communication between classroom and home is essential for a child's success.

Humans have always aspired to be more, to do more, and to better ourselves and our communities. This is where education lies, right at the heart of humanity's desire to be all that we can be. Education helps us strive for higher goals and better treatment of ourselves and others. I shudder to think what would become of us if education ceased to be the "last bastion of civility." We must be unapologetic about expecting excellence from our students—our very existence depends upon it.

12. Which of the following best summarizes the author's main point?
    a. Education as we know it is over-valued in modern society, and we should find alternative solutions.
    b. The survival of the human race depends on the educational system, and it is worth fighting for to make it better.
    c. The government should do away with all public schools and require parents to homeschool their children instead.
    d. While education is important, some children simply are not capable of succeeding in a traditional classroom.
    e. Students are learning new ways to learn while teachers are learning to adapt to their needs.

13. Based on this passage, which of the following can be inferred about the author?
    a. The author feels passionately about education.
    b. The author does not feel strongly about their point.
    c. The author is angry at the educational system.
    d. The author is unsure about the importance of education.
    e. The author does not trust the government.

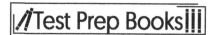
14. Based on this passage, which of the following conclusions could be drawn about the author?
   a. The author would not support raising taxes to help fund much-needed reforms in education.
   b. The author would support raising taxes to help fund much-needed reforms in education, as long as those reforms were implemented in higher socio-economic areas first.
   c. The author would support raising taxes to help fund much-needed reforms in education for all children in all schools.
   d. The author would support raising taxes only in certain states to help fund much-needed reforms in education.
   e. The author would not support raising taxes unless the people in the communities agreed to it.

15. According to the passage, which of the following is NOT mentioned as an important factor in education today?
   a. Parent involvement
   b. Communication between parents and teachers
   c. Impact of technology
   d. Cost of textbooks
   e. Safe and healthy children

For question 16, use the following graphics.

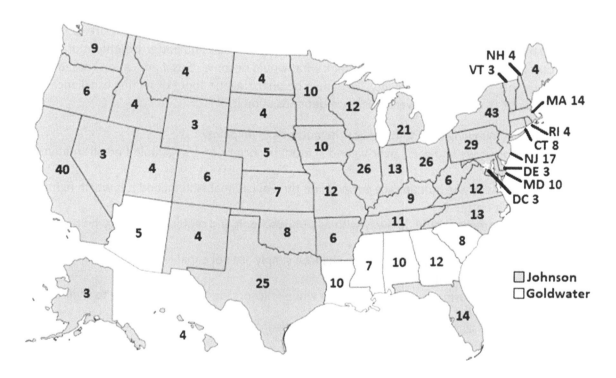

162

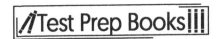

1964 Election Results			
Candidate	Party	Electoral Votes	Popular Votes
Lyndon B. Johnson	Democratic	486	42,825,463
Barry M. Goldwater	Republican	52	27,146,969

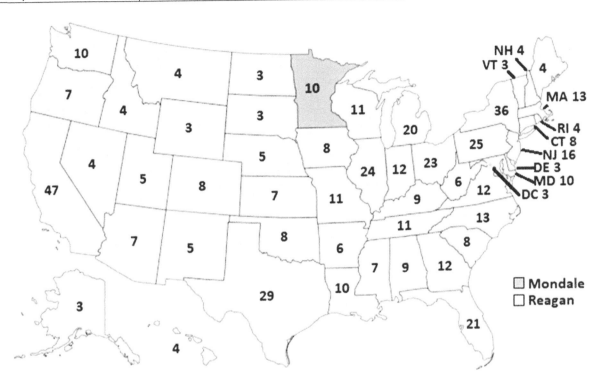

1984 Election Results			
Candidate	Party	Electoral Votes	Popular Votes
Ronald Reagan (I)	Republican	525	54,455,000
Walter F. Mondale	Democratic	13	37,577,000

16. Based on the two maps, which of the following statements is true?
    a. Over twenty years, the country's voter turnout for a presidential election stayed the exact same.
    b. Over twenty years, there was a noticeable decrease in voter turnout during a presidential election.
    c. Over twenty years, the electoral vote swung from almost completely Democrat to almost completely Republican.
    d. There was very little change in the number of electoral votes won for each party from 1964 to 1984.
    e. Over twenty years, the electoral vote swung from almost completely Republican to almost completely Democrat.

163

For question 17, use the following graphic.

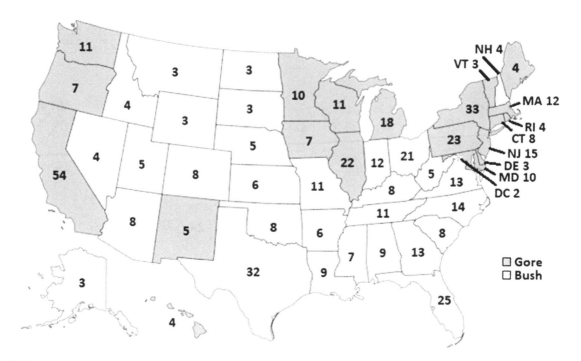

2000 Election Results			
Candidate	**Party**	**Electoral Votes**	**Popular Votes**
George W. Bush	Republican	271	50,456,062
Albert Gore, Jr.	Democratic	266	50,996,582

17. Based on the map, which of the following statements is NOT true?
    a. In 2000, the Democratic candidate won the popular vote, which means he won more the electoral votes of more states.
    b. In 2000, the Republican candidate won the presidential election because he won the electoral vote even though he did not win the popular vote.
    c. In 2000, the Democratic candidate won the popular vote but not the electoral vote, which reveals a discrepancy in the electoral system.
    d. In 2000, the Republican candidate won more states but did not win the popular vote.
    e. In 2000, the Republican candidate won 271 electoral votes, and the Democratic candidate won 266 electoral votes.

18. If you were asked to write a comprehensive research paper about life during the Great Depression in the United States, which of the following would be a reliable primary source?
    a. Wikipedia article titled "Life in Depression America"
    b. Diary entry from Elsie May Long published in the article "The Great Depression: Two Kansas Diaries" by C. Robert Haywood in *Great Plains Quarterly*
    c. Article titled "The Great Depression Begins: the Stock Market Crash of 1929," found at http://www.history.com/topics/great-depression
    d. Book by Glen H. Elder, Jr., titled *Children of the Great Depression: Social Change in Life Experience*, published in 1999 by the American Psychological Association
    e. Analysis of a diary entry titled "The Country's Depression: Oklahoma in a Time of Crisis"

164

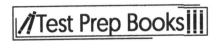

19. "Excuse me, sir," the host of the party declared, "this matter is not *any* of your business." The use of italics in this sentence indicates which of the following?
   a. Dialogue
   b. Thoughts
   c. Emphasis
   d. Volume
   e. A title

20. Snails, clams, mussels, and squid are mollusks, i.e., invertebrates with soft, unsegmented bodies that live in aquatic or damp habitats and have calcareous shells.

Which of the following does the abbreviation i.e. stand for in the preceding sentence?
   a. For example
   b. In error
   c. In addition
   d. That is
   e. Excepting

Questions 21–25 are based upon the following passage:

This excerpt is adapted from Charles Dickens' speech in Birmingham in England on December 30, 1853 on behalf of the Birmingham and Midland Institute.

> My Good Friends,—When I first imparted to the committee of the projected Institute my particular wish that on one of the evenings of my readings here the main body of my audience should be composed of working men and their families, I was animated by two desires; first, by the wish to have the great pleasure of meeting you face to face at this Christmas time, and accompany you myself through one of my little Christmas books; and second, by the wish to have an opportunity of stating publicly in your presence, and in the presence of the committee, my earnest hope that the Institute will, from the beginning, recognise one great principle—strong in reason and justice—which I believe to be essential to the very life of such an Institution. It is, that the working man shall, from the first unto the last, have a share in the management of an Institution which is designed for his benefit, and which calls itself by his name.
>
> I have no fear here of being misunderstood—of being supposed to mean too much in this. If there ever was a time when any one class could of itself do much for its own good, and for the welfare of society—which I greatly doubt—that time is unquestionably past. It is in the fusion of different classes, without confusion; in the bringing together of employers and employed; in the creating of a better common understanding among those whose interests are identical, who depend upon each other, who are vitally essential to each other, and who never can be in unnatural antagonism without deplorable results, that one of the chief principles of a Mechanics' Institution should consist. In this world a great deal of the bitterness among us arises from an imperfect understanding of one another. Erect in Birmingham a great Educational Institution, properly educational; educational of the feelings as well as of the reason; to which all orders of Birmingham men contribute; in which all orders of Birmingham men meet; wherein all orders of Birmingham men are faithfully

represented—and you will erect a Temple of Concord here which will be a model edifice to the whole of England.

Contemplating as I do the existence of the Artisans' Committee, which not long ago considered the establishment of the Institute so sensibly, and supported it so heartily, I earnestly entreat the gentlemen—earnest I know in the good work, and who are now among us,—by all means to avoid the great shortcoming of similar institutions; and in asking the working man for his confidence, to set him the great example and give him theirs in return. You will judge for yourselves if I promise too much for the working man, when I say that he will stand by such an enterprise with the utmost of his patience, his perseverance, sense, and support; that I am sure he will need no charitable aid or condescending patronage; but will readily and cheerfully pay for the advantages which it confers; that he will prepare himself in individual cases where he feels that the adverse circumstances around him have rendered it necessary; in a word, that he will feel his responsibility like an honest man, and will most honestly and manfully discharge it. I now proceed to the pleasant task to which I assure you I have looked forward for a long time.

21. Based upon the contextual evidence provided in the passage above, what is the meaning of the term *enterprise* in the third paragraph?
    a. Company
    b. Courage
    c. Game
    d. Honesty
    e. Cause

22. The speaker addresses his audience as "My Good Friends." What function does this salutation serve for the speaker?
    a. The speaker is an employer addressing his employees, so the salutation is a way for the boss to bridge the gap between himself and his employees.
    b. The speaker's salutation is one from an entertainer to his audience and uses the friendly language to connect to his audience before a serious speech.
    c. The salutation gives the serious speech that follows a somber tone, as it is used ironically.
    d. The speech is one from a politician to the public, so the salutation is used to grab the audience's attention.
    e. The salutation is one from a man on trial to his peers, so he is trying to evoke their empathy.

23. According to the passage, what is the speaker's second desire for his time in front of the audience?
    a. To read a Christmas story
    b. To support the idea that the "working man" should have a say in an institution that is designed for his benefit
    c. To have an opportunity to stand in their presence
    d. For the life of the institution to be essential to the audience as a whole
    e. To join them one day in the working forces

24. The speaker's tone in the passage can be described as:
   a. Happy and gullible
   b. Lazy and entitled
   c. Confident and informed
   d. Angry and frustrated
   e. Ceremonious and stern

25. Which of the following is one of the main purposes of the last paragraph?
   a. To persuade the audience to support the Institute no matter what, since it provided so much support to the working class
   b. To market the speaker's new book, while at the same time, supporting the activities of the Institute
   c. To inform the audience that the Institute is corrupt and will not help them out when the time comes to give them compensation
   d. To provide credibility to the working man and share confidence in their ability to take on responsibilities
   e. To improve his standing with the audience because he has kept them waiting through his speech for a long time

26. Consider the following headings that might be found under the entry for "Basketball" in an electronic encyclopedia.

   • Introduction
   • Basic Rules
   • Professional Basketball
   • College Basketball
   • Similarities to Lacrosse
   • Olympic and International Basketball
   • Women's Basketball
   • Bibliography

Which one does not belong?
   a. Women's Basketball
   b. Similarities to Lacrosse
   c. Basic Rules
   d. Bibliography
   e. College Basketball

27. The guidewords at the top of a dictionary page are *receipt* and *reveal*. Which of the following words is NOT an entry on this page?
   a. Receive
   b. Retail
   c. Revere
   d. Reluctant
   e. Reception

Use the nutrition label below for questions 28–30.

Nutrition Facts

Serving Size 2/3 cup (55g)
Servings Per Container About 8

Amount Per Serving

Calories 230   Calories from Fat 72

	% Daily Value*
Total Fat 8g	**12**%
Saturated Fat 1g	**5**%
Trans Fat 0g	
Cholesterol 0mg	**0**%
Sodium 160mg	**7**%
Total Carbohydrate 37g	**12**%
Dietary Fiber 4g	**16**%
Sugars 1g	
Protein 3g	
Vitamin A	10%
Vitamin C	8%
Calcium	20%
Iron	45%

* Percent Daily Values are based on a 2,000 calorie diet.
  Your daily value may be higher or lower depending on
  your calorie needs.

	Calories:	2,000	2,500
Total Fat	Less than	65g	80g
Sat Fat	Less than	20g	25g
Cholesterol	Less than	300mg	300mg
Sodium	Less than	2,400mg	2,400mg
Total Carbohydrate		300g	375g
Dietary Fiber		25g	30g

28. Based on the information provided on the nutrition label, approximately what percent of the total calories come from fat?
    a. 12%
    b. 33%
    c. 5%
    d. 0%
    e. 25%

29. If Alex ate two cups of this product, approximately how many calories did he consume?
    a. Almost 700 calories
    b. A little more than 200 calories
    c. Around 450 calories
    d. A little more than 70
    e. Around 300 calories

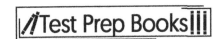

30. Based on the information from the nutrition label above, which of the following statements is true?
    a. Someone eating this food item would not need to worry for the rest of the day about getting more of Vitamins A and C.
    b. This food item is not a good source of iron.
    c. For someone consuming 2,000 calories a day, this food item contains too much dietary fiber.
    d. Someone on a low-sodium diet would not need to worry about this food item being high in sodium.
    e. The trans-fat found in this food would exceed the appropriate amounts per day.

31. In her famous poem "Because I Could Not Stop for Death," Emily Dickinson writes, "Because I could not stop for Death / He kindly stopped for me." Her mention of death is an example of which of the following?
    a. Hyperbole
    b. Personification
    c. Allusion
    d. Alliteration
    e. Simile

32. In the poem quoted above, what does the slash mark between the words *Death* and *He* represent?
    a. The break between two stanzas
    b. The end of one sentence and the start of another
    c. A punctuation mark that stands in for a comma
    d. The shift from one speaker to another
    e. The break between two lines of poetry

Use the following three quotations from Thomas Jefferson to answer questions 33 and 34.

"The tree of liberty must be refreshed from time to time with the blood of patriots and tyrants."

"In matters of style, swim with the current; in matters of principle, stand like a rock."

"I hold it, that a little rebellion, now and then, is a good thing, and as necessary in the political world as storms in the physical."

33. What is Jefferson's opinion on conflict?
    a. It is unavoidable and necessary.
    b. It must be avoided at all costs.
    c. Staying true to your principles is never worth the price you might pay.
    d. It will lead to ultimate destruction.
    e. It is unnecessary though not avoidable.

34. The "tree of liberty" is an example of which of the following?
    a. Personification
    b. Allusion
    c. Analogy
    d. Idiom
    e. Hyperbole

169

35. If you were looking for the most reliable and up-to-date information regarding the safety of travel overseas, which of the following websites would be the most accurate?
   a. http://www.nomadicmatt.com/travel-blog/
   b. https://en.wikipedia.org/wiki/Tourism
   c. http://gizmodo.com/how-to-travel-internationally-for-the-very-first-time
   d. http://www.state.gov/travel/
   e. https://travel.usnews.com/rankings/usa/

Use the following excerpt for questions 36 and 37.

> Evidently, our country has overlooked both the importance of learning history and the appreciation of it. But why is this a huge problem? Other than historians, who really cares how the War of 1812 began, or who Alexander the Great's tutor was? Well, not many, as it turns out. So, *is* history really that important? Yes! History is *critical* to help us understand the underlying forces that shape decisive events, to prevent us from making the same mistakes twice, and to give us context for current events.

36. The above is an example of which type of writing?
   a. Expository
   b. Persuasive
   c. Narrative
   d. Poetry
   e. Technical

37. In the above passage, what does the use of italics for the word "critical" indicate?
   a. Dialogue
   b. Volume
   c. Emphasis
   d. Misspelling
   e. Inaccurate information

38. The guidewords at the top of a dictionary page are *able-bodied* and *about-face*. Which of the following words appear as an entry on this page?
   a. Abolition
   b. Abundant
   c. Able
   d. Ability
   e. Abuse

39. Synonyms of the word *spurious* are *feigned* and *fraudulent*. Which of the following is an antonym for *spurious*?
   a. Phony
   b. Impersonated
   c. Misleading
   d. Genuine
   e. Contrived

40. Which of the following sentences contains an opinion statement?
    a. In 1819, the Supreme Court ruled that Congress could create a national bank.
    b. Marshall also ruled that the states did not have the right to tax the bank or any other agency created by the federal government.
    c. John Marshall was one of the most intelligent chief justices in the United States.
    d. The chief justice is the head of the judicial branch of the government.
    e. John Marshall was the fourth Chief Justice of the United States.

41. Which of the following sentences is a factual statement?
    a. Many nutritionists believe a low-carbohydrate, high-protein diet is the healthiest diet.
    b. Legislation should be passed mandating that cell phones be banned in all public-school classrooms.
    c. Spanish is an easier language to learn than Japanese.
    d. College students would benefit greatly from participating in intramural sports on their campuses.
    e. Macbook computers are easier to use than PC.

42. Follow the numbered instructions to transform the starting word into a different word.
    1. Start with the word *CARLOAD*.
    2. Move the first letter to the end of the word.
    3. Switch the first and second letters.
    4. Switch the third and sixth letters.
    5. Change the fourth letter to an *i*.
    6. Move the last letter before the second *a*.

What is the new word?
    a. Carpool
    b. Radical
    c. Ordeal
    d. Railroad
    e. Rainbow

Questions 43 and 44 refer to the following quote from Martin Luther King Jr.'s Nobel Peace Prize acceptance speech in Oslo on December 10, 1964.

> "I refuse to accept the view that mankind is so tragically bound to the starless midnight of racism and war that the bright daybreak of peace and brotherhood can never become a reality ... I believe that unarmed truth and unconditional love will have the final word."

43. Which of the following statements is NOT accurate based on this quote?
    a. Martin Luther King Jr. felt that the fight against racism was ultimately hopeless due to mankind's primitive instincts.
    b. Martin Luther King Jr. was eternally optimistic about mankind's ability to overcome racism.
    c. Martin Luther King Jr. believed that the war against racism could be won with truth and love.
    d. Martin Luther King Jr. believed that the goodness of mankind would prevail.
    e. Martin Luther King Jr. felt that "bright daybreak" was a proper metaphor for peace and brotherhood.

44. By referring to the "starless midnight of racism," Martin Luther King means:
   a. Racism involves prejudices against people with dark skin.
   b. Racism is evil and blinds people to the truth.
   c. It is easier to be racist on a starless night.
   d. The problem of racism is not as bad during the day.
   e. Racism has historically been associated with the Moon.

Questions 45–48 refer to the following passage.

At the end of the Civil War, Moses Carver, the slave owner who owned George's parents, decided to keep George and his brother and raise them on his farm. As a child, George was driven to learn and he loved painting. He even went on to study art while in college but was encouraged to pursue botany instead. He spent much of his life helping others by showing them better ways to farm; his ideas improved agricultural productivity in many countries. One of his most notable contributions to the newly emerging class of Black farmers was to teach them the negative effects of agricultural monoculture (i.e., growing the same crops in the same fields year after year, depleting the soil of much needed nutrients and resulting in a lesser crop yield). Carver was an innovator, always thinking of new and better ways to do things, and is most famous for his over three hundred uses for the peanut. Toward the end of his career, Carver returned to his first love of art. Through his artwork, he hoped to inspire people to see the beauty around them and to do great things themselves. When Carver died, he left his money to help fund ongoing agricultural research. Today, people still visit and study at the George Washington Carver Foundation at Tuskegee Institute.

45. Which of the following describes the kind of writing used in the above passage?
   a. Narrative
   b. Persuasive
   c. Technical
   d. Expository
   e. Poetry

46. According to the passage, what was George Washington Carver's first love?
   a. Plants
   b. Music
   c. Animals
   d. Soil
   e. Art

47. According to the passage, what is the best definition for agricultural monoculture?
   a. The practice of producing or growing a single crop or plant species over a wide area and for a large number of consecutive years
   b. The practice of growing a diversity of crops and rotating them from year to year
   c. The practice of growing crops organically to avoid the use of pesticides
   d. The practice of charging an inflated price for cheap crops to obtain a greater profit margin
   e. A place where farmers come together and sell their goods to the public

48. Which of the following is the best summary of this passage?
    a. George Washington Carver was born at a time when scientific discovery was at a virtual standstill.
    b. Because he was African American, there were not many opportunities for George Washington Carver.
    c. George Washington Carver was an intelligent man whose research and discoveries had an impact worldwide.
    d. George Washington Carver was far more successful as an artist than he was as a scientist.
    e. George Washington Carver placed duty above passion for the good of the people.

Questions 49–50 are based upon the following passage:

This excerpt is adapted from *The Life-Story of Insects,* by Geo H. Carpenter.

> Insects as a whole are preeminently creatures of the land and the air. This is shown not only by the possession of wings by a vast majority of the class, but by the mode of breathing to which reference has already been made, a system of branching air-tubes carrying atmospheric air with its combustion-supporting oxygen to all the insect's tissues. The air gains access to these tubes through a number of paired air-holes or spiracles, arranged segmentally in series.
>
> It is of great interest to find that, nevertheless, a number of insects spend much of their time under water. This is true of not a few in the perfect winged state, as for example aquatic beetles and water-bugs ('boatmen' and 'scorpions') which have some way of protecting their spiracles when submerged, and, possessing usually the power of flight, can pass on occasion from pond or stream to upper air. But it is advisable in connection with our present subject to dwell especially on some insects that remain continually under water till they are ready to undergo their final moult and attain the winged state, which they pass entirely in the air. The preparatory instars of such insects are aquatic; the adult instar is aerial. All may-flies, dragon-flies, and caddis-flies, many beetles and two-winged flies, and a few moths thus divide their life-story between the water and the air. For the present we confine attention to the stone-flies, the may-flies, and the dragon-flies, three well-known orders of insects respectively called by systematists the Plecoptera, the Ephemeroptera, and the Odonata.
>
> In the case of many insects that have aquatic larvae, the latter are provided with some arrangement for enabling them to reach atmospheric air through the surface-film of the water. But the larva of a stone-fly, a dragon-fly, or a may-fly is adapted more completely than these for aquatic life; it can, by means of gills of some kind, breathe the air dissolved in water.

49. Which statement best details the central idea in this passage?
    a. It introduces certain insects that transition from water to air.
    b. It delves into entomology, especially where gills are concerned.
    c. It defines what constitutes insects' breathing.
    d. It invites readers to have a hand in the preservation of insects.
    e. It explains the life expectancy of the boatman and the scorpion.

50. Which definition most closely relates to the usage of the word *moult* in the passage?
  a. An adventure of sorts, especially underwater
  b. Mating act between two insects
  c. The act of shedding part or all of the outer shell
  d. Death of an organism that ends in a revival of life
  e. The last stage before the insect becomes an adult

Mathematics

1. If $6t + 4 = 16$, what is t?
  a. 1
  b. 2
  c. 3
  d. 4
  e. 5

2. The variable y is directly proportional to x. If $y = 3$ when $x = 5$, then what is y when $x = 20$?
  a. 10
  b. 12
  c. 14
  d. 16
  e. 18

3. A line passes through the point $(1,2)$ and crosses the y-axis at $y = 1$. Which of the following is an equation for this line?
  a. $y = 2x$
  b. $y = 3x$
  c. $x + y = 1$
  d. $y = \frac{x}{2} - 2$
  e. $y = x + 1$

4. There are $4x + 1$ treats in each party favor bag. If a total of $60x + 15$ treats are distributed, how many bags are given out?
  a. 15
  b. 16
  c. 20
  d. 22
  e. 25

5. Apples cost $2 each, while bananas cost $3 each. Maria purchased 10 fruits in total and spent $22. How many apples did she buy?
  a. 5
  b. 6
  c. 7
  d. 8
  e. 9

6. What are the roots of the polynomial $x^2 + x - 2$?
   a. 1 and −2
   b. −1 and 2
   c. 2 and −2
   d. 9 and 13
   e. 4 and 13

7. What is the y-intercept of $y = x^{\frac{5}{3}} + (x - 3)(x + 1)$?
   a. 3.5
   b. 7.6
   c. −3
   d. −15.1
   e. −5.5

8. $x^4 - 16$ can be simplified to which of the following?
   a. $(x^2 + 2)(x^2 - 4)$
   b. $(x^2 + 4)(x^2 + 4)$
   c. $(x^2 - 4)(x^2 - 4)$
   d. $(x^2 - 2)(x^2 + 4)$
   e. $(x^2 - 4)(x^2 + 4)$

9. $(4x^2y^4)^{\frac{3}{2}}$ can be simplified to which of the following?
   a. $8x^3y^6$
   b. $4x^{\frac{5}{2}}y$
   c. $4xy$
   d. $32x^{\frac{7}{2}}y^{\frac{11}{2}}$
   e. $8x^2y^3$

10. If $\sqrt{1 + x} = 4$, what is x?
   a. 10
   b. 15
   c. 20
   d. 25
   e. 30

11. Suppose $\frac{x+2}{x} = 2$. What is x?
   a. −1
   b. 0
   c. 2
   d. 4
   e. 5

175

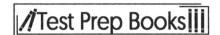
12. A ball is thrown from the top of a high hill, so that the height of the ball as a function of time is $h(t) = -16t^2 + 4t + 6$, in feet. What is the maximum height of the ball in feet?

    a. 6
    b. 6.25
    c. 6.5
    d. 6.75
    e. 7.25

13. A rectangle has a length that is 5 feet longer than three times its width. If the perimeter is 90 feet, what is the length in feet?

    a. 10
    b. 20
    c. 25
    d. 35
    e. 45

14. Five students take a test. The scores of the first four students are 80, 85, 75, and 60. If the median score is 80, which of the following could NOT be the score of the fifth student?

    a. 60
    b. 80
    c. 85
    d. 100
    e. 110

15. In an office, there are 50 workers. A total of 60% of the workers are women. 50% of the women (and none of the other workers) are wearing skirts. How many workers are wearing skirts?

    a. 12
    b. 15
    c. 16
    d. 20
    e. 22

16. Ten students take a test. Five students get a 50. Four students get a 70. If the average score is 55, what was the last student's score?

    a. 20
    b. 40
    c. 50
    d. 60
    e. 70

17. A company invests $50,000 in a building where they can produce saws. If the cost of producing one saw is $40, then which function expresses the amount of money the company pays? The variable y is the money paid and x is the number of saws produced.

    a. $y = 50{,}000x + 40$
    b. $y + 40 = x - 50{,}000$
    c. $y = 40x - 50{,}000$
    d. $y = 50x - 400{,}000$
    e. $y = 40x + 50{,}000$

18. A six-sided die is rolled. What is the probability that the roll is 1 or 2?

a. $\frac{1}{6}$

b. $\frac{1}{4}$

c. $\frac{1}{3}$

d. $\frac{1}{2}$

e. $\frac{5}{2}$

19. A line passes through the origin and through the point $(-3,4)$. What is the slope of the line?

a. $-\frac{4}{3}$

b. $-\frac{3}{4}$

c. $\frac{4}{3}$

d. $\frac{3}{4}$

e. $-\frac{1}{2}$

20. An equilateral triangle has a perimeter of 18 feet. The sides of a square have the same length as the triangle's sides. What is the area of the square?

a. 6 square feet
b. 36 square feet
c. 256 square feet
d. 1,000 square feet
e. 1,200 square feet

21. Change $3\frac{3}{5}$ to a decimal.

a. 3.6
b. 4.67
c. 5.3
d. 0.28
e. 1.77

22. If a car can travel 300 miles in 4 hours, how far can it go in an hour and a half?

a. 100 miles
b. 112.5 miles
c. 135.5 miles
d. 150 miles
e. 223 miles

23. Which measure for the center of a small sample set is most affected by outliers?
    a. Mean
    b. Median
    c. Mode
    d. Range
    e. None of the above

24. Given the value of a given stock at monthly intervals, which graph should be used to best represent the trend of the stock?
    a. Box plot
    b. Line plot
    c. Line graph
    d. Circle graph
    e. Pie chart

25. Before a race of four horses, you make a random guess of which horse will get first place and which will get second place. What is the probability that both your guesses will be correct?
    a. $\frac{1}{4}$
    b. $\frac{1}{2}$
    c. $\frac{1}{16}$
    d. $\frac{1}{12}$
    e. $\frac{1}{15}$

26. Which of the following could be used in the classroom to show $\frac{3}{7} < \frac{5}{6}$ is a true statement?
    a. A bar graph
    b. A number line
    c. An area model
    d. Base 10 blocks
    e. A line graph

27. Add $103,678 + 487$.
    a. 103,191
    b. 103,550
    c. 104,265
    d. 104,165
    e. 105,270

28. Add $1.001 + 5.629$.
    a. 4.472
    b. 4.628
    c. 5.630
    d. 6.628
    e. 6.630

29. Add $143.77 + 5.2$.
    a. 138.57
    b. 148.97
    c. 138.97
    d. 148.57
    e. 149.67

30. What is the next number in the following sequence: $1, 3, 6, 10, 15, 21, \ldots$
    a. 26
    b. 27
    c. 28
    d. 29
    e. 31

31. Add and express in reduced form: $\frac{14}{33} + \frac{10}{11}$
    a. $\frac{2}{11}$
    b. $\frac{6}{11}$
    c. $\frac{4}{3}$
    d. $\frac{44}{33}$
    e. $\frac{1}{120}$

32. 32 is 25% of what number?
    a. 64
    b. 128
    c. 12.65
    d. 8
    e. 15

33. Which of the following is NOT a way to write 40 percent of N?
    a. $(0.4)N$
    b. $\frac{2}{5}N$
    c. $40N$
    d. $\frac{4N}{10}$
    e. $\frac{8}{20}N$

34. Subtract $112{,}076 - 1{,}243$.
    a. 109,398
    b. 113,319
    c. 113,833
    d. 110,319
    e. 110,833

179

35. Carey bought 184 pounds of fertilizer to use on her lawn. Each segment of her lawn required $11\frac{1}{2}$ pounds of fertilizer to do a sufficient job. If a student was asked to determine how many segments could be fertilized with the amount purchased, what operation would be necessary to solve this problem?
   a. Multiplication
   b. Division
   c. Addition
   d. Subtraction
   e. Exponentiation

36. Subtract $701.1 - 52.33$.
   a. 753.43
   b. 648.77
   c. 652.77
   d. 638.43
   e. 524.87

37. Which of the following expressions best exemplifies the additive and subtractive identity?
   a. $5 + 2 - 0 = 5 + 2 + 0$
   b. $6 + x = 6 - 6$
   c. $9 - 9 = 0$
   d. $8 + 2 = 10$
   e. $7 + 2 = 8x - 9$

38. Which of the following is an equivalent measurement for 1.3 cm?
   a. 0.13 m
   b. 0.013 m
   c. 0.13 mm
   d. 0.013 mm
   e. 1.3 mm

39. Divide $1,015 \div 1.4$.
   a. 7,250
   b. 0.725
   c. 7.25
   d. 72.50
   e. 725

40. At the store, Jan spends $90 on apples and oranges. Apples cost $1 each and oranges cost $2 each. If Jan buys the same number of apples as oranges, how many oranges did she buy?
   a. 20
   b. 25
   c. 30
   d. 35
   e. 40

41. Multiply 12.4×0.2.
    a. 12.6
    b. 2.48
    c. 12.48
    d. 2.6
    e. 18.2

42. Multiply $1,987 \times 0.05$.
    a. 9.935
    b. 99.35
    c. 993.5
    d. 999.35
    e. 87.99

43. Which item taught in the classroom would allow students to correctly find the solution to the following problem: A clock reads 5:00 am. What is the measure of the angle formed by the two hands of that clock?
    a. Each time increment on an analog clock measures 90 degrees.
    b. Each time increment on an analog clock measures 30 degrees.
    c. Two adjacent angles sum up to 180 degrees.
    d. Two complementary angles sum up to 180 degrees.
    e. Two complementary angles sum up to 90 degrees.

44. Divide, express with a fractional remainder $1,202 \div 44$.
    a. $27\frac{2}{7}$
    b. $2\frac{7}{22}$
    c. $7\frac{2}{7}$
    d. $27\frac{7}{22}$
    e. $9\frac{2}{27}$

45. A box with rectangular faces is 5 feet long, 6 feet wide, and 3 feet high. What is its volume?
    a. 60 cubic feet
    b. 75 cubic feet
    c. 90 cubic feet
    d. 14 cubic feet
    e. 5 cubic feet

46. Divide $702 \div 2.6$.
    a. 27
    b. 207
    c. 2.7
    d. 3.7
    e. 270

47. A train traveling 50 miles per hour takes a trip lasting 3 hours. If a map has a scale of 1 inch per 10 miles, how many inches apart are the train's starting point and ending point on the map?
    a. 14
    b. 12
    c. 13
    d. 15
    e. 17

48. A traveler takes an hour to drive to a museum, spends 3 hours and 30 minutes there, and takes half an hour to drive home. What percentage of their time was spent driving?
    a. 15%
    b. 30%
    c. 40%
    d. 60%
    e. 65%

49. A truck is carrying three cylindrical barrels. Their bases have a diameter of 2 feet, and they have a height of 3 feet. What is the total volume of the three barrels in cubic feet?
    a. 3π
    b. 9π
    c. 12π
    d. 15π
    e. 20π

50. Greg buys a $10 lunch with 5% sales tax. He leaves a $2 tip after his bill. How much money does he spend?
    a. $12.50
    b. $12
    c. $13
    d. $13.25
    e. $11.50

Writing

First Essay Prompt

Directions: The Writing section of the CBEST will require test takers to write two essays based on provided prompts. The first essay has a referential aim so that test takers can showcase their analytical and expository writing skills. The second essay will have an expressive aim, with a topic relating to the test taker's past lived experience.

Please read the prompt below and answer in an essay format.

> Albert Einstein said that "Everybody is a genius. But if you judge a fish by its ability to climb a tree, it will live its whole life believing that it is stupid." What do you think Einstein meant by this statement? Support your answer with details and observations.

Second Essay Prompt

Please read the prompt below and answer in an essay format.

> Write an essay detailing your experience with loss and how you dealt with it. Talk about the process of the loss and if or how it changed you. How do you view life today in light of that loss?

The following pages are provided for writing your essay.

Answer Explanations for Practice Test #1

Reading

1. C: All the details in this paragraph suggest that Brookside is a great place to live, plus the last sentence states that it is an *idyllic neighborhood*, meaning it is perfect, happy, and blissful. Choices *A* and *B* are incorrect, because although they do contain specific details from the paragraph that support the main idea, they are not the main idea. Choice *D* is incorrect because there is no reference in the paragraph to the crime rate in Brookside. Choice *E* is incorrect; the author does think Brookside is a great place, but they don't try and convince the audience to move there.

2. E: A passage like this one would likely appear in some sort of community profile, highlighting the benefits of living or working there. Choice *A* is incorrect because nothing in this passage suggests that it is fictional. It reads as non-fiction, if anything. Choice *B* is incorrect; it is more an informational passage than a creative passage. Choice *C* is incorrect because it does not report anything particularly newsworthy, and Choice *D* is incorrect because it has absolutely nothing to do with a movie review.

3. D: In the first sentence, it states very clearly that the Brookside neighborhood is one of the nation's first planned communities. This makes it unique, as many other neighborhoods are old, many other neighborhoods exist in Kansas City, and many other neighborhoods have shopping areas. For these reasons, all the other answer choices are incorrect.

4. B: Chapter 4 would have information for a research paper about the problem of child neglect in disproportionately affected communities. The title of this chapter is "Reducing Child Abuse and Neglect Deaths in Disproportionately Affected Communities."

5. A: The chapter on page 52 is called "Addressing the Needs of American Indian/Alaska Native Children." Choice *B* is the chapter related to child abuse in disproportionately affected communities. Choice *C* is related to law enforcement and CPS. Choice *D* is related to support for families. Choice *E* is related to a solution or recommendation for the problems. Thus, Choice *A* is the correct answer choice.

6. C: Child abuse and neglect is alive and rampant in our communities, and this chapter outlines those who are in dire need of our attention. Choice *A* has more to do with Chapter 2, "Saving Children's Lives Today and Into the Future," and thus is incorrect. Choice *B* relates to Chapter 4, "Reducing Child Abuse and Neglect Deaths in Disproportionately Affected Communities," and is also incorrect. Choice *D* relates to Chapter 7, "Multidisciplinary Support for Families," which is incorrect. Choice *E* relates to Chapter 6, "Decisions Grounded in Better Data and Research."

7. E: Choice *E* is correct because a *simile* is a comparison between two unlike things using the words *like* or *as*. Choice *A* is incorrect because *hyperbole* is an exaggeration for effect. Choice *B* is incorrect; since the simile uses "like," the comparison cannot be considered a metaphor. Choice *C* is incorrect because *personification* attributes human characteristics to an inanimate object. Choice *D* is incorrect because *alliteration* is a poetic device in which several words begin with the same letter or letters. It is used to add emphasis or effect.

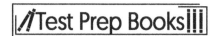

8. A: Choice *A* is correct because there is evidence in the passage to support it, specifically when he mentions catching "a mess of black-fish, which you couldn't buy in New York for a dollar—large fat fellows, with meat on their bones that it takes a pretty long fork to stick through." Choice *E* is a detail at the beginning of the passage, but it's not a summary of the passage as a whole.

9. B: *Prodigious* means great in extent, size, or degree. In this passage, Whitman is comparing the easternmost part of Long Island to a very large alligator. Therefore, the other answer choices are incorrect.

10. C: Choice *C* is correct because it states the fact that education has a positive impact on lowering crime rates, and it tells your reader what you will cover in that paragraph without providing specific details yet. That's what the remainder of the paragraph is for. Choice *A* is incorrect because the paragraph is not about the verification of crime statistics. Choice *B* is incorrect because it is a broad generalization that is simply not true. Choice *D*, while it is on topic, is too specific to be a topic sentence, but it would be an excellent supporting detail. Choice *E* acts as the beginning of a counterargument so this cannot be the topic sentence.

11. E: This sentence would not be a good thesis statement because it conveys one very specific detail. All the other answer choices would be good thesis statements because they are general enough for an entire essay but specific enough that the reader knows exactly what the essay will cover.

12. B: The author clearly states that education is crucial to the survival of the human race, and it can be easily inferred that if this is true, then improvements to our educational system are certainly worth fighting for. Choices *A* and *C* are incorrect because there is nothing in the passage that relates to these statements. Choice *D* is incorrect because it directly contradicts what the author states about all children's ability to learn. Choice *E* is mentioned in the passage, but it is not the main point.

13. A: Clearly, this author feels passionately about the importance of education. This is evident especially in the word choices. For this reason, all the other answer choices are incorrect.

14. C: Based on the author's passionate stance about the importance of education for all children, this answer choice makes the most sense. For this reason, all the other answer choices are incorrect.

15. D: The author mentions the importance of parent involvement and communication between school and home. He also devotes one full paragraph to the impact of technology on education. Nowhere in the passage does the author mention the cost of textbooks, so Choice *D* is correct.

16. C: In 1964, the Democratic candidate won 486 electoral votes while the Republican candidate only won 52, and in 1984, almost the complete opposite was true—the Republican candidate won 525 electoral votes, while the Democratic candidate only won 13. Clearly, this was an almost total swing from one party to the other. Choices *A* and *B* are incorrect because the voter turnout, as indicated by the popular vote numbers, did not remain the same or decrease over this twenty-year period. The popular vote turnout increased by approximately twenty thousand over this twenty-year period. Choice *D* is incorrect because the electoral votes won by each party did change during this twenty-year period. Choice *E* is incorrect; this is the opposite of the correct answer.

17. A: The Democratic candidate did win the popular vote, but he lost the electoral votes by five, and a closer look at the map reveals that he only won 21 out of the possible 50 states. All the other statements are correct.

188

18. B: Primary sources are original, firsthand accounts of events or time periods as they are happening or very close to the time they occurred. Diary entries are excellent primary sources, as are newspaper articles, works of art and literature, interviews, and live recordings. Choice *A* is incorrect because a Wikipedia article is not a reliable source due to the fact that multiple authors can access and manipulate the information. Choices *C* and *D* are incorrect because they are examples of secondary sources. While they might be very reliable and useful, they are not primary sources. Choice *E* describes an analysis of a primary source, which is a secondary source, so this is incorrect.

19. C: Italics are often used to indicate emphasis. Choice *A* is incorrect because quotation marks, not italics, are used to indicate dialogue. Choice *B* is incorrect because although italics can also indicate someone's interior thoughts, in this case, it would not make sense for the word *any* to be a thought rather than spoken aloud. Choice *D* is incorrect because volume is typically indicated by capital letters. Choice *E* is incorrect; sometimes the use of italics indicates a title of a film or novel, but the context here tells us that someone is emphasizing speech rather than giving us a title.

20. D: The abbreviation *i.e.* stands for the Latin phrase, "id est" meaning "that is." It is used to clarify an idea, in this case, the term "mollusk." Choice *A* is incorrect because the abbreviation meaning "for example" is *e.g.* Choices *B, C,* and *E* are incorrect because there are no abbreviations in English for these phrases.

21. E: *Enterprise* most closely means *cause.* Choices *A, B,* and *C* are all related to the term *enterprise.* However, Dickens speaks of a *cause* here, not a company, courage, or a game. "He will stand by such an enterprise" is a call to stand by a cause to enable the working man to have a certain autonomy over his own economic standing. The very first paragraph ends with the statement that the working man *shall* "...have a share in the management of an institution which is designed for his benefit."

22. B: Recall from the first paragraph that the speaker is there to "accompany [the audience] ... through one of my little Christmas books," making him an author there to entertain the crowd with his own writing. The speech preceding the reading is the passage itself, and, as the tone indicates, it is a serious speech addressing the "working man." Although the passage speaks of employers and employees, the speaker himself is not an employer of the audience, so Choice *A* is incorrect. Choice *C* is also incorrect, as the salutation is not used ironically, but sincerely, as the speech addresses the wellbeing of the crowd. Choice *D* is incorrect because the speech is not given by a politician, but by a writer. Choice *E* is incorrect, as there is no indication the speaker is on trial.

23. B: For the working man to have a say in his institution Choice *A* is incorrect because that is the speaker's first desire, not his second. Choices *C* and *D* are tricky because the language of both of these is mentioned after the word second. However, the speaker doesn't get to the second wish until the next sentence. Choices C and D are merely preliminary remarks before the statement of the main clause, Choice *B.* Choice *E* is not in the passage.

24. C: The speaker's tone can best be described as *confident and informed.* The speaker addresses the audience as "My good friends," and says, "I have no fear of being misunderstood," which implies confidence. Additionally, the speaker's knowledge of the proposal and topic can be seen in the text as well, especially in the second paragraph.

25. D: The speaker provides credibility by saying "he will stand by such an enterprise with the utmost of his patience," and displays their responsibilities by saying "he will feel his responsibility like an honest man."

26. B: While lacrosse does develop some similar skill sets as basketball, it does not belong in an encyclopedia entry about basketball. All the other answer choices do contain relevant information that would likely appear in an encyclopedia entry under "Basketball."

27. C: The word *revere* would not be an entry on this page because the letters *rever* would come after *revea* in alphabetical order. All the other answer choices contain letters that would come between *receipt* and *reveal* and would therefore appear as entries on this page.

28. B: According to the label, 72 calories out of the total 230 calories come from fat. This is approximately a third of 230, or 33%. Choice *A* is incorrect because 12% is the percentage of the daily value of total fat found in a serving of this product. Choice *C* is incorrect because 5% is the percentage of the daily value of saturated fat found in a serving of this product. Choice *D* is incorrect because 0% represents the number of grams of trans fat found in a serving of this product. Choice *E* is incorrect because it is just a random number.

29. A: This is the correct answer because if Alex ate two cups, that would be exactly three full servings, based on the label information that 2/3 cup is one serving size. One serving contains 230 calories, so three servings would be three times that amount, or 690 calories. Choice *B* is incorrect because that reflects the number of calories in one serving. Choice *C* is incorrect because that reflects the number of calories in two servings. Choice *D* is incorrect because that reflects the number of calories from fat in one serving. Choice *E* does not equal a certain amount of servings here.

30. D: This is the correct answer because this product only contains 160 mg, or 7% of the daily value of sodium, so this item would be perfectly fine for someone on a low-sodium diet to consume. Choice *A* is incorrect because the values of Vitamins A and C are relatively low, meaning someone should try to consume more of those throughout the day. Choice *B* is incorrect because this item contains 45% of the daily value of iron, so it is a good source of iron. Choice *C* is incorrect because this item is not too high in dietary fiber for someone consuming 2,000 calories a day. Choice *E* is incorrect; there is no trans-fat in this food.

31. B: The correct answer is *personification* because Dickinson gives death characteristics of a human person. In addition, by capitalizing the word, she has made "Death" a proper noun or name. Choice *A* is incorrect because *hyperbole* is an exaggeration for effect. Choice *C* is incorrect because an *allusion* is a brief or indirect reference to a person, place, or thing from history, culture, literature, or politics. Choice *D* is incorrect because *alliteration* is a poetic device in which several words begin with the same letter or letters. It is used to add emphasis or effect. Choice *E* is incorrect because a simile compares two things using the words "like" or "as."

32. E: This is the correct answer because the slash mark represents the break between the first line of this poem and the second. A slash mark would not be used to indicate any of the other answer choices.

33. A: This is the correct answer because he makes it clear that sometimes conflict must happen, and that it can even be a good thing.

34. C: *Analogy* is the correct answer because an analogy is a comparison between two seemingly unlike things, used to help clarify meaning. In this case, Jefferson is comparing what it takes to keep the ideal of liberty alive to a tree. Choice *A* is incorrect because *personification* attributes human traits or characteristics to an inanimate object. Choice *B* is incorrect because an *allusion* is a brief or indirect reference to a person, place, or thing from history, culture, literature, or politics. Choice *D* is incorrect

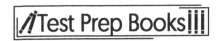

because an *idiom* is an expression whose meaning is not to be taken literally. Choice *E, hyperbole,* is an exaggeration.

35. D: This is the correct answer because the "gov" indicates that this is a government website. If you are traveling overseas, the U.S. government would be a reliable and up-to-date source of information, especially in regard to travel safety. While the other websites may contain some helpful information, and may indeed be worth reading, blogs and wikis may not be as reliable.

36. B: Persuasive is the correct answer because the author is clearly trying to convey the point that history education is very important. Choice *A* is incorrect because expository writing is more informational and less emotional. Choice *C* is incorrect because narrative writing involves storytelling. Choice *D* is incorrect because this is a piece of prose, not poetry. Choice *E* is incorrect because technical writing represents instruction manuals and proposals and is mostly neutral and objective.

37. C: This is the correct answer because italics is often used to indicate emphasis.

Choice *A* is incorrect because quotation marks are used to indicate dialogue. Choice *B* is incorrect because volume is typically indicated by the use of capital letters. Choices *D* and *E* are incorrect because there is no way to indicate misspelling or inaccurate information by altering the text.

38. A: Choice *A* is correct because the letters *abol* fall between the two guidewords in alphabetical order. All the other answer choices are incorrect because they do not fall between the two guidewords in alphabetical order.

39. D: An antonym is a word that means the opposite, so *genuine* is the antonym of *feigned,* which means falsified or pretended. All the other answer choices are synonyms for the word *feigned*.

40. C: This answer choice is correct because "one of the most intelligent" is a matter of opinion, not a quantifiable fact. All the other answer choices are factual statements.

41. A: This answer choice is correct because it is the only statement that is not based on opinion. Nutritionists' belief in one certain diet might be a matter of opinion, but the statement that many do believe in the health benefits of this particular diet is a fact.

42. B: Following the steps in order will change the word *carload* into the word *radical*.

43. A: This is the correct answer choice because there is evidence to the contrary that Martin Luther King Jr. refused to believe that mankind would be bound to the darkness of racism.

44. B: This is the correct answer choice because Martin Luther King Jr. is using an analogy, comparing the evil of racism to the darkness one would experience on a starless night. He is also making the point that just as one cannot see in the dark, racism blinds one to the truth.

45. D: Expository writing involves straightforward, factual information and analysis. It is unbiased and does not rely on the writer's personal feelings or opinions. Choice *A* is incorrect because narrative writing tells a story. Choice *B* is incorrect because persuasive writing is intended to change the reader's mind or position on a topic. Choice *C* is incorrect because technical writing attempts to outline a complex object or process. Choice *E* is incorrect because poetry usually has line breaks within stanzas, and the formatting usually does not look like a single paragraph with objective information.

46. E: The passage begins by describing Carver's childhood fascination with painting and later returns to this point when it states that at the end of his career, "Carver returned to his first love of art." For this reason, all the other answer choices are incorrect.

47. A: This is the correct answer choice because the passage contains a definition of the term, *agricultural monoculture*, which is very similar to this answer.

48. C: There is ample evidence in the passage that refers to Carver's brilliance and the fact that his discoveries had a far-reaching impact both then and now. There is no evidence in the passage to support any of the other answer choices.

49. A: The passage's purpose is to introduce certain insects that transition from water to air. Choice *B* is incorrect because although the passage talks about gills, it is not the central idea of the passage. Choices *C* and *D* are incorrect because the passage does not "define" or "invite," but only serves as an introduction to stoneflies, dragonflies, and mayflies and their transition from water to air. Choice *E* is incorrect; the passage mentions "boatmen" and "scorpions" but does not explain their life expectancy.

50. C: The act of shedding part or all of the outer shell. Choices *A*, *B*, *D*, and *E* are incorrect.

Mathematics

1. B: First, subtract 4 from each side. This yields $6t = 12$. Now, divide both sides by 6 to obtain $t = 2$.

2. B: The variable y is directly proportional to x, which means that whenever x is multiplied by a number, y is multiplied by that same number. When x changes from 5 to 20, it is multiplied by 4, so the original y value must also be multiplied by 4. That means $y = 3 \times 4 = 12$.

3. E: We can use slope-intercept form, $y = mx + b$. We are told that the y-intercept (b) is 1, which gives us $y = mx + 1$. Now we can plug in the x and y values from our point, (1,2), to find the slope: $2 = m(1) + 1$, so m=1. This gives us $y = x + 1$.

4. A: Each bag has $4x + 1$ treats. The total number of treats for n bags will be $n(4x + 1)$, or $4nx + n$. We know the total number of treats is $60x + 15$, which means that $60x + 15 = 4nx + n$. Looking at this, we can see that the equation only works when $n = 15$.

5. D: Let a be the number of apples, and let b represent the number of bananas. The total number of fruits is $a + b = 10$, and the total cost is $2a + 3b = 22$. To solve this pair of equations, we can multiply the first equation by –3:

$$-3(a + b) = -3(10)$$

$$-3a - 3b = -30$$

Now we can add this to the other equation, and the b terms cancel out:

$$(-3a - 3b = -30) + (2a + 3b = 22)$$

$$= (-a = -8)$$

This simplifies to $a = 8$.

6. A: Finding the roots means finding the values of x that make the polynomial equal zero. The quadratic formula could be used, but in this case, it is possible to factor by hand, since the numbers –1 and 2 add to 1 and multiply to –2. So, factor $x^2 + x - 2 = (x - 1)(x + 2) = 0$, then set each factor equal to zero. Solving for each value gives the values $x = 1$ and $x = -2$.

7. C: To find the y-intercept, substitute zero for x, which gives us:

$$y = 0^{\frac{5}{3}} + (0 - 3)(0 + 1) = 0 + (-3)(1) = -3$$

8. E: This has the form $t^2 - y^2$, with $t = x^2$ and $y = 4$. It's also known that $t^2 - y^2 = (t + y)(t - y)$, and substituting the values for t and y into the right-hand side gives:

$$(x^2 - 4)(x^2 + 4)$$

9. A: Simplify this to:

$$(4x^2 y^4)^{\frac{3}{2}} = 4^{\frac{3}{2}}(x^2)^{\frac{3}{2}}(y^4)^{\frac{3}{2}}$$

Now:

$$4^{\frac{3}{2}} = (\sqrt{4})^3 = 2^3 = 8$$

For the rest, recall that the exponents must be multiplied, so this yields:

$$8x^{2 \cdot \frac{3}{2}} y^{4 \cdot \frac{3}{2}} = 8x^3 y^6$$

10. B: Start by squaring both sides to get $1 + x = 16$. Then subtract 1 from both sides to get $x = 15$.

11. C: Multiply both sides by x to get $x + 2 = 2x$. Then, subtract x from both sides to get $2 = x$.

12. B: The independent variable's coordinate at the vertex of a parabola (which is the highest point when the coefficient of the squared independent variable is negative) is given by $x = -\frac{b}{2a}$. Substitute and solve for x to get:

193

$$x = -\frac{4}{2(-16)} = \frac{1}{8}$$

Using this value of x, the maximum height of the ball (y), can be calculated. Substituting $\frac{1}{8}$ into the equation for x yields:

$$h(t) = -16\left(\frac{1}{8}\right)^2 + 4\frac{1}{8} + 6 = 6.25$$

13. D: Denote the width as w and the length as l. Then:

$$l = 3w + 5$$

The perimeter is:

$$2w + 2l = 90$$

Substituting the first expression for l into the second equation yields:

$$2(3w + 5) + 2w = 90$$

$$6w + 10 + 2w = 90$$

$$8w = 80$$

$$w = 10$$

Putting this into the first equation, it yields:

$$l = 3(10) + 5 = 35$$

14. A: Putting the scores in order from least to greatest, we have 60, 75, 80, and 85, as well as one unknown. The median is 80, so 80 must be the middle data point out of these five. Therefore, the unknown data point must be the fourth or fifth data point, meaning it must be greater than or equal to 80. The only answer that fails to meet this condition is 60.

15. B: If 60% of 50 workers are women, then there are 30 women working in the office. If half of them are wearing skirts, then that means 15 women wear skirts. Since nobody else wears skirts, this means there are 15 people wearing skirts.

16. A: Let the unknown score be x. The average will be:

$$\frac{5 \times 50 + 4 \times 70 + x}{10} = \frac{530 + x}{10} = 55$$

Multiply both sides by 10 to get $530 + x = 550$, or $x = 20$.

17. E: The total amount the company pays, y, equals the cost of the building ($50,000) plus the cost of the saws. Since the saws cost $40 each, the overall cost of the saws is $40 times x, where x is the number of saws. Putting all this together, we have $y = 50,000 + 40x$, which is equivalent to Choice D.

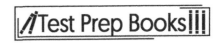

18. C: When a die is rolled, each outcome is equally likely. Since it has six sides, each outcome has a probability of $\frac{1}{6}$. The chance of a 1 or a 2 is therefore:

$$\frac{1}{6} + \frac{1}{6} = \frac{1}{3}$$

19. A: The slope is given by:

$$m = \frac{y_2 - y_1}{x_2 - x_1} = \frac{0 - 4}{0 - (-3)} = -\frac{4}{3}$$

20. B: An equilateral triangle has three sides of equal length, so if the total perimeter is 18 feet, each side must be 6 feet long. A square with sides of 6 feet will have an area of $6^2 = 36$ square feet.

21. A: 3.6

Divide 3 by 5 to get 0.6 and add that to the whole number 3, to get 3.6. An alternative is to incorporate the whole number 3 earlier on by creating an improper fraction: $\frac{18}{5}$. Then divide 18 by 5 to get 3.6.

22. B: 300 miles in 4 hours is $\frac{300}{4} = 75$ miles per hour. In 1.5 hours, the car will go 1.5×75 miles, or 112.5 miles.

23. A: An outlier is a data value that is either far above or far below the majority of values in a sample set. The mean is the average of all the values in the set. In a small sample set, a very high or very low number could drastically change the average of the data points. Outliers will have no more of an effect on the median (the middle value when arranged from lowest to highest) than any other value above or below the median. If the same outlier does not repeat, outliers will have no effect on the mode (value that repeats most often).

24. C: The scenario involves data consisting of two variables, month and stock value. Box plots display data consisting of values for one variable. Therefore, a box plot is not an appropriate choice. Both line plots and circle graphs are used to display frequencies within categorical data. Neither can be used for the given scenario. Line graphs display two numerical variables on a coordinate grid and show trends among the variables. Pie charts usually show proportional data.

25. D: The probability of picking the winner of the race is $\frac{1}{4}$, or $\left(\frac{\text{number of favorable outcomes}}{\text{number of total outcomes}}\right)$. Assuming the winner was picked on the first selection, three horses remain from which to choose the runner-up (these are dependent events). Therefore, the probability of picking the runner-up is $\frac{1}{3}$. To determine the probability that multiple events all happen, multiply the probabilities of the events:

$$\frac{1}{4} \times \frac{1}{3} = \frac{1}{12}$$

26. B: This inequality can be seen with the use of a number line. $\frac{3}{7}$ is close to $\frac{1}{2}$. $\frac{5}{6}$ is close to 1, but less than 1. Therefore, $\frac{3}{7}$ is less than $\frac{5}{6}$.

27. D: 104,165

195

Set up the problem and add each column, starting on the far right (ones). Add, carrying anything over 9 into the next column to the left. Solve from right to left.

28. E: 6.630

Set up the problem, with the larger number on top and numbers lined up at the decimal. Add, carrying anything over 9 into the next column to the left. Solve from right to left.

29. B: 148.97

Set up the problem, with the larger number on top and numbers lined up at the decimal. Insert 0 in any blank spots to the right of the decimal as placeholders. Add, carrying anything over 9 into the next column to the left.

30. C: Starting with 1, we get the next number in the sequence by adding 2, then 3, 4, 5, and 6. So to find the next number, we take our latest number and add 7, getting $21 + 7 = 28$.

31. C: To find a common denominator, look for a number that has both denominators (33 and 11) as factors. 33 works. Multiply the top and bottom of each fraction by whatever number will make the denominator 33.

$$\frac{14}{33} \times \frac{1}{1} = \frac{14}{33} \text{ and } \frac{10}{11} \times \frac{3}{3} = \frac{30}{33}$$

Now that we have a common denominator, add the numerators.

$$\frac{14}{33} + \frac{30}{33} = \frac{14 + 30}{33} = \frac{44}{33}$$

Since 31 and 36 have no common factors except 1, this fraction can't be reduced. Reduce by dividing both the numerator and denominator by 11.

$$\frac{44 \div 11}{33 \div 11} = \frac{4}{3}$$

32. B: This question involves the percent formula.

$$\frac{32}{x} = \frac{25}{100}$$

We multiply the diagonal numbers, 32 and 100, to get 3,200. Dividing by the remaining number, 25, gives us 128.

There is an additional way to solve this problem without using the percent formula. Since 25% is $\frac{1}{4}$ of 100, you know that 32 needs to be multiplied by 4, which yields 128.

33. C: $40N$ would be 4,000% of N. $\frac{40}{100}$.

34. E: 110,833

Set up the problem, with the larger number on top. Begin subtracting with the far-right column (ones). Borrow 10 from the column to the left, when necessary.

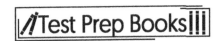

35. B: This is a division problem because the original amount needs to be split up into equal amounts. Although it's not required to answer the test question, we could solve Carey's problem as follows. The mixed number $11\frac{1}{2}$ should be converted to an improper fraction first:

$$11\frac{1}{2} = \frac{(11 \times 2) + 1}{2} = \frac{23}{2}$$

Carey needs to determine how many times $\frac{23}{2}$ goes into 184. This is a division problem:

$$184 \div \frac{23}{2} = ?$$

The fraction can be flipped, and the problem turns into multiplication:

$$184 \times \frac{2}{23} = \frac{368}{23}$$

This improper fraction can be simplified into 16 because $368 \div 23 = 16$. Carey would be able to fertilize 16 lawn segments.

36. B: 648.77

Set up the problem, with the larger number on top and numbers lined up at the decimal. Insert 0 in any blank spots to the right of the decimal as placeholders. Begin subtracting with the far-right column. Borrow 10 from the column to the left, when necessary.

37. A: The additive and subtractive identity is 0. When added to or subtracted from any number, 0 does not change the original number.

38. B: 100 cm is equal to 1 m. 1.3 divided by 100 is 0.013. Therefore, 1.3 cm is equal to 0.013 m. Because 1 cm is equal to 10 mm, 1.3 cm is equal to 13 mm.

39. E: Set up the division problem.

$$1.4\overline{)1\,0\,1\,5}$$

Move the decimal point over one place to the right in both numbers.

$$14\overline{)1\,0\,1\,5\,0}$$

14 does not go into 1 or 10 but does go into 101, so start there.

$$
\begin{array}{r}
725 \\
14\overline{)10150} \\
-98 \\
\hline
35 \\
-28 \\
\hline
70 \\
-70 \\
\hline
0
\end{array}
$$

The result is 725.

40. C: The best way to solve this problem is by using a system of equations. We know that Jan bought $90 worth of apples ($a$) and oranges ($o$) at $1 and $2 respectively. That means our first equation is:

$$1(a) + 2(o) = 90$$

We also know that she bought an equal number of apples and oranges, which gives us our second equation $a = o$. We can then replace a with o in the first equation to give:

$$1(o) + 2(o) = 90 \text{ or } 3(o) = 90$$

Which yields:

$$o = 30$$

Thus, Jan bought 30 oranges (and 30 apples).

41. B: 2.48

Set up the problem, with the larger number on top. Multiply as if there are no decimal places. Add the answer rows together. Count the number of decimal places that were in the original numbers ($1 + 1 = 2$). Place the decimal 2 places to the right for the final solution.

42. B: 99.35

Set up the problem, with the larger number on top. Multiply as if there are no decimal places. Add the answer rows together. Count the number of decimal places that were in the original numbers (2).

Place the decimal in that many spots from the right for the final solution.

43. B: Each hour on the clock represents 30 degrees. For example, 3:00 represents a right angle. Therefore, 5:00 represents 150 degrees. We know that each hour does not represent 90 degrees, because there are 12 angles on a clock face. The 360 degrees in a circle, divided by the 12 angles, gives us 30 degrees for each hour.

44. D: Set up the division problem.

$$44\overline{)1202}$$

44 does not go into 1 or 12 but will go into 120 so start there.

$$
\begin{array}{r}
27 \\
44\overline{)1202} \\
-88 \\
\hline
322 \\
-308 \\
\hline
14
\end{array}
$$

The answer is $27\frac{14}{44}$.

Reduce the fraction for the final answer.

$$27\frac{7}{22}$$

45. C: The formula for the volume of a box with rectangular faces is the length times the width times the height, so:

$$5 \times 6 \times 3 = 90 \text{ cubic feet}$$

46. E: Set up the division problem.

$$2.6\overline{)702}$$

Move the decimal over one place to the right in both numbers.

$$26\overline{)7020}$$

26 does not go into 7 but does go into 70 so start there.

$$
\begin{array}{r}
270 \\
26\overline{)7020} \\
-52 \\
\hline
182 \\
-182 \\
\hline
0
\end{array}
$$

The result is 270

47. D: First, the train's journey in the real world is:

$$3 \text{ h} \times 50\frac{\text{mi}}{\text{h}} = 150 \text{ mi}$$

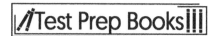

On the map, 1 inch corresponds to 10 miles, so that is equivalent to:

$$150 \text{ mi} \times \frac{1 \text{ in}}{10 \text{ mi}} = 15 \text{ in}$$

Therefore, the start and end points are 15 inches apart on the map.

48. B: The total trip time is $1 + 3.5 + 0.5 = 5$ hours. The total time driving is $1 + 0.5 = 1.5$ hours. So, the fraction of time spent driving is $\frac{1.5}{5}$ or $\frac{3}{10}$. To convert this to a percentage, multiply the top and bottom by 10 to make the denominator 100. We find $\frac{3}{10} \times \frac{10}{10} = \frac{30}{10}$. Since the denominator is 100, the numerator is our percentage: 30%.

49. B: The formula for the volume of a cylinder is $\pi r^2 h$, where r is the radius and h is the height. The diameter is twice the radius, so these barrels have a radius of 1 foot. That means each barrel has a volume of:

$$\pi \times 1^2 \times 3 = 3\pi \text{ ft}^3$$

Since there are three of them, the total is:

$$3 \times 3\pi = 9\pi \text{ ft}^3$$

50. A: The tip is not taxed, so he pays 5% tax only on the $10. To find 5% of $10, calculate $0.05 \times \$10 = \$0.50$. Add up $10 + \$0.50 + \$2$ to get $12.50.

Reading

1. After reading *To Kill a Mockingbird*, Louise has been asked to write an expository piece that explores the life, significant achievements, and societal impact of Harper Lee, the book's author. Which of the following sources would yield the most information about the author?
   a. A dictionary
   b. A newspaper article about the author
   c. A study guide for *To Kill a Mockingbird*
   d. A biographical account
   e. An analysis on the life's work of the author

2. Read the following words:

   mixed
   thrown
   are
   grown
   beaten
   jumped

Analyze the list and determine which word does not belong.
   a. Mixed
   b. Are
   c. Grown
   d. Jumped
   e. Beaten

3. Read the following words:

   formaldehyde
   forward
   foliage
   follicle
   format
   fort

Which of the following words would not be found in a dictionary between the guide words focus and fortitude?
   a. Formaldehyde
   b. Forge
   c. Format
   d. Fort
   e. Forward

4. Asbestos was an *insidious* yet popular product, mass produced for over one hundred years. Due to its durability and fire resistance, it was used in a wide range of products, such as houses, cars, and ships. As with tobacco, evidence was presented early on that asbestos was dangerous and had cumulative adverse effects, but production didn't decline until the 1970s.

A dictionary provides four different definitions for *insidious*. Based on the above passage, which definition would fit best?
   a. Awaiting a chance to trap or ensnare
   b. Damaging or deadly but attractive
   c. Having incremental or gradual build-up of harmful effects
   d. Causing catastrophic harm
   e. Causing a sudden explosion

5. After applying for a job multiple times, Bob was finally granted an interview. During the interview, he fumbled several questions, mispronounced his potential supervisor's name, and forgot the name of the company. Soon it was clear he knew he wouldn't be working there. At the end of the interview, he stood up and, with *spurious* confidence, shook the interviewer's hand firmly.

Based on the context of the word *spurious*, a good substitution might be:
   a. Extreme
   b. Mild
   c. Proud
   d. Genuine
   e. Fake

6. Follow the numbered instructions to transform the starting word into a different word.

   1. Start with the word KAKISTOCRACY.
   2. Remove the first K.
   3. Change the Y to an I.
   4. Move the last C to the right of the last I.
   5. Add a T between the last A and the last I.
   6. Change the K to R.

What is the new word?
   a. Aristocrat
   b. Artistic
   c. Aristocratic
   d. Artifact
   e. Antidote

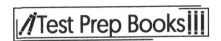

Question 7 is based upon the following table.

Name brand diaper #1	Name brand diaper #2	U-Save discount diaper	Online diaper
88 diapers for $29.99	30 diapers for $12.00	50 diapers for $13.00	100 diapers for $45.00
$4.00 in tax	$2.00 in tax	$3.00 in tax	No tax

7. Marge, who is a new parent, is trying to find the best deal on diapers. She has priced them from several different locations. Based on the chart above, which product offers the best deal?
   a. Name brand diaper #1
   b. Name brand diaper #2
   c. U-Save discount diaper
   d. Online diaper
   e. They all come out the same

Refer to the map below for questions 8–11.

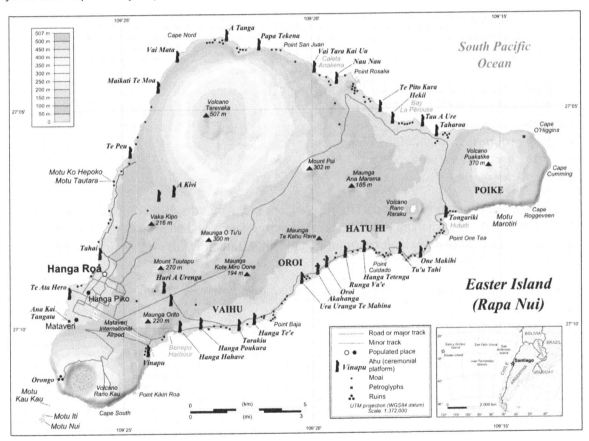

(Eric Gaba, *Wikimedia*, 2016)

8. How many land masses are represented on this map?
   a. One
   b. Two
   c. Three
   d. Four
   e. Five

9. How many locations are at or above 300 meters?
   a. Four
   b. Five
   c. Six
   d. Seven
   e. Eight

10. Where is the most populated area of the island?
    a. In the northwest corner
    b. Centrally located
    c. In the southwest corner
    d. Near the coastline
    e. In the north central area

11. Where are most ceremonial platforms on the island?
    a. In the northwest corner of the island
    b. Centrally located
    c. In the southwest corner of the island
    d. In the north central area
    e. Near the coastline

12. Reggie had been preparing for his part in the play for several months. His mother had even knitted him a costume. That night when he went on stage, his entire family and all his friends were there to watch, and he was *mortified* when his costume split in half. Afterwards, his mother admitted that she was not the best of seamstresses.

The best substitute for *mortified* would be which of the following?
    a. Inhibited
    b. Humiliated
    c. Annoyed
    d. Afraid
    e. Elated

Questions 13–16 are based on the following passage.

Science fiction has been a part of the American fabric for a long time. During the Great Depression, many Americans were looking for an escape from dismal circumstances, and their escape often took the form of reading. Outlandish stories of aliens and superheroes were printed on cheap, disposable paper stock, hence the name *pulp* (as in paper) *fiction*. Iconic heroes like Buck Rogers, the Shadow, and Doc Rogers got their start in throwaway magazines and pulp novels.

204

As time went on, science fiction evolved, presenting better plots and more sophisticated questions, and, consequently, it garnered more respect. Authors like Kurt Vonnegut and Ray Bradbury, now household names and respected American authors, emerged from the science fiction fringe. Thanks to works like Vonnegut's 1961 short story "Harrison Bergeron," in which mediocrity is the law and exceptional ability is punished, and Bradbury's 1953 novel *Fahrenheit 451*, in which books are illegal and burned on sight, science fiction rose to a serious genre.

In the late 1970s, the genre that begun in the medium of pulp fiction and crossed into serious literature had a resurgence in the medium of film. The new prominence of science fiction film was spearheaded by the first *Star Wars* movie, which harkened to pulp fiction roots. The tide of science fiction films hasn't really slowed since. *Blade Runner, Jurassic Park, The Matrix, I Am Legend*, even Disney's *Wall-E* all continue the tradition of unrealized futures and alternate realities. Modern science fiction movies can trace their roots back to the pulp fiction published during the Great Depression.

13. The main purpose of this passage is to:
    a. Describe
    b. Inform
    c. Persuade
    d. Entertain
    e. Instruct

14. This passage was written with a _____ structure.
    a. Compare/contrast
    b. Sequential
    c. Cause/effect
    d. Problem/solution
    e. Descriptive

15. Which of the following passages from the above text best summarizes the main idea?
    a. "Science fiction has been a part of the American fabric for a long time."
    b. "As time went on, science fiction evolved, posing better plots and more sophisticated questions."
    c. "Outlandish stories of aliens and superheroes were printed on cheap, disposable paper stock, hence the name *pulp* (as in paper) *fiction*."
    d. "Modern science fiction movies can trace their roots back to the pulp fiction published during the Great Depression."
    e. "Thanks to works like Vonnegut's 1961 short story 'Harrison Bergeron,' in which mediocrity is the law and exceptional ability is punished, and Bradbury's 1953 novel *Fahrenheit 451*, in which books are illegal and burned on sight, science fiction rose to a serious genre."

16. "These outlandish stories of aliens and superheroes were printed on cheap, disposable paper stock, hence the name *pulp* (as in paper) *fiction*." The author most likely wrote this sentence because:
   a. He or she wants the reader to understand that science fiction was not always taken seriously.
   b. He or she wants the reader to understand that science fiction is not a new medium.
   c. He or she wants to demonstrate that science fiction was constrained by the technology of the time.
   d. He or she wants to demonstrate that even those in the past imagined what the future might hold.
   e. He or she wants the reader to understand the importance that pulp fiction carried during its time.

Use the following definition to answer questions 17–19.

A dictionary provides the following information for the word *involve*: in volve (in-volv') v.t. [INVOLVED (-volvd'), INVOLVING], [M.E. *enoulen*; Ofr. *Involver*; L. *involvere*; *in-*, in + *volvere*, to roll up]

17. What does v.t. indicate?
   a. The origin(s) of the word
   b. How to pronounce the word
   c. How to use the word
   d. How many syllables are present
   e. In what region the word was used

18. What does the hyphen in the word *in-volve* indicate?
   a. The origins of the word
   b. How to pronounce the word
   c. How to use the word
   d. How many syllables are present
   e. How many letters are present

19. What are the oldest origins for the word *involve*?
   a. Middle English
   b. Old French
   c. Old Germanic
   d. Old English
   e. Latin

Use the table below to answer questions 20–23.

	Car 1	Car 2	Car 3	Car 4
Distance Traveled	100 miles	50 miles	70 miles	200 miles
Gallons Needed	4.23 gallons needed	2.083 gallons needed	3.181 gallons needed	8 gallons needed
Size of Tank	12-gallon tank	13-gallon tank	16-gallon tank	14-gallon tank

20. Based on the information above, which car gets the best gas mileage?
    a. Car 1
    b. Car 2
    c. Car 3
    d. Car 4
    e. Cars 3 & 4

21. Which car gets the worst gas mileage?
    a. Car 1
    b. Car 2
    c. Car 3
    d. Car 4
    e. Cars 1 & 2

22. Which car has the greatest range on one tank of gas?
    a. Car 1
    b. Car 2
    c. Car 3
    d. Car 4
    e. Cars 2 & 3

23. Which car has the least range on one tank of gas?
    a. Car 1
    b. Car 2
    c. Car 3
    d. Car 4
    e. Cars 1 & 3

Questions 24–27 are based on the following passage.

The more immediately after the commission of a crime a punishment is inflicted, the more just and useful it will be. It will be more just, because it spares the criminal the cruel and superfluous torment of uncertainty, which increases in proportion to the strength of his imagination and the sense of his weakness; and because the privation of liberty, being a punishment, ought to be inflicted before condemnation, but for as short a time as possible. Imprisonments, I say, being only the means of securing the person of the accused, until he be tried, condemned, or acquitted, ought not only to be of as short duration, but attended with as little severity as possible. The time should be determined by the necessary preparation for the trial, and the right of priority in the oldest prisoners. The confinement ought not to be closer than is requisite to prevent his flight,

or his concealing the proofs of the crime; and the trial should be conducted with all possible expedition. Can there be a more cruel contrast than that between the indolence of a judge, and the painful anxiety of the accused; the comforts and pleasures of an insensible magistrate, and the filth and misery of the prisoner? In general, as I have before observed, *the degree of the punishment, and the consequences of a crime, ought to be so contrived, as to have the greatest possible effect on others, with the least possible pain to the delinquent*. If there be any society in which this is not a fundamental principle, it is an unlawful society; for mankind, by their union, originally intended to subject themselves to the least evils possible.

An immediate punishment is more useful; because the smaller the interval of time between the punishment and the crime, the stronger and more lasting will be the association of the two ideas of *Crime* and *Punishment;* so that they may be considered, one as the cause, and the other as the unavoidable and necessary effect. It is demonstrated, that the association of ideas is the cement which unites the fabric of the human intellect; without which, pleasure and pain would be simple and ineffectual sensations. The vulgar, that is, all men who have no general ideas or universal principles, act in consequence of the most immediate and familiar associations; but the more remote and complex only present themselves to the minds of those who are passionately attached to a single object, or to those of greater understanding, who have acquired an habit of rapidly comparing together a number of objects, and of forming a conclusion; and the result, that is, the action in consequence, by these means, becomes less dangerous and uncertain.

It is, then, of the greatest importance, that the punishment should succeed the crime as immediately as possible, if we intend, that, in the rude minds of the multitude, the seducing picture of the advantage arising from the crime, should instantly awake the attendant idea of punishment. Delaying the punishment serves only to separate these two ideas; and thus affects the minds of the spectators rather as being a terrible sight than the necessary consequence of a crime; the horror of which should contribute to heighten the idea of the punishment.

There is another excellent method of strengthening this important connexion between the ideas of crime and punishment; that is, to make the punishment as analogous as possible to the nature of the crime; in order that the punishment may lead the mind to consider the crime in a different point of view, from that in which it was placed by the flattering idea of promised advantages.

Crimes of less importance are commonly punished, either in the obscurity of a prison, or the criminal is *transported*, to give, by his slavery, an example to societies which he never offended; an example absolutely useless, because distant from the place where the crime was committed. Men do not, in general, commit great crimes deliberately, but rather in a sudden gust of passion; and they commonly look on the punishment due to a great crime as remote and improbable. The public punishment, therefore, of small crimes will make a greater impression, and, by deterring men from the smaller, will effectually prevent the greater.

Cesare Beccaria, "Punishments, Advantages of Immediate," *The Criminal Recorder,* 1810

24. What is the main purpose of this passage?
    a. To describe
    b. To inform
    c. To persuade
    d. To entertain
    e. To instruct

25. What text structure is this passage using?
    a. Compare/contrast
    b. Sequential
    c. Cause/effect
    d. Problem-solution
    e. Descriptive

26. Which of the following excerpts best exemplifies the main idea of this passage?
    a. "The vulgar, that is, all men who have no general ideas or universal principles, act in consequence of the most immediate and familiar associations."
    b. "Crimes of less importance are commonly punished, either in the obscurity of a prison, or the criminal is *transported*, to give, by his slavery, an example to societies which he never offended."
    c. "Men do not, in general, commit great crimes deliberately, but rather in a sudden gust of passion; and they commonly look on the punishment due to a great crime as remote and improbable."
    d. "The more immediately after the commission of a crime a punishment is inflicted, the more just and useful it will be."
    e. "The public punishment, therefore, of small crimes will make a greater impression, and, by deterring men from the smaller, will effectually prevent the greater."

27. With which of the following statements would the author most likely DISAGREE?
    a. Criminals are incapable of connecting crime and punishment.
    b. A punishment should quickly follow the crime.
    c. Most criminals do not think about the consequences of their actions.
    d. Where a criminal is punished is just as important as when.
    e. A criminal should not be published in public.

Questions 28–30 are based on the following table.

Cellular Phone 1	Cellular Phone 2	Cellular Phone 3	Cellular Phone 4
Cost of phone: $200	Cost of phone: $100	Cost of phone: $50	Cost of phone: free
Monthly plan: $35	Monthly plan: $25	Monthly plan: $50	Monthly plan: $65
Monthly insurance: $20	Monthly insurance: $30	Monthly insurance: $25	Monthly insurance: $7

28. Taking into consideration the cost of the phone and payments per month, which contract would offer the best value over the course of two months?
    a. Cellular phone 1
    b. Cellular phone 2
    c. Cellular phone 3
    d. Cellular phone 4
    e. Both cellular phones 1 & 2

29. Taking into consideration the cost of the phone and payments per month, which contract would offer the best value over the course of a year?
    a. Cellular phone 1
    b. Cellular phone 2
    c. Cellular phone 3
    d. Cellular phone 4
    e. Both cellular phones 3 & 4

30. If someone were accident prone and needed the monthly insurance, which phone would offer the best value over the course of a year?
    a. Cellular phone 1
    b. Cellular phone 2
    c. Cellular phone 3
    d. Cellular phone 4
    e. Both cellular phones 1 & 3

Questions 31–32 are based on the following passage.

Dear Brand-X Employees:

Over the past ten years, Brand-X has been happy to provide free daycare to Brand-X employees. Based on the dedication, long workdays, and professionalism shown daily, it's the least Brand-X management can do. Brand-X wouldn't be where it is today without the hard work of countless unsung heroes and is truly blessed to have such an amazing staff.

Unfortunately, Brand-X is subject to the same economic forces as any other company. We regret to inform you that, beginning March 15th, Brand-X has decided to discontinue the childcare program. This was a difficult decision to make, one that was arrived at only with the greatest of deliberation. Many other options were discussed, and this seemed to be the only one that allowed Brand-X to still stay competitive while not reducing staff.

Fortunately, all other programs—employee rewards, vacation and sick days, retirement options, volunteer days—have not been impacted. In addition, on Friday we'll be hosting a free lunch buffet. Employees are welcome to wear jeans.

Hope to see you there,

Brand-X Management

31. Which of the following words best describe the tone in the first, second, and third paragraphs?
   a. Relieved; conciliatory; ominous
   b. Conciliatory; ominous; relieved
   c. Proud; apologetic; placating
   d. Placating; apologetic; proud
   e. Apologetic; placating; relieved

32. "Unfortunately, Brand-X is subject to the same economic forces as any other company." This line was most likely provided to do what?
   a. Emphasize that Brand-X is no worse than other companies.
   b. Redirect blame from Brand-X to outside forces.
   c. Encourage staff to look for work elsewhere.
   d. Intimidate staff into cooperating.
   e. Insult Brand-X to make the employees feel better.

   For his American literature course next fall, Benito's professor submits a required summer reading list to all students. Before the first day of class, Benito is required to read *The Sound and the Fury*, "Barn Burning," *For Whom the Bell Tolls*, *The Grapes of Wrath*, and "A&P."

33. How many books is Benito required to read during the summer?
   a. One
   b. Two
   c. Three
   d. Four
   e. Five

34. How many short stories is Benito required to read during the summer?
   a. One
   b. Two
   c. Three
   d. Four
   e. Five

35. Carl's chore for the day was to clean out a little-used storage shed. When he unlocked the door and walked through it, he got a mouthful of spider web. Brushing his mouth and sputtering, he reached for the light's pull chain. As soon as the bulb went on, a mouse ran between his legs and out the door. *This place is worse than a zoo*, thought Carl as he reached *reluctantly* for a box.

The best replacement for *reluctantly* would be which of the following?
   a. Angrily
   b. Suspiciously
   c. Fearfully
   d. Excitingly
   e. Hesitantly

36. Jason had never been the best student. He had flunked three math tests and turned in only half of his homework. Worrying about his graduation, Jason's mother signed him up for tutoring. Even after several sessions, it was unclear whether he would pass. In the last week of math class, Jason buckled down and passed. Jason's mother marveled at his gumption.

The best substitute for gumption would be which of the following?
   a. Stubbornness
   b. Laziness
   c. Initiative
   d. Ambition
   e. Courage

Questions 37 and 38 are based on the following table.

Ship 1	Ship 2	Ship 3	Ship 4
Depart: 1:10 p.m.	Depart: 1:00 p.m.	Depart: 1:30 p.m.	Depart: 12:30 p.m.
Arrive: 2:30 p.m.	Arrive: 2:45 p.m.	Arrive: 2:20 p.m.	Arrive: 1:50 p.m.
Return: 4:40 p.m.	Return: 5:30 p.m.	Return: 5:30 p.m.	Return: 5:45 p.m.

37. Lucy and Bob both enjoy fishing and want to take a charter ship to an island, but they have different schedules. Lucy, who works mornings, can't leave until 12:45 p.m. She needs thirty minutes to arrive at the dock. Bob, on the other hand, starts work at 6:30 p.m. and needs an hour to get from the docks to his job. There are four different charter ships available. Based on their schedules, which ship would meet both Lucy and Bob's needs?
   a. Ship 1
   b. Ship 2
   c. Ship 3
   d. Ship 4
   e. Ship 1 & 2

38. If Lucy and Bob didn't have any time restraints, which boat would give them the most time on the island to fish?
   a. Ship 1
   b. Ship 2
   c. Ship 3
   d. Ship 4
   e. Ship 3 & 4

Questions 39–42 are based on the following two passages.

Passage 1

In the modern classroom, cell phones have become indispensable. Cell phones, which are essentially handheld computers, allow students to take notes, connect to the web, perform complex computations, teleconference, and participate in surveys. Most importantly, though, due to their mobility and excellent reception, cell phones are necessary in emergencies. Unlike tablets, laptops, or computers, cell phones are a readily available and free resource—most school district budgets are already strained to begin with—and since today's student is already strongly rooted in technology, when teachers incorporate cell phones, they're "speaking" the student's language, which increases the chance of higher engagement.

Passage 2

As with most forms of technology, there is an appropriate time and place for the use of cell phones. Students are comfortable with cell phones, so it makes sense when teachers allow cell phone use at their discretion. Allowing cell phone use can prove advantageous if done correctly. Unfortunately, if that's not the case—and often it isn't—then a sizable percentage of students pretend to pay attention while *surreptitiously* playing on their phones. This type of disrespectful behavior is often justified by the argument that cell phones are not only a privilege but also a right. Under this logic, confiscating phones is akin to rummaging through students' backpacks. This is in stark contrast to several decades ago when teachers regulated where and when students accessed information.

39. With which of the following statements would both the authors of Passages 1 and 2 agree?
   a. Teachers should incorporate cell phones into curriculum whenever possible.
   b. Cell phones are useful only when an experienced teacher uses them properly.
   c. Cell phones and, moreover, technology are a strong part of today's culture.
   d. Despite a good lesson plan, cell phone disruptions are impossible to avoid.
   e. Cell phones are necessary in an emergency.

40. Which of the following reasons is NOT listed in Passage 1 as a reason for students to have cell phones?
   a. Cell phones are a free, readily available resource.
   b. Cell phones incorporate others forms of technology.
   c. Due to their mobility, cell phones are excellent in an emergency.
   d. Cell phones allow teachers to "speak" clearly with students.
   e. Cell phones allow higher engagement between students and teachers.

41. Passage 2 includes the statement, "confiscating phones is akin to rummaging through students' backpacks." The author most likely included this statement to do which of the following?
   a. Indicate how unlikely students are to change their minds.
   b. Exemplify how strongly students believe this is a right.
   c. Exemplify how easily the modern student is offended.
   d. Demonstrate how illogical most students' beliefs are.
   e. Explain how the rules of education are rapidly changing.

213

42. Based on the context of Passage 2, the best substitute for *surreptitiously* would most likely be which of the following?
  a. Privately
  b. Casually
  c. Obstinately
  d. Defiantly
  e. Slyly

Questions 43 and 44 are based on the following table.

Cooking Oils	Smoking Point F°	Neutral Taste?
Clarified Butter	485°	No
Peanut Oil	450°	Yes
Lard	374°	No
Safflower Oil	510°	Yes
Coconut Oil	350°	No

43. Zack is getting ready to heat some cooking oil. He knows that if an oil goes above its smoking point, it doesn't taste good. For his recipe, he must get the oil to reach 430° F. Zack has a peanut allergy and would prefer a neutral-tasting oil. Which oil should he use?
  a. Clarified butter
  b. Peanut oil
  c. Safflower oil
  d. Coconut oil
  e. Lard

44. If Zack still needed the oil to reach 430° F but he didn't have a peanut allergy and preferred a flavored oil, which oil would he use?
  a. Clarified butter
  b. Peanut oil
  c. Safflower oil
  d. Coconut oil
  e. Lard

45. After many failed attempts, Julio made a solemn promise to his mother to clean his room. When she came home from a long day of work, she found her son playing video games, his room still a disaster. Her fists clenched, her eyebrows knitted, she stared down her son and delivered a *vituperative* speech that made him hang his head regretfully.

The best substitute for *vituperative* would be which of the following?
  a. Annoyed
  b. Abusive
  c. Passionate
  d. Sorrowful
  e. Virtuous

Questions 46–48 are based on the following passage.

   Random Lake Advertisement

214

Who needs the hassle of traveling far away? This summer, why not rent a house on Random Lake? Located conveniently ten miles away from Random City, Random Lake has everything a family needs. Swimming, kayaking, boating, fishing, volleyball, mini-golfing, go-cart racing, eagle watching, nature trail hiking—there are enough activities here to keep a family busy for a month, much less a week.

Random Lake hotels are available for every lifestyle and budget. Prefer a pool or free breakfast? Prefer quiet? Historical? Modern? No problem. The Random Lake area has got you covered. House rentals are affordable too. During the summer months, rentals can go as cheaply as 600 dollars a week. Even better deals can be found during the off season. Most homes come fully furnished, and pontoon boats, kayaks, and paddle boats are available for rental. With the Legends and the Broadmoor developments slated for grand openings in March, the choices are endless!

46. The main purpose of this passage is to do what?
   a. Describe
   b. Inform
   c. Narrate
   d. Entertain
   e. Persuade

47. Which of the following sentences is out of place and should be removed?
   a. "This summer, why not rent a house on Random Lake?"
   b. "There are enough activities here to keep a family busy for a month."
   c. "Pontoon boats, kayaks, and paddle boats are available for rental."
   d. "Random Lake hotels are available for every lifestyle and budget."
   e. "With the Legends and the Broadmoor developments slated for grand openings in March, the choices are endless!"

48. Which of the following can be deduced from the passage?
   a. Random City is more populated than Random Lake.
   b. The Random Lake area is newer than Random City.
   c. The Random Lake area is growing.
   d. Random Lake prefers families to couples.
   e. You can go kayaking at a Random Lake Hotel.

Questions 49–50 are based upon the following passage:

Fellow-citizens, pardon me, allow me to ask, why am I called upon to speak here to-day? What have I, or those I represent, to do with your national independence? Are the great principles of political freedom and of natural justice, embodied in that Declaration of Independence, extended to us? And am I, therefore, called upon to bring our humble offering to the national altar, and to confess the benefits and express devout gratitude for the blessings resulting from your independence to us?

Would to God, both for your sakes and ours, that an affirmative answer could be truthfully returned to these questions! Then would my task be light, and my burden easy and delightful. For who is there so cold, that a nation's sympathy could not warm him? Who so obdurate and dead to the claims of gratitude, that would not thankfully

acknowledge such priceless benefits? Who so stolid and selfish, that would not give his voice to swell the hallelujahs of a nation's jubilee, when the chains of servitude had been torn from his limbs? I am not that man. In a case like that, the dumb may eloquently speak, and the lame man leap as an hart.

But, such is not the state of the case. I say it with a sad sense of the disparity between us. I am not included within the pale of this glorious anniversary. Your high independence only reveals the immeasurable distance between us. The blessings in which you, this day, rejoice, are not enjoyed in common. The rich inheritance of justice, liberty, prosperity, and independence, bequeathed by your fathers, is shared by you, not by me. The sunlight that brought life and healing to you, has brought stripes and death to me.red by you, not by me. The sunlight that brought life and healing to you, as brought stripes and death to me. This Fourth [of] July is yours, not mine. You may rejoice, I must mourn. To drag a man in fetters into the grand illuminated temple of liberty, and call upon him to join you in joyous anthems, were inhuman mockery and sacrilegious irony. Do you mean, citizens, to mock me, by asking me to speak to-day? If so, there is a parallel to your conduct. And let me warn you that it is dangerous to copy the example of a nation whose crimes, lowering up to heaven, were thrown down by the breath of the Almighty, burying that nation in irrecoverable ruin! I can to-day take up the plaintive lament of a peeled and woe-smitten people!

By the rivers of Babylon, there we sat down. Yea! we wept when we remembered Zion. We hanged our harps upon the willows in the midst thereof. For there, they that carried us away captive, required of us a song; and they who wasted us required of us mirth, saying, 'Sing us one of the songs of Zion.' How can we sing the Lord's song in a strange land? If I forget thee, O Jerusalem, let my right hand forget her cunning. If I do not remember thee, let my tongue cleave to the roof of my mouth.

"What to the Slave is the Fourth of July?" Rochester, New York, July 5, 1852

49. What is the tone of the first paragraph of this passage?
    a. Incredulous
    b. Inclusive
    c. Contemplative
    d. Nonchalant
    e. Irate

50. Which word is NOT a synonym for "obdurate" as it is used in the sentence below?

    Who so obdurate and dead to the claims of gratitude, that would not thankfully acknowledge such priceless benefits?

    a. Steadfast
    b. Stubborn
    c. Adamant
    d. Unwavering
    e. Contented

Mathematics

1. Add 5,089 + 10,323.
   a. 15,402
   b. 15,412
   c. 5,234
   d. 15,234
   e. 10,534

2. A teacher is showing students how to evaluate $5 \times 6 + 4 \div 2 - 1$. Which operation should be completed first?
   a. Multiplication
   b. Addition
   c. Division
   d. Subtraction
   e. Exponentiation

3. A factor of 36 is defined as:
   a. A whole number that can be divided by 36 and have no remainder
   b. A number that can be added to 36 with no remainder
   c. A prime number that is multiplied by 36
   d. An even number that is multiplied by 36
   e. A whole number that 36 can be divided by and have no remainder

4. Which of the following is the definition of a prime number?
   a. A number whose only factors are itself and 1
   b. A number greater than 1 whose only factors are itself and 1
   c. A number less than 10
   d. A number divisible by 10
   e. A number divisible by 0

5. Add and express in reduced form $\frac{5}{12} + \frac{4}{9}$.
   a. $\frac{9}{17}$
   b. $\frac{1}{3}$
   c. $\frac{31}{36}$
   d. $\frac{3}{5}$
   e. $\frac{9}{21}$

6. Which of the following is the correct order of operations that could be used on a difficult math problem that contained grouping symbols?
    a. Parentheses, Exponents, Multiplication & Division, Addition & Subtraction
    b. Exponents, Parentheses, Multiplication & Division, Addition & Subtraction
    c. Parentheses, Exponents, Addition & Multiplication, Division & Subtraction
    d. Parentheses, Exponents, Division & Addition, Subtraction & Multiplication
    e. Division, Exponents, Addition & Parentheses, Subtraction & Multiplication

7. Convert $\frac{5}{8}$ to a decimal.
    a. 0.62
    b. 1.05
    c. 0.63
    d. 1.60
    e. 2.38

8. Subtract $9{,}576 - 891$.
    a. 10,467
    b. 9,685
    c. 8,325
    d. 7,833
    e. 8,685

9. If a teacher was showing a class how to round 245.2678 to the nearest thousandth, which place value would be used to decide whether to round up or round down?
    a. Ten-thousandth
    b. Thousandth
    c. Hundredth
    d. Thousand
    e. Tenth

10. Subtract $50.888 - 13.091$.
    a. 63.799
    b. 63.979
    c. 37,979
    d. 33,817
    e. 37.797

11. Students should line up the decimal places of the numbers before doing which of the following?
    a. Multiplication
    b. Division
    c. Subtraction
    d. Calculating exponents
    e. Addition

12. Subtract and express in reduced form: $\frac{23}{24} - \frac{1}{6}$

   a. $\frac{22}{18}$

   b. $\frac{11}{9}$

   c. $\frac{19}{24}$

   d. $\frac{4}{5}$

   e. $\frac{5}{6}$

13. Subtract and express in reduced form $\frac{43}{45} - \frac{11}{15}$.

   a. $\frac{10}{45}$

   b. $\frac{16}{15}$

   c. $\frac{32}{30}$

   d. $\frac{2}{9}$

   e. $\frac{1}{3}$

14. Change 0.56 to a fraction.

   a. $\frac{5.6}{100}$

   b. $\frac{14}{25}$

   c. $\frac{56}{1,000}$

   d. $\frac{56}{10}$

   e. $\frac{100}{56}$

15. Multiply $13,114 \times 191$.

   a. 2,504,774

   b. 250,477

   c. 150,474

   d. 2,514,774

   e. 2,515,774

16. Marty wishes to save $150 over a 4-day period. How much must Marty save each day on average?

   a. $37.50

   b. $35

   c. $45.50

   d. $41

   e. $42

17. A teacher cuts a pie into 6 equal pieces and takes one away. What topic would she be introducing to the class by using such a visual?
    a. Decimals
    b. Addition
    c. Subtraction
    d. Measurement
    e. Fractions

18. Multiply and reduce $\frac{15}{23} \times \frac{54}{127}$.
    a. $\frac{810}{2,921}$

    b. $\frac{81}{292}$

    c. $\frac{69}{150}$

    d. $\frac{810}{2929}$

    e. $\frac{30}{882}$

19. Which of the following represents one hundred eighty-two billion, thirty-six thousand, four hundred twenty-one and three hundred fifty-six thousandths?
    a. 182,036,421.356
    b. 182,036,421.0356
    c. 182,000,036,421.0356
    d. 182,000,036,421.356
    e. 182,036,000,421.356

20. Divide, express with a fractional remainder $188 \div 16$.
    a. $1\frac{3}{4}$

    b. $111\frac{3}{4}$

    c. $10\frac{3}{4}$

    d. $11\frac{3}{4}$

    e. $3\frac{1}{111}$

21. What other operation could be utilized to teach the process of dividing 9,453 by 24 besides division?
    a. Multiplication
    b. Addition
    c. Exponents
    d. Subtraction
    e. Parentheses

22. Bernard can make $80 per day. If he needs to make $300 and only works full days, how many days will this take?
    a. 6
    b. 3
    c. 5
    d. 4
    e. 2

23. A couple buys a house for $150,000. They sell it for $165,000. By what percentage did the house's value increase?
    a. 18%
    b. 13%
    c. 15%
    d. 17%
    e. 10%

24. What operation are students taught to repeat to evaluate an expression involving an exponent?
    a. Addition
    b. Multiplication
    c. Division
    d. Subtraction
    e. Parentheses

25. Which of the following formulas would correctly calculate the perimeter of a legal-sized piece of paper that is 14 inches long and $8\frac{1}{2}$ inches wide?
    a. $P = 14 + 8\frac{1}{2}$
    b. $P = 14 + 8\frac{1}{2} + 14 + 8\frac{1}{2}$
    c. $P = 14 \times 8\frac{1}{2}$
    d. $P = 14 \times \frac{17}{2}$
    e. $P = 8 \times 14 + \frac{1}{2}$

26. Which of the following are units that would be taught in a lecture covering the metric system?
    a. Inches, feet, miles, pounds
    b. Millimeters, centimeters, meters, pounds
    c. Kilograms, grams, kilometers, meters
    d. Teaspoons, tablespoons, ounces
    e. Minutes, seconds, milliseconds

27. Which important mathematical property is shown in the expression: $(7 \times 3) \times 2 = 7 \times (3 \times 2)$?
    a. Distributive property
    b. Commutative property
    c. Additive inverse
    d. Multiplicative inverse
    e. Associative property

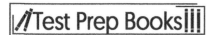

28. A grocery store is selling individual bottles of water, and each bottle contains 750 milliliters of water. If 12 bottles are purchased, what conversion will correctly determine how many liters that customer will take home?
    a. 100 milliliters equals 1 liter
    b. 1,000 milliliters equals 1 liter
    c. 1,000 liters equals 1 milliliter
    d. 10 liters equals 1 milliliter
    e. 1 liter equals 2,000 milliliters

29. If a student evaluated the expression $(3 + 7) - 6 \div 2$ to equal 2 on an exam, what error did she most likely make?
    a. She performed the operations from left to right instead of following order of operations.
    b. There was no error. 2 is the correct answer.
    c. She did not perform the operation within the grouping symbol first.
    d. She divided first instead of doing the addition within the grouping symbol.
    e. She performed the operations from right to left instead of following order of operations.

30. What is $(2 \times 20) \div (7 + 1) + (6 \times 0.01) + (4 \times 0.001)$?
    a. 5.064
    b. 5.64
    c. 5.0064
    d. 48.064
    e. 52.587

31. A cereal box has a base 3 inches by 5 inches and is 10 inches tall. Another box has a base 5 inches by 6 inches. Students are trying to calculate how tall the second box must be to hold the same amount of cereal as the first box. What formula should they use?
    a. Area of a rectangle
    b. Area of a circle
    c. Volume of a cube
    d. Perimeter of a square
    e. Volume of a rectangular solid

32. An angle measures 54 degrees. To correctly determine the measure of its complementary angle, what concept is necessary?
    a. Two complementary angles sum up to 180 degrees.
    b. Complementary angles are always acute.
    c. Two complementary angles sum up to 90 degrees.
    d. Complementary angles sum up to 360 degrees.
    e. Two complementary angles are always obtuse.

33. Which is closest to 17.8×9.9?
    a. 140
    b. 180
    c. 200
    d. 350
    e. 400

34. A school's faculty consists of 15 teachers and 20 teaching assistants. They have 200 students. What is the ratio of faculty to students?

    a. $3 : 20$
    b. $4 : 17$
    c. $5 : 54$
    d. $7 : 40$
    e. $8 : 40$

35. $\frac{3}{4}$ of a pizza remains on the stove. Katie eats $\frac{1}{3}$ of the remaining pizza. In order to determine how much of the pizza is left, what topic must be introduced to the students?

    a. Converting fractions to decimals
    b. Subtraction of fractions with like denominators
    c. Addition of fractions with unlike denominators
    d. Division of fractions
    e. Adding exponents

36. Taylor works two jobs. The first pays $20,000 per year. The second pays $10,000 per year. She donates 15% of her income to charity. How much does she donate each year?

    a. $4,500
    b. $5,000
    c. $5,500
    d. $6,000
    e. $6,500

37. Joshua collected 12,345 nickels over a span of 8 years. He took them to a bank to deposit into his bank account. Students are asked to determine how much money he deposited. For what mathematical topic would this problem be a good introduction?

    a. Adding decimals
    b. Multiplying decimals
    c. Geometry
    d. The metric system
    e. Fractions

38. A box with rectangular sides is 24 inches wide, 18 inches deep, and 12 inches high. What is the volume of the box in cubic feet?

    a. 2
    b. 6
    c. 4
    d. 5
    e. 3

39. What is the solution to $9 \times 9 \div 9 + 9 - 9 \div 9$?

    a. 0
    b. 13
    c. 81
    d. 9
    e. 17

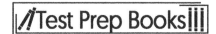

40. A student answers a problem with the following fraction: $\frac{3}{15}$. Why would this be considered incorrect?
    a. It is not expressed in decimal form.
    b. It is not simplified.
    c. It needs to be converted to a mixed number.
    d. It is in the correct form, and there is no problem with it.
    e. It does not have an exponent.

41. The hospital has a nurse-to-patient ratio of $1:25$. If a maximum of 325 patients may be admitted at a time, how many nurses are there?
    a. 13 nurses
    b. 25 nurses
    c. 325 nurses
    d. 12 nurses
    e. 50 nurses

42. A hospital has a bed-to-room ratio of $2:1$. If there are 145 rooms, how many beds are there?
    a. 145 beds
    b. 2 beds
    c. 90 beds
    d. 290 beds
    e. 300 beds

43. Solve for x:

$$\frac{2x}{5} - 1 = 59$$

    a. 60
    b. 145
    c. 150
    d. 115
    e. 130

44. A National Hockey League store in the state of Michigan advertises 50% off all items. Sales tax in Michigan is 6%. How much would a hat originally priced at $32.99 and a jersey originally priced at $64.99 cost during this sale? Round to the nearest penny.
    a. $97.98
    b. $103.86
    c. $51.93
    d. $48.99
    e. $44.98

45. Store-brand coffee beans cost $1.23 per pound. A local coffee bean roaster charges $1.98 per 1 $\frac{1}{2}$ pounds. How much more would 5 pounds from the local roaster cost than 5 pounds of the store brand?
   a. $0.55
   b. $1.55
   c. $1.45
   d. $0.45
   e. $2.15

46. Paint Inc. charges $2,000 for painting the first 1,800 feet of trim on a house and $1.00 per foot for each foot after. How much would it cost to paint a house with 3,125 feet of trim?
   a. $3,125
   b. $2,000
   c. $5,125
   d. $3,325
   e. $3,500

47. A bucket can hold 11.4 liters of water. A kiddie pool needs 35 gallons of water to be full. How many times will the bucket need to be filled to fill the kiddie pool? 1 gallon = 3.78541 liters
   a. 12
   b. 35
   c. 11
   d. 45
   e. 50

48. Mom's car drove 72 miles in 90 minutes. There are 5,280 feet per mile. How fast did she drive in feet per second?
   a. 0.8 feet per second
   b. 48.9 feet per second
   c. 0.009 feet per second
   d. 70.4 feet per second
   e. 9 feet per second

49. Convert 0.351 to a percentage.
   a. 3.51%
   b. 35.1%
   c. $\frac{351}{100}$
   d. 0.00351%
   e. $\frac{1}{351}$

50. Convert $\frac{2}{9}$ to a percentage.
   a. 22%
   b. 4.5%
   c. 450%
   d. 0.22%
   e. 78%

225

Writing

First Essay Prompt

Directions: The Writing section of the CBEST will require test takers to write two essays based on provided prompts. The first essay has a referential aim so that test takers can showcase their analytical and expository writing skills. The second essay will have an expressive aim, with a topic relating to the test taker's past lived experience.

Please read the prompt below and answer in an essay format.

> Margaret Atwood says "war is what happens when language fails." In an essay that is going to be read by educated adults, explain whether you agree or disagree with this observation. Support your argument with details and examples.

Second Essay Prompt

Please read the prompt below and answer in an essay format.

> Students and teachers alike have had mentors who have changed the course of their lives for the better. Name someone who was a mentor to you. Explain what they were like and how their experience and encouragement changed the course of your life.

The following pages are provided for writing your essay.

Answer Explanations for Practice Test #2

Reading

1. D: To find the correct answer, ask what yields the most information and is relevant to the task at hand: finding out about Harper Lee. A dictionary's main purpose is to define words, provide tenses, and establish pronunciation. A newspaper article might offer some information about Harper Lee, but it would be limited in scope to a specific topic or time period. A study guide would focus on literary elements of *To Kill a Mockingbird*, not Harper Lee's life. A biography would be the most comprehensive. It would cover the author, from birth to death, and touch on topics such as upbringing, significant achievements, and societal impacts. An analysis of the author's life's work would be about her work, not her life.

2. B: Unlike all the other words on the list, the word *are* is a being verb. In addition, *are* is in the present tense. The words *mixed*, *thrown*, *grown*, *beaten*, and *jumped* are all action verbs, and they are all in the past tense. The past tense of *are*, of course, is *were*. Therefore, *are* does not fit for two reasons: verb type and tense.

3. E: *Forward* is the correct answer. Since *focus* and *fortitude* are the guide words, all words that fall between them must correspond alphabetically. *Formaldehyde*, beginning with an *f, o,* and *r*, falls after focus, but the next letter, *a*, places it before *fortitude*. In *forge*, the *f* and *o* falls after focus, but then the *g* comes before the *t* in *fortitude*. The *f, o,* and *r* in *format* are similar to *formaldehyde*, and, again, the *m* places it before *fortitude*. Then there's *fort*. Since the first four letters match fortitude but there's no additional letters, it would precede fortitude as an entry.

4. C: "Having incremental or gradual build-up of harmful effects" is the correct answer. To find the correct answer, try replacing or substituting words. Here, one might try saying "Damaging or deadly but attractive"; this answer is incorrect because, although the paragraph says the product was popular, it does not indicate that *insidious* means *popular*. "Awaiting a chance to entrap or ensnare" is incorrect because asbestos is an inanimate object. "Causing catastrophic harm" doesn't work because the level of harm was not specified in the paragraph, and "Causing a sudden explosion" is incorrect because the passage says that it was fire resistant.

5. E: To arrive at the correct answer, find the best synonym for *spurious*. *Fake* makes the most sense because Bob is trying to hide his true emotions. Based on his horrible performance, he understands that he didn't get the job, so the reader can infer that his confidence is not at an all-time high. Therefore, *fake* would make just as much sense in this case as *spurious*. *Extreme* would indicate that Bob is euphoric and the interview went well. *Mild* would indicate that Bob thought he had a slight chance at getting hired. In this instance, *genuine* would be an antonym (i.e., the exact opposite of what Bob is feeling). *Proud* would also not fit here, because Bob's interview went poorly.

6. C:

1. Start with the word KAKISTOCRACY
2. Replace the first K with the first A (akistocracy)
3. Change the Y to an I. (akistocraci)
4. Move the last C to the right of the last I (akistocraic)
5. Add a T between the last A and the last I. (akistocratic)
6. Change the K to R. (aristocratic)

7. C: U-Save discount diaper offers the best deal. To arrive at the correct answer, take the price of the diaper in each column and divide by the number of diapers. Next, take the cost of tax in each column and divide by the numbers of diapers. Add these two totals together to arrive at the total cost per individual diaper. (Note: for the online diaper column, there is no tax to calculate.) The u-save diaper has a total cost of $.26 cents per diaper and $.06 cents tax, totaling $.32 cents per diaper. The first name brand diaper has a cost of $.34 cents per diaper with $.04 cents tax per diaper, totaling $.38 cents per diaper. The second name brand diaper has $.40 cents per diaper and $.06 cents tax per diaper, totaling $.46 cents total per diaper. The online diaper has a cost of $.45 cents per diaper.

8. D: There are four land masses depicted on the map: Easter Island, Motu Kau Kau, Motu Iti, and Motu Nui.

9. A: According to both the number markings and the colored topography, there are four areas above 300 meters: Volcano Terevaka, Volcano Puakatike, Maunga O Tu'u, and Volcano Rano Kau.

10. C: Taking into consideration both the number of roads and the population marker (o) at Hanga Roa, the southwest corner of the island is the most heavily populated.

11. E: Most ahus (ceremonial platforms) which feature the moai (Easter Island's statues) are located near the coastline, as indicated by the ahu markers on the key.

12. B: *Humiliated* would be the best substitute for *mortified*. *Inhibited* is a general characteristic of a person unable to act in a relaxed or natural manner; it might be true of Reggie in general but does not describe his acute emotional state at that moment described in the anecdote. *Annoyed* is also too mild a word. *Afraid* is not a synonym of *mortified*. *Elated* means happy so this is incorrect.

13. B: The main purpose of this passage is to inform. It wants the reader to understand how American science fiction evolved. Choice *A* is incorrect because the passage is not very descriptive; there is not an abundance of adjectives and adverbs painting a picture in the reader's mind. The passage is not persuasive, Choice *C*; the author is not asking the reader to adopt a stance or argument. For Choice *D,* it might be mildly entertaining, but the entertainment aspect of the passage takes a back seat to its informative aspects. Choice *E, instruct*, is something an instruction manual or a technical paper would do, so this isn't the *best* answer.

14. B: This passage begins with the oldest (the pulp fiction magazines of the Great Depression), moves forward to the science fiction of the fifties and sixties via names like Ray Bradbury and Kurt Vonnegut, and ends with a discussion of modern science fiction movies—*Jurassic Park, The Matrix, I am Legend*. It follows a sequential timeline of American science fiction.

15. A: All other concepts discussed throughout this passage connect to the main idea: "Science fiction has been a part of the American fabric for a long time." Choice *B* states: "As time went on, science

fiction evolved, posing better plots and more sophisticated questions." This is only a portion of the entire history of American science fiction. The same is true of Choice *C*: "These outlandish stories of aliens and superheroes were printed on cheap, disposable paper stock, hence the name *pulp* (as in paper) *fiction*." Choice *D*, though it ties together the Great Depression and modern American cinema, doesn't touch on the period in between. Choice *E* presents some supporting details of the main idea.

16. A: There are several clues that support Choice *A*. First, the fact that the stories were printed on disposable paper proves that these stories were, at the time, not considered serious literature. Furthermore, it's noted later in the passage that science fiction was taken seriously as authors like Kurt Vonnegut and Ray Bradbury gained prominence. This further reinforces the notion that at the beginning it was considered only fanciful and for children. Choice *B* is incorrect. Even though the statement is true of the passage, it's not supported by the individual sentence. Choice *C* is incorrect because the sentence never states directly or hints at this, and, in addition, movies and radio were available during this time period. Choice *D* is incorrect. The premise of the whole passage is that the medium of science fiction is not new. It doesn't spend any time discussing how science fiction was written and what those authors believed.

17. C: V.t. means the verb is transitive (v.t. is short for the Latin words *verbum transitivum*).

18. D: The hyphen in *involve* is present to indicate how many syllables are present. When people pronounce the word *involve*, there's a break between the *in* and *volve*. The hyphen is there to indicate that break.

19. E: Latin is the oldest origins for the word *involve*. The origins can be traced back through the entry. In Middle English it was *enoulen*; old French used *involver*, and the most ancient version (Latin) is *involvere*.

20. D: Car 4 gets the best mileage at 25 mpg. This is calculated by taking the miles (200) and dividing by the number of gallons needed (8). For car 1, divide 100 by 4.23; it gets 23.6 mpg. For car 2, divide 50 by 2.083; it gets 24 mpg. For car 3, divide 70 by 3.181; it gets 22 mpg.

21. C: Car 3 gets the worst mileage at 22 mpg. This is calculated by taking the miles (200) and dividing by the number of gallons needed (8). For car 1, divide 100 by 4.23; it gets 23.6 mpg. For car 2, divide 50 by 2.083; it gets 24 mpg. For car 3, divide 70 by 3.181; it gets 22 mpg.

22. C: To get the number of miles a car can drive on one tank, calculate the mpg by multiplying miles (200) by gallons needed. Next, multiply the mpg by the size of the tank. First, calculate the number of miles for car 1:

$$23.6 \text{ mpg} \times 12 \text{ gal} = 283.2 \text{ mi}$$

Car 2:

$$24 \text{ mpg} \times 13 \text{ gal} = 312 \text{ mi}$$

Car 3:

$$22 \text{ mpg} \times 16 \text{ gal} = 352 \text{ mi}$$

Car 4:

$$25 \text{ mpg} \times 14 \text{ gal} = 350 \text{ mi}$$

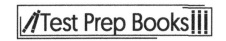

Therefore, car 3 can travel the greatest distance on one tank of gas.

23. A: To get the number of miles a car can drive on one tank, calculate the mpg by multiplying miles (200) by gallons needed. Next, multiply the mpg by the size of the tank. First, calculate the number of miles for car 1:

$$23.6 \text{ mpg} \times 12 \text{ gal} = 283.2 \text{ mi}$$

Car 2:

$$24 \text{ mpg} \times 13 \text{ gal} = 312 \text{ mi}$$

Car 3:

$$22 \text{ mpg} \times 16 \text{ gal} = 352 \text{ mi}$$

Car 4:

$$25 \text{ mpg} \times 14 \text{ gal} = 350 \text{ mi}$$

Therefore, car 1 can travel the least amount with a range of only 283.2 miles.

24. C: Throughout the entire text, the author maintains a persuasive tone. He argues that punishment should quickly follow the crime and gives a host of reasons why: it's more humane; it helps the prisoner to understand the nature of their crimes; it makes a better example for society. To confirm it's a persuasive stance, try reversing the argument. If the position cannot be reversed, then it's not persuasive. In this instance, the reader could argue in rebuttal that the punishment does not have to quickly follow the crime. Regardless of the veracity of this argument, simply creating it proves that the passage is persuasive.

25. C: This passage was written with a cause/effect structure. The cause is that the length between incarceration and trial should be as short as possible. The author, then, lists multiple effects of this cause. There are several key words that indicate this is a cause/effect argument. For instance, the author states, "The degree of the punishment, and the consequences of a crime, ought to be so contrived, as to have the greatest possible effect on others, with the least possible pain to the delinquent." The key words *as to have* indicate that changing the manner of punishment will change the outcome. Similarly, the authors states, "An immediate punishment is more useful; because the smaller the interval of time between the punishment and the crime, the stronger and more lasting will be the association of the two ideas of Crime and Punishment." Similar to *as to have* in the previous excerpt, *because* shows causation. In this instance, the author argues that the shorter the duration between crime and punishment, the more criminals will grasp the consequences of their actions. In general, for cause-effect passages, keep a lookout for words like *because*, *since*, *consequently*, *so*, and *as a result*.

26. D: "The more immediately after the commission of a crime a punishment is inflicted, the more just and useful it will be," best exemplifies the main idea of this passage. All subsequent discussion links back to this main idea and plays the role of supporting details. "The vulgar, that is, all men who have no general ideas or universal principles, act in consequence of the most immediate and familiar associations," supports this idea because the "vulgar," criminals, in other words, are used to making quick associations and are not used to delaying gratification or ignoring their impulses. "Crimes of less importance are commonly punished, either in the obscurity of a prison, or the criminal is transported, to give, by his slavery, an example to societies which he never offended," supports the main idea because

233

the author argues that this is the wrong way to punish because if the punishment occurs in the same area the crime was committed, then the punishment will have more effect, since criminals will associate the areas with their crimes.

Furthermore, transferring a prisoner takes time and delays punishment. For Choice *C*, the author states, "Men do not, in general, commit great crimes deliberately, but rather in a sudden gust of passion; and they commonly look on the punishment due to a great crime as remote and improbable." To reduce the sense of punishments being remote and improbable, criminals must, according to the author, receive an immediate punishment. Therefore, by removing a lengthy gap between crime and punishment, a criminal's punishment will be close and probable, which the author argues is the most humane way to punish and the mark of a civilized society. Choice *E* states "The public punishment, therefore, of small crimes will make a greater impression, and, by deterring men from the smaller, will effectually prevent the greater." This sentence is more of an add-on to the main idea, not the main idea itself.

27. A: The author would disagree most strongly with the statement "criminals are incapable of connecting crime and punishment." Though the author states that criminals are often passionate and consider punishment unlikely in the heat of the crime, the entire premise of the passage is that reducing the time between crime and punishment increases the likelihood of an association. He also argues that if a society does this consistently, the probability that individuals will consider the consequences of their actions increases. "A punishment should quickly follow the crime" is a restatement of the main idea, supported by evidence throughout the passage. Though the author makes it clear that "Most criminals do not think about the consequences of their actions," he goes on to say that, in general, reducing the time between crime and punishment will have the most positive effect on the prisoner and on society. The statement that "Where a criminal is being punished is just as important as when" supports what the author argues in the passage, that a punishment should be immediate and near where the crime originally occurred. The author also argues that offenders should be punished publicly for small crimes.

28. D: Cellular phone 4 offers the best value for two months. Since there's no cost for the cell phone, take $65 \times 2 = \$130$.

Cellular phone 1: $\$200 + \$35 \times 2 = \$270$
Cellular phone 2: $\$100 + \$25 \times 2 = \$150$
Cellular phone 3: $\$50 + \$45 \times 2 = \$140$
Cellular phone 4: $\$65 \times 2 = \$130$

29. B: Cellular phone 2 offers the best value.

Cellular phone 2: $\$100 + \$25 \times 12 = \$400$
Cellular phone 1: $\$200 + \$35 \times 12 = \$620$
Cellular phone 3: $\$50 + \$45 \times 12 = \$590$
Cellular phone 4: $\$65 \times 12 = \$744$

30. B: Cellular phone 2 offers the best value:

Cellular phone 2: $\$100 + (\$25 + \$30) \times 12 = \$760$
Cellular phone 1: $\$200 + (\$35 + \$20) \times 12 = \$860$
Cellular phone 3: $\$50 + (\$45 + \$25) \times 12 = \$890$
Cellular phone 4: $(\$65 + \$7) \times 12 = \$864$

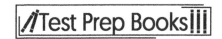

31. C: Brand-X Management uses a proven technique to deliver bad news: sandwich it between good. The first paragraph extolls the virtue of its employees: "Brand-X wouldn't be where it is today without the hard work of countless unsung heroes and is truly blessed to have such an amazing staff." The management of Brand-X is proud of its employees. The second paragraph delivers the bad news. Along with the announcement of the termination of the childcare program, Brand-X management provides several reasons why, such as they're "subject to the same economic forces as any other company" and their decision "allowed Brand-X to still stay competitive while not reducing staff."

The passage implies that they didn't want to—they had to. The tone of the second paragraph is apologetic. The third paragraph ends on a positive note. Management reminds staff that other services—employee rewards, vacation and sick days, retirement options, volunteer days—have not been impacted, and on Friday employees will have a luncheon and be allowed to wear jeans. This passage is there to not only remind employees why it's still beneficial to work there, but also to provide evidence that Brand-X wants its employees to be happy by hosting luncheons and letting employees wear jeans. It's designed to reduce their hostilities about cancelling the program or, in other words, placate or appease them.

32. B: "Unfortunately, Brand-X is subject to the same economic forces as any other company." This line was most likely provided to redirect blame from Brand-X to outside forces. Throughout the second paragraph, Brand-X consistently defends its decision to cancel the childcare program. Based on the context of the paragraph, it's continually implied that management was left with no choice. While it might be true that Brand-X is no worse than other companies (others are forced to do the same), this statement supports the idea that it's beyond their control, a message reiterated throughout the paragraph. Nowhere in the paragraph does Brand-X encourage employees to look for work elsewhere. In fact, management does the opposite by reminding employees why they want to continue working there: employee rewards, vacation and sick days, retirement options, and volunteer days. The tone of the passage is not intimidating. No threats are made, implied or otherwise. For example, when management makes reference to reducing staff, it's described as an undesirable choice, not a viable option. The Brand-X memo does not attempt to insult itself, so Choice *E* is incorrect.

33. C: In modern formatting, longer works, such as books, are indicated through the use of italics. Shorter works, such as poems or short stories, are indicated through the use of quotation marks. Accordingly, *The Sound and the Fury*, *For Whom the Bell Tolls*, and *The Grapes of Wrath* are full-length books, while "A&P" and "Barn Burning" are short stories.

34. B: In modern formatting, longer works, such as books, are indicated through the use of italics. Shorter works, such as poems or short stories, are indicated through the use of quotation marks. Accordingly, *The Sound and the Fury*, *For Whom the Bell Tolls*, and *The Grapes of Wrath* are full-length books, while "A&P" and "Barn Burning" are short stories.

35. E: Based on what Carl has encountered—a spider web and a mouse—he would be hesitant, lest he encounter another critter. *Fearfully* is too strong a word to replace *reluctantly* and would indicate something more serious, like mortal danger. Nowhere in the passage does it indicate Carl is angry, and for Carl to be suspicious, he would have to assume that someone in his life was trying to deceive him. There's no evidence of deception here. *Excitingly* does not fit the context here because Carl has run into one unfortunate event after another.

36. C: *Initiative* would be the best replacement for *gumption*. Both words indicate a strong desire to complete a task and overcome obstacles. *Stubbornness* would imply that Jason was resistant to

changing his behavior despite it being good or beneficial for him. Despite Jason being lazy, at the end of the passage, he finds the intrinsic motivation necessary to pass the class. The word *ambition* indicates not only a desire for success but also a desire to gain power and influence. Though Jason eventually wants to succeed, he's not trying to gain power or influence. *Courage* is close, but it's not quite as relevant as the word *initiative* here.

37. C: To arrive at the correct answer, first calculate the actual times Lucy and Bob could arrive at and depart from the dock. Lucy needs an additional thirty minutes, so that equates to 1:15 p.m., not 12:45. Bob works at 6:30 p.m. and needs an hour subtracted to get to work on time, so that means he would have to leave the dock by 5:30 p.m. Ship 3 leaves at 1:30 p.m., which gives Lucy an additional fifteen minutes' leeway, then returns at 5:30 p.m., which gives Bob the hour he needs to arrive at work on time. Ships 1 and 2 depart at 1:10 p.m. and 1:00 p.m., respectively. Both departure times are too early for Lucy. Ship 4 returns at 5:45 p.m., which is later than Bob can leave the dock for work.

38. D: To arrive at the correct answer, subtract the return times from the arrival times. Assuming it takes approximately the same amount of time for each ship to return, the biggest number should indicate the most amount of time spent on each respective island. Ship 4 provides the most amount of time with 3 hours, 55 minutes. Ship 1 allows 2 hours, 10 minutes; ship 2 is 2 hours, 45 minutes, and ship 3 is 2 hours, 50 minutes.

39. C: Despite the opposite stances in Passages 1 and 2, both authors establish that cell phones are a strong part of culture. In Passage 1 the author states, "Today's student is already strongly rooted in technology." In Passage 2 the author states, "Students are comfortable with cell phones." The author of Passage 2 states that cell phones have a "time and place." The author of Passage 2 would disagree with the statement that *teachers should incorporate cell phones into curriculum whenever possible. Cell phones are useful only when an experienced teacher uses them properly*—this statement is implied in Passage 2, but the author in Passage 1 says cell phones are "indispensable."

In other words, no teacher can do without them. *Despite a good lesson plan, cell phone disruptions are impossible to avoid*. This is not supported by either passage. Even though the author in the second passage is more cautionary, the author states, "This can prove advantageous if done correctly." Therefore, there is a possibility that a classroom can run properly with cell phones. *Cell phones are necessary in an emergency*. The author of Passage 1 would agree with this statement, but the author of Passage 2 does not think cell phones are appropriate in a classroom setting.

40. D: Here, *speaking* has nothing to do with *communication*. The original quotation from Passage 1 reads, "Since today's student is already strongly rooted in technology, when teachers incorporate cell phones, they're '*speaking*' the student's language." The first dependent clause makes reference to technology, then uses the word *speaking* as an analogy. The "language" the author refers to is *culture*. The author never intended the word speak to imply actual communication. "Cell phones are a free, readily available resource;" "cell phones incorporate other forms of technology;" and "due to their mobility, cell phones are excellent in an emergency" are all listed as reasons in Passage 1 to have cell phones.

41. B: The author states in Passage 2, "Confiscating phones is akin to rummaging through students' backpacks." The author most likely included this passage to exemplify how strongly students believe this is a right. This quotation is the evidence or example, and it ties to the previous sentence: "This type of disrespectful behavior is often justified by the argument that cell phones are not only a privilege but also a right." The backpack example illustrates how students believe it's a right. *Indicate how unlikely*

236

students are to change their minds; exemplify how easily the modern student is offended; demonstrate how illogical most students' beliefs are; and *explain how the rules of education are rapidly changing;* are not supported by Passage 2.

42. E: The best substitute for *surreptitiously* would be *slyly.* Let's look at the context of the sentence: "a sizable percentage of a classroom pretends to pay attention while surreptitiously playing on their phones." The key word here is *pretends.* The students in the classroom, therefore, want to use their cell phones but are afraid of getting caught. *Privately* and *casually* don't work because they leave out the connotation of hiding a wrong act or ulterior motive. *Obstinately* and *defiantly* are also incorrect since students are hiding their disobedience.

43. C: Safflower oil has a smoking point of 510° Fahrenheit. Since Zack's recipe doesn't exceed 430° F, it won't reach the smoking point. In addition, safflower oil doesn't contain peanuts, and safflower oil has a neutral taste. Though clarified butter has a high smoke point, too, it doesn't have a neutral taste. Zack is allergic to peanut oil. Lard, at 374° F, has too low a smoking point and doesn't have a neutral taste. Coconut oil has a smoking point of 350° F and doesn't have a neutral taste.

44. A: Clarified butter has a high smoke point (485°), which would be well above 430° F and doesn't have a neutral taste, which in this scenario Zack prefers. Here, peanut oil is a neutral flavor. Lard, at 374° F, has too low a smoking point. Safflower oil has a smoking point of 510° F, but, here, the flavor is neutral, and he wants a flavored oil. Coconut oil is not neutral, but the smoking point of 350° F is too low.

45. B: *Abusive* would be the best substitute for *vituperative.* Based on the context clues of "long day of work," "fists clenched," and "eyebrows knitted," Julio's mother is angry with her son. Therefore, one can infer that her language will match her nonverbal behavior. *Annoyed* is simply too mild of a word and does not match with her enraged posture. *Passionate* is too vague of a word that can be matched to a different number of moods. *Sorrowful* contradicts the angry posture she's adopted. *Virtuous* means innocent so this is incorrect.

46. E: This passage is designed to persuade. The whole purpose of the passage is to convince vacationers to come to Random Lake. There are some informative aspects of the passage, such as what's available – boating, house rentals, pontoon boats, but an extremely positive spin is put on the area, a spin that's designed to attract visitors. To prove it's persuasive, the argument can be reversed: Random Lake is not a good place to vacation. With a lack of adjectives and adverbs, there's a lack of descriptive detail, and this passage doesn't delight or entertain like a witty narrative might. positive spin is put on the area, a spin that's designed to attract visitors. To prove it's persuasive, the argument can be reversed: Random Lake is *not* a good place to vacation. With a lack of adjectives and adverbs, there's a lack of descriptive detail, and this passage doesn't delight or entertain like a witty narrative might.

47. C: "Pontoon boats, kayaks, and paddle boats are available for rental" is out of place. The sentence before refers to fully furnished homes, and the sentence after refers to new developments. This sentence would have fit much better near, "Swimming, kayaking, boating, fishing, volleyball, mini-golfing, go-cart racing, eagle watching, nature trail hiking," because the activities of the area are described. "This summer, why not rent a house on Random Lake?" is followed, logically, by a description of where Random Lake is. "There are enough activities there to keep a family busy for a month," is preceded by a listing of all those activities. "Random Lake hotels are available for every lifestyle and budget." is followed by questions to find out the customer's preferences, which connects back to "every lifestyle and budget". "With the Legends and the Broadmoor developments slated for grand openings in

237

March, the choices are endless!" This is an effective conclusion to the passage, so Choice *E* is not out of place.

48. C: The fact that the Random Lake area is growing can be deduced with the sentence, "With the Legends and The Broadmoor developments slated for grand openings in March, the choices are endless!" Considering buildings are being added, not razed, the Random Lake area would have to be growing. While Random City may seem more populated than Random Lake at first glance, the word city is not necessarily indicative of size. There's simply not enough information to determine the size of either Random City or Random Lake. Though the Random Lake area may logically seem newer than Random City with the addition of new buildings at Random Lake, there's no way to confirm this. The reader simply doesn't know enough about Random City to draw a comparison. Finally, Random Lake does not necessarily prefer families to couples. The ad definitely appeals to families but, "There are hotels available for every lifestyle and budget;" this proves that Random Lake is trying to appeal to everyone. Furthermore, "Prefer quiet? Historical? Modern?" shows that there are accommodations for every lifestyle.

49. A: While contemplative is an option because of the inquisitive nature of the text, Choice *A* is correct because the speaker expresses frustration over being asked to celebrate liberty that he and members of his race do not have. Choice *B* is incorrect because Frederick Douglass is drawing contrasts between two groups of people rather than being inclusive. He is neither nonchalant nor accepting of the circumstances which he describes.

50. E: Choice *C, contented*, is the only word that has a different meaning. Furthermore, the speaker expresses objection and disdain throughout the entire text.

Mathematics

1. B: 15,412

Set up the problem and add each column, starting on the far right (ones). Add, carrying anything over 9 into the next column to the left. Solve from right to left.

2. A: The order of operations (PEMDAS) is: parentheses, exponents, multiplication and division (from left to right), and addition and subtraction (from left to right). This question has parentheses, so those should be completed first.

3. E: If 36 can be divided by a whole number and have no remainder, then that number is a factor of 36. In other words, a factor of 36 is a whole number that can be multiplied by another whole number to make 36. The number 36 equals $1 \times 36, 2 \times 18, 3 \times 12, 4 \times 9,$ and 6×6, so it has nine unique factors: 1, 2, 3, 4, 6, 9, 12, 18, and 36.

4. B: A prime number is a number whose only factors are itself and 1, but only numbers greater than 1 can be considered prime.

5. C: Set up the problem and find a common denominator for both fractions.

$$\frac{5}{12} + \frac{4}{9}$$

238

Multiply each fraction across by a fraction equivalent to 1 to convert to a common denominator.

$$\frac{5}{12} \times \frac{3}{3} + \frac{4}{9} \times \frac{4}{4}$$

Once over the same denominator, add across the top. The total is over the common denominator.

$$\frac{15 + 16}{36} = \frac{31}{36}$$

6. A: Order of operations follows PEMDAS: Parentheses, Exponents, Multiplication and Division from left to right, and Addition and Subtraction from left to right.

7. C: Divide 5 by 8, which results in 0.625. This rounds up to 0.63.

8. E: Set up the problem, with the larger number on top. Begin subtracting with the far-right column (ones). Borrow 10 from the column to the left, when necessary.

9. A: The place value to the right of the thousandth place, which would be the ten-thousandth place, is what gets used. The value in the thousandth place is 7. The number in the place value to its right is 5 or greater, so the 7 gets bumped up to 8. Everything to its right turns to a zero, and the final zero is dropped because it is part of the decimal. 245.2678 rounded to the nearest thousandth is 245.268.

10. E: 37.797

Set up the problem, larger number on top and numbers lined up at the decimal. Begin subtracting with the far-right column. Borrow 10 from the column to the left, when necessary.

11. C: Numbers should be lined up by decimal places before subtraction is performed. Subtraction only works when the place value on top is the same as on the bottom. With the other operations—multiplying, dividing, and calculating exponents (which is a form of multiplication)—we ignore the decimal places at first and then include them at the end.

12. C: To find a common denominator, look for a number that has both denominators (24 and 6) as factors. 24 works. Multiply the top and bottom of each fraction by whatever number will make the denominator 24:

$$\frac{23}{24} \times \frac{1}{1} = \frac{23}{24} \text{ and } \frac{1}{6} \times \frac{4}{4} = \frac{4}{24}$$

Now that we have a common denominator, subtract the numerators:

$$\frac{23}{24} - \frac{4}{24} = \frac{23 - 4}{24} = \frac{19}{24}$$

Since 19 and 24 have no common factors except 1, this fraction can't be reduced.

13. D: Set up the problem and find a common denominator for both fractions.

$$\frac{43}{45} - \frac{11}{15}$$

Multiply each fraction across by a fraction equivalent to 1 to convert to a common denominator.

239

$$\frac{43}{45} \times \frac{1}{1} - \frac{11}{15} \times \frac{3}{3}$$

Once over the same denominator, subtract across the top.

$$\frac{43 - 33}{45} = \frac{10}{45}$$

Reduce.

$$\frac{10 \div 5}{45 \div 5} = \frac{2}{9}$$

14. B: $\frac{14}{25}$

Since 0.56 goes to the hundredths place, it can be placed over 100:

$$\frac{56}{100}$$

Essentially, the way we got there is by multiplying the numerator and denominator by 100:

$$\frac{0.56}{1} \times \frac{100}{100} = \frac{56}{100}$$

Then, the fraction can be simplified down to $\frac{14}{25}$:

$$\frac{56}{100} \div \frac{4}{4} = \frac{14}{25}$$

15. A: 2,504,774

Line up the numbers (the number with the most digits on top) to multiply. Begin with the right column on top and the right column on bottom.

Move one column left on top and multiply by the far-right column on the bottom. Remember to add the carry over after you multiply. Continue that pattern for each of the numbers on the top row.

Starting on the far-right column on top repeat this pattern for the next number left on the bottom. Write the answers below the first line of answers; remember to begin with a zero placeholder. Continue for each number in the top row.

Starting on the far-right column on top, repeat this pattern for the next number left on the bottom. Write the answers below the first line of answers. Remember to begin with zero placeholders.

Once completed, ensure the answer rows are lined up correctly, then add.

16. A: Divide the total amount by the number of days: $\frac{150}{4} = 37.5$. She needs to save an average of $37.50 per day.

17. E: The teacher would be introducing fractions. If a pie was cut into 6 pieces, each piece would represent $\frac{1}{6}$ of the pie. If one piece was taken away, $\frac{5}{6}$ of the pie would be left over.

240

18. A: $\frac{810}{2921}$

Line up the fractions.

$$\frac{15}{23} \times \frac{54}{127}$$

Multiply across the top and across the bottom.

$$\frac{15 \times 54}{23 \times 127} = \frac{810}{2921}$$

19. D: There are no millions, so the millions period consists of all zeros. 182 is in the billions period, 36 is in the thousands period, and 421 is in the ones period. After the decimal point, 356 is positioned with its last digit in the thousandths place (the third digit).

20. D: Set up the division problem.

$$16\overline{)188}$$

16 does not go into 1 but does go into 18 so start there.

$$
\begin{array}{r}
11 \\
16\overline{)188} \\
-16 \\
\hline
28 \\
-16 \\
\hline
12
\end{array}
$$

The result is $11\frac{12}{16}$

Reduce the fraction for the final answer.

$$11\frac{3}{4}$$

21. D: Division can be computed as a repetition of subtraction problems by subtracting multiples of 24.

22. D: The number of days can be found by taking the total amount Bernard needs to make and dividing it by the amount he earns per day:

$$\frac{300}{80} = \frac{30}{8} = \frac{15}{4} = 3.75$$

But Bernard is only working full days, so he will need to work 4 days since 3 days is not a sufficient amount of time.

23. E: The value went up by $165,000 − $150,000 = $15,000. Out of $150,000, this is:

241

$$\frac{15,000}{150,000} = \frac{1}{10}$$

Convert this to having a denominator of 100, the result is $\frac{10}{100}$, or 10%.

24. B: A number raised to an exponent is a compressed form of multiplication. For example:

$$10^3 = 10 \times 10 \times 10$$

25. B: The perimeter of a rectangle is the sum of all four sides. Therefore, the answer is:

$$P = 14 + 8\frac{1}{2} + 14 + 8\frac{1}{2}$$

$$14 + 14 + 8 + \frac{1}{2} + 8 + \frac{1}{2} = 45 \text{ square inches}$$

26. C: Kilograms, grams, kilometers, and meters. Variants of "gram" (including kilograms) and variants of "meter" (including kilometers, centimeters, and millimeters) belong to the metric system. The other units listed above are not part of the metric system.

27. E: It shows the associative property of multiplication. The order of multiplication does not matter, and the grouping symbols do not change the final result once the expression is evaluated.

28. B: The amount of water in one bottle is measured in milliliters but the question asks for an amount in liters. Therefore, the conversion from milliliters to liters is needed. There are 1,000 milliliters in 1 liter.

29. A: According to order of operations, the operation within the parentheses must be completed first. Division is completed next, and then subtraction. Therefore, the expression is evaluated as:

$$(3 + 7) - 6 \div 2 = 10 - 6 \div 2 = 10 - 3 = 7$$

In order to incorrectly obtain 2 as the answer, the student must have performed the operations from left to right, instead of following the order of operations.

30. A: Operations within the parentheses must be completed first. Division is completed next, and finally, addition. When adding decimals, digits within each place value are added together. Therefore, the expression is evaluated as:

$$(2 \times 20) \div (7 + 1) + (6 \times 0.01) + (4 \times 0.001)$$

$$40 \div 8 + 0.06 + 0.004 = 5 + 0.06 + 0.004 = 5.064$$

31. E: The formula for the volume of a rectangular solid would need to be used. The volume of the first box is:

$$V = 3 \times 5 \times 10 = 150 \text{ cubic inches}$$

The second box needs to hold cereal that would take up the same space. The volume of the second box is:

$$V = 5 \times 6 \times h = 30 \times h$$

In order for this to equal 150, h must equal 5 inches.

32. C: The measure of two complementary angles sums up to 90 degrees. $90 - 54 = 36$. Therefore, the complementary angle is 36 degrees.

33. B: Instead of multiplying these out, we can estimate the product by using $18 \times 10 = 180$.

34. D: The total faculty is:

$$15 + 20 = 35$$

So, the ratio is $35 : 200$. Then, divide both of these numbers by 5, since 5 is a common factor to both, with a result of $7 : 40$.

35. B: Katie eats $\frac{1}{3}$ of $\frac{3}{4}$ of the pizza. That means she eats $\frac{1}{3} \times \frac{3}{4} = \frac{3}{12} = \frac{1}{4}$ of the pizza. Therefore, $\frac{3}{4} - \frac{1}{4} = \frac{2}{4} = \frac{1}{2}$ of the pizza remains. This problem involves subtraction of fractions with like denominators.

36. A: Taylor's total income is $\$20,000 + \$10,000 = \$30,000$. Fifteen percent of this is $\frac{15}{100} = \frac{3}{20}$. So:

$$\frac{3}{20} \times \$30,000 = \frac{\$90,000}{200} = \frac{\$9,000}{2}$$

37. B: Each nickel is worth $\$0.05$. Therefore, Joshua deposited:

$$12,345 \times \$0.05 = \$617.25$$

Working with change is a great way to teach decimals to children, so this problem would be a good introduction to multiplying decimals.

38. E: Since the answer will be in cubic feet rather than inches, the first step is to convert from inches to feet for the dimensions of the box. There are 12 inches per foot, so the box is 24/12 = 2 feet wide, 18/12 = 1.5 feet deep, and 12/12 = 1 foot high. The volume is the product of these three together:

$$2 \times 1.5 \times 1 = 3 \text{ cubic feet}$$

39. E: According to the order of operations, multiplication and division must be completed first from left to right. Then, addition and subtraction are completed from left to right. Therefore:

$$9 \times 9 \div 9 + 9 - 9 \div 9$$

$$81 \div 9 + 9 - 9 \div 9$$

$$9 + 9 - 9 \div 9$$

$$9 + 9 - 1$$

$$18 - 1$$

$$17$$

40. B: When giving an answer to a math problem that is in fraction form, it always should be simplified. Both 3 and 15 have a common factor of 3 that can be divided out, so the correct answer is:

$$\frac{3 \div 3}{15 \div 3} = \frac{1}{5}$$

41. A: Using the given information of 1 nurse to 25 patients and 325 patients, set up an equation to solve for the number of nurses (N):

$$\frac{N}{325} = \frac{1}{25}$$

Multiply both sides by 325 to get N by itself on one side.

$$\frac{N}{1} = \frac{325}{25} = 13 \text{ nurses}$$

42. D: Using the given information of 2 beds to 1 room and 145 rooms, set up an equation to solve for number of beds (B):

$$\frac{B}{145} = \frac{2}{1}$$

Multiply both sides by 145 to get B by itself on one side.

$$\frac{B}{1} = \frac{290}{1} = 290 \text{ beds}$$

43. C: Set up the initial equation.

$$\frac{2x}{5} - 1 = 59$$

Add 1 to both sides.

$$\frac{2x}{5} - 1 + 1 = 59 + 1$$

Multiply both sides by $\frac{5}{2}$.

$$\frac{2x}{5} \times \frac{5}{2} = 60 \times \frac{5}{2} = 150$$

$$x = 150$$

44. C: List the givens.

$$\text{Tax} = 6.0\% = 0.06$$

$$\text{Sale} = 50\% = 0.5$$

$$\text{Hat} = \$32.99$$

$$\text{Jersey} = \$64.99$$

244

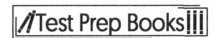
Calculate the sales prices.

$$\text{Hat Sale} = 0.5\,(32.99) = 16.495$$

$$\text{Jersey Sale} = 0.5\,(64.99) = 32.495$$

Total the sales prices.

$$\text{Hat sale} + \text{jersey sale} = 16.495 + 32.495 = 48.99$$

Calculate the tax and add it to the total sales prices.

$$\text{Total after tax} = 48.99 + (48.99 \times 0.06) = \$51.93$$

45. D: 5 pounds of store-brand coffee would cost $\frac{\$1.23}{1\,lbs} \times 5\,lbs = \$6.15$. For 5 pounds of local coffee, the cost would be $\frac{\$1.98}{1.5\,lbs} \times 5\,lbs = \$6.60$. Calculate the price difference: $\$6.60 - \$6.15 = \$0.45$.

46. D: List the givens.

$$1,800\ \text{ft} = \$2,000$$

$$\text{Cost after } 1,800\ \text{ft} = \$1.00/\text{ft}.$$

Find how many feet left after the first 1,800 feet.

$$\begin{array}{r} 3,125\ \text{ft} \\ -1,800\ \text{ft} \\ \hline 1,325\ \text{ft} \end{array}$$

Calculate the cost for the feet over 1,800 feet.

$$1,325\ \text{ft} \times \frac{\$1.00}{1\ \text{ft}} = \$1,325$$

Add these together to find the total for the entire cost.

$$\$2,000 + \$1,325 = \$3,325$$

47. A: Calculate how many gallons the bucket holds.

$$11.4\ \text{L} \times \frac{1\ \text{gal}}{3.8\ \text{L}} = 3\ \text{gal}$$

Next, calculate how many buckets are needed to fill the 35-gallon pool.

$$\frac{35}{3} = 11.67$$

Since the amount is more than 11 but less than 12, we must fill the bucket 12 times.

48. D: This problem can be solved by using unit conversion. The initial units are miles per minute. The final units need to be feet per second. Converting miles to feet uses the equivalence statement 1 mi =

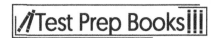

5,280 ft. Converting minutes to seconds uses the equivalence statement 1 min = 60 s. Setting up the ratios to convert the units is shown in the following equation:

$$\frac{72 \text{ mi}}{90 \text{ min}} \times \frac{1 \text{ min}}{60 \text{ s}} \times \frac{5{,}280 \text{ ft}}{1 \text{ mi}} = 70.4 \frac{\text{ft}}{\text{s}}$$

The initial units cancel out, and the new units are left.

49. B: To convert from a decimal to a percentage, the decimal needs to be moved two places to right. In this case, that makes 0.351 become 35.1%.

50. A: Converting from a fraction to a percentage generally involves two steps. First, the fraction needs to be converted to a decimal.

Divide 2 by 9 which results in $0.\overline{22}$. The top line indicates that the decimal actually goes on forever with an endless amount of 2s.

Second, the decimal needs to be moved two places to the right:

$$22\%$$

CBEST Practice Tests #3 & #4

To keep the size of this book manageable, save paper, and provide a digital test-taking experience, the 3rd and 4th practice tests can be found online. Scan the QR code or go to this link to access it:

testprepbooks.com/bonus/cbest

The first time you access the tests, you will need to register as a "new user" and verify your email address.

If you have any issues, please email support@testprepbooks.com

Dear CBEST Test Taker,

Thank you again for purchasing this study guide for your CBEST exam. We hope that we exceeded your expectations.

Our goal in creating this study guide was to cover all of the topics that you will see on the test. We also strove to make our practice questions as similar as possible to what you will encounter on test day. With that being said, if you found something that you feel was not up to your standards, please send us an email and let us know.

We would also like to let you know about other books in our catalog that may interest you.

CSET English

This can be found on Amazon: amazon.com/dp/1628458941

CSET Multiple Subject

amazon.com/dp/1628458739

NES Elementary Education

amazon.com/dp/1628459239

CSET Mathematics

amazon.com/dp/1628459158

We have study guides in a wide variety of fields. If the one you are looking for isn't listed above, then try searching for it on Amazon or send us an email.

Thanks Again and Happy Testing!
Product Development Team
info@studyguideteam.com

FREE Test Taking Tips Video/DVD Offer

To better serve you, we created videos covering test taking tips that we want to give you for FREE. **These videos cover world-class tips that will help you succeed on your test.**

We just ask that you send us feedback about this product. Please let us know what you thought about it—whether good, bad, or indifferent.

To get your **FREE videos**, you can use the QR code below or email freevideos@studyguideteam.com with "Free Videos" in the subject line and the following information in the body of the email:

a. The title of your product

b. Your product rating on a scale of 1-5, with 5 being the highest

c. Your feedback about the product

If you have any questions or concerns, please don't hesitate to contact us at info@studyguideteam.com.

Thank you!

Made in the USA
Las Vegas, NV
18 March 2024

87409107R00142